SCHOLASTIC

Terms and conditions

IMPORTANT – PERMITTED USE AND WARNINGS – READ CAREFULLY BEFORE USING

Recommended system requirements:

- Windows: XP (Service Pack 3), Vista (Service Pack 2), Windows 7 or Windows 8 with 2.33GHz processor
- Mac: OS 10.6 to 10.8 with Intel Core™ Duo processor
- 1GB RAM (recommended)
- 1024 x 768 Screen resolution
- CD-ROM drive (24x speed recommended)
- 16-bit sound card
- Adobe Reader (version 9 recommended for Mac users)
- Broadband internet connections (for installation and updates)

For all technical support queries, please phone Scholastic Customer Services on 0845 6039091.

SCHOLASTIC

Book End, Range Road, Witney, Oxfordshire, OX29 0YD
www.scholastic.co.uk

© 2014, Scholastic Ltd

1 2 3 4 5 6 7 8 9   4 5 6 7 8 9 0 1 2 3

British Library Cataloguing-in-Publication Data
A catalogue record for this book is available from the
British Library.

ISBN 978-1407-12855-9
Printed by Bell & Bain Ltd, Glasgow

Extracts from *The National Curriculum in English, History
Programme of Study* © Crown Copyright. Reproduced
under the terms of the Open Government Licence
(OGL). http://www.nationalarchives.gov.uk/doc/open-
government-licence/open-government-licence.htm

Author
Helen Lewis

Editorial team
Jenny Wilcox, Rachel Morgan, Vicky Butt,
Roanne Charles and Margaret Eaton

Cover Design
Andrea Lewis

Design
Andrea Lewis

CD-ROM development
Hannah Barnett, Phil Crothers, MWA Technologies
Private Ltd

Illustrations
Phillip Hood

Acknowledgements
The publishers gratefully acknowledge permission
to reproduce the following copyright material:
Canadian Museum of History 'Mystery of the Maya'
virtual exhibit.

Crown Copyright for the use of 'Biography of
Ethelred II: the Unready' from its website:
www.royal.gov.uk. Reproduced under the terms
of the Open Government Licence (OGL).
http://www.nationalarchives.gov.uk/doc/open-
government-licence/version/2

East of England Broadband for the recipes
'Beancakes' and 'Baked apples' from
http://cookit.e2bn.org/historycookbook

Imperial War Museum for the use of 'Hurricane
versus Messerschmitt' from an interview with
Roland Beamont © Imperial War Museum

The Mint Museum for use of 'Maya creation story'

RAF museum for the use of an extract 'Air-raid
shelters'

Scholastic Ltd for the use of an extract from My
Story: Workhouse by Pamela Oldfield. Text © 2004,
Pamela Oldfield. Published by Scholastic Ltd.
All Rights Reserved

Science Museum for the use of 'History of
hospitals' and 'Smallpox' © Board of Trustees of the
Science Museum

David White for the use of the text extract 'The
Mayan Ball Game'. Copyright © David White
www.socialstudiesforkids.com

Every effort has been made to trace copyright
holders for the works reproduced in this book,
and the publishers apologise for any inadvertent
omissions.

Contents

Introduction

The *100 History Lessons* series is designed to meet the requirements of the 2014 Curriculum, History Programmes of Study. There are three books in the series, Years 1–2, 3–4 and 5–6, and each book contains lesson plans, resources and ideas matched to the new curriculum. It can be a complex task to ensure that a progressive and appropriate curriculum is followed in all year groups; this series has been carefully structured to ensure that a progressive and appropriate curriculum is followed throughout.

About the new curriculum

The 2014 National Curriculum for Key Stages 1 and 2 explains the purpose and aims of history as follows: *A high-quality history education will help pupils gain a coherent knowledge and understanding of Britain's past and that of the wider world. It should inspire pupils' curiosity to know more about the past. Teaching should equip pupils to ask perceptive questions, think critically, weigh evidence, sift arguments, and develop perspective and judgement. History helps pupils to understand the complexity of people's lives, the process of change, the diversity of societies and relationships between different groups, as well as their own identity and the challenges of their time.*

The National Curriculum for History aims to ensure that all children:
- *know and understand the history of these islands as a coherent, chronological narrative, from the earliest times to the present day: how people's lives have shaped this nation and how Britain has influenced and been influenced by the wider world*
- *know and understand significant aspects of the history of the wider world: the nature of ancient civilisations; the expansion and dissolution of empires; characteristic features of past non-European societies; achievements and follies of mankind*
- *gain and deploy a historically grounded understanding of abstract terms such as 'empire', 'civilisation', 'parliament' and 'peasantry'*
- *understand historical concepts such as continuity and change, cause and consequence, similarity, difference and significance, and use them to make connections, draw contrasts, analyse trends, frame historically valid questions and create their own structured accounts, including written narratives and analyses*
- *understand the methods of historical enquiry, including how evidence is used rigorously to make historical claims, and discern how and why contrasting arguments and interpretations of the past have been constructed*
- *gain historical perspective by placing their growing knowledge into different contexts, understanding the connections between local, regional, national and international history; between cultural, economic, military, political, religious and social history; and between short- and long-term timescales.*

The curriculum goes on to state that *children are expected to know, apply and understand the matters, skills and processes specified in the relevant Programme of Study.* There are two Programmes of Study in the primary history curriculum: one for Key Stage 1 and one for Key Stage 2. On its own, the content of the programmes of study is insufficient to create exciting and effective learning experiences. This series of books is designed to help provide guidance and support for schools and teachers, through a coherent, challenging, engaging and enjoyable scheme of work.

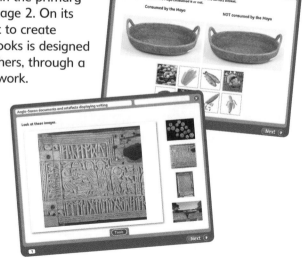

Terminology
- **Curriculum objectives:** These are the statutory programme of study statements or objectives.

■SCHOLASTIC
www.scholastic.co.uk

About the book

This book is divided into twelve chapters; six for each year group. Each chapter contains a half-term's work and is based around a topic or theme. Each chapter follows the same structure:

Chapter introduction

At the start of each chapter there is a summary of what is covered. This includes:

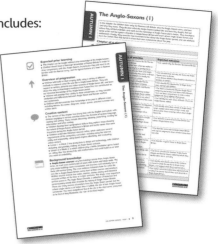

- **Introduction:** A description of what is covered in the chapter.
- **Chapter at a glance:** This is a table that summarises the content of each lesson, including: the curriculum objectives, a summary of the activities and the outcome.
- **Expected prior learning:** What the children are expected to know before starting the work in the chapter.
- **Overview of progression:** A brief explanation of how the children progress through the chapter.
- **Creative context:** How the chapter could link to other curriculum areas.
- **Background knowledge:** A section explaining grammatical terms and suchlike to enhance your subject knowledge, where required.

Lessons

Each chapter contains six weeks' of lessons, each week contains two lessons. At the start of each week there is an introduction about what is covered. The lesson plans then include the relevant combination of headings from below.

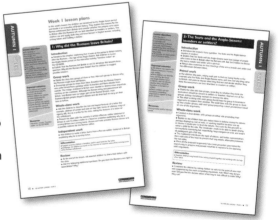

- **Lesson objectives:** Objectives that are based upon the Curriculum objectives, but are more specific broken-down steps to achieve them.
- **Expected outcomes:** What you should expect all, most and some children to know by the end of the lesson.
- **Resources:** What you require to teach the lesson.
- **Introduction:** A short and engaging activity to begin the lesson.
- **Whole-class work:** Working together as a class.
- **Group/Paired/Independent work:** Children working independently of the teacher in pairs, groups or alone.
- **Differentiation:** Ideas for how to support children who are struggling with a concept or how to extend those children who understand a concept without taking them onto new work.
- **Review:** A chance to review the children's learning and ensure the outcomes of the lesson have been achieved.

Assess and review

At the end of each chapter are activities for assessing and reviewing the children's understanding. These can be conducted at the end of the chapter or at a later date. They all follow the same format:

- **Curriculum objectives:** These are the areas of focus for the assess and review activity.
- **Resources:** What you require to conduct the activities.
- **Revise:** A series of short activities or one longer activity to revise and consolidate the children's learning and ensure they understand the concept(s).
- **Assess:** An assessment activity to provide a chance for the children to demonstrate their understanding and for you to check this.
- **Further practice:** Ideas for further practice on the focus, whether children are insecure in their learning or you want to provide extra practice or challenge.

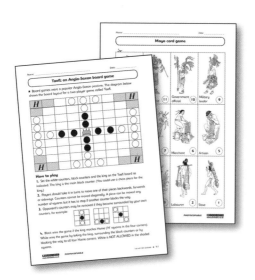

Photocopiable pages

At the end of each chapter are some photocopiable pages that will have been referred to in the lesson plans. These sheets are for the children to use. There is generally a title, an instruction, an activity and an 'I can' statement at the bottom. The children should be encouraged to complete the 'I can' statements by colouring in the traffic lights to say how they think they have done (red – not very well, amber – ok, green – very well).

These sheets are also provided on the CD-ROM alongside additional pages as referenced in the lessons (see page 7 About the CD-ROM).

About the CD-ROM

The CD-ROM contains:
- Printable versions of the photocopiable sheets from the book and additional photocopiable sheets as referenced in the lesson plans.
- Interactive activities for children to complete or to use on the whiteboard.
- Media resources to display.
- Printable versions of the lesson plans.
- Digital versions of the lesson plans with the relevant resources linked to them.

Getting started
Put the CD-ROM into your CD-ROM drive.
- For Windows users, the install wizard should autorun, if it fails to do so then navigate to your CD-ROM drive. Then follow the installation process.
- For Mac users, copy the disk image file to your hard drive. After it has finished copying double-click it to mount the disk image. Navigate to the mounted disk image and run the installer. After installation the disk image can be unmounted and the DMG can be deleted from the hard drive.
- To complete the installation of the program you need to open the program and click 'Update' in the pop-up. Please note – this CD-ROM is web-enabled and the content will be downloaded from the internet to your hard-drive to populate the CD-ROM with the relevant resources. This only needs to be done on first use, after this you will be able to use the CD-ROM without an internet connection. If at any point any content is updated you will receive another pop-up upon start up with an internet connection.

Navigating the CD-ROM
There are two options to navigate the CD-ROM either as a Child or as a Teacher.

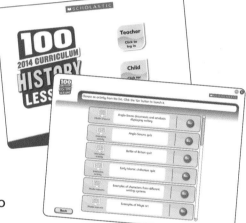

Child
- Click on the 'Child' button on the first menu screen.
- In the second menu click on the relevant class (please note only the books installed on the machine or network will be accessible. You can also rename year groups to match your school's naming conventions via the Teacher > Settings > Rename books area).
- A list of interactive activities will be displayed, children need to locate the correct one and click 'Go' to launch it.
- There is the opportunity to print or save a PDF of the activity at the end.

Teacher
- Click on the Teacher button on the first menu screen and you will be taken to a screen showing which of the 100 History books you have purchased. From here, you can also access information about getting started and the credits.
- To enter the product click 'Next' in the bottom right.
- You then need to enter a password (the password is: login).
  - On first use: Enter as a Guest by clicking on the 'Guest' button.
  - If desired, create a profile for yourself by adding your name to the list of users. Profiles allow you to save favourites and to specify which year group(s) you wish to be able to view.
  - Go to 'Settings' to create a profile for yourself – click 'Add user' and enter your name. Then choose the year groups you wish to have access to (you can return to this screen to change this at any time). Click on 'Login' at the top of the screen to re-enter the disk under your new profile.
- On subsequent uses you can choose your name from the drop-down list. The 'Guest' option will always be available if you, or a colleague, wish to use this.
- You can search the CD-ROM using the tools or save favourites.

For more information about how to use the CD-ROM, please refer to the help file which can be found in the teacher area of the CD-ROM. It is a red button with a question mark on it on the right-hand side of the screen just underneath the 'Settings' tab.

The Anglo-Saxons (1)

In this chapter the children learn why the Romans left Britain, who the Anglo-Saxons were, and how and why they came. They discover what the Anglo-Saxons looked like and how they fought, find out where they settled in Britain, and work out the meanings of Anglo-Saxon place names. They investigate social order and the system of justice in Anglo-Saxon Britain and learn about Anglo-Saxon homes and settlements. Finally, they consider how historians know about the Anglo-Saxon period, and use artefacts from the Sutton Hoo ship burial to draw their own conclusions about the past.

Chapter at a glance

Curriculum objective

• Britain's settlement by Anglo-Saxons and Scots.

Week	Lesson	Summary of activities	Expected outcomes
1	1	• Children explore the reasons for the Roman withdrawal from Britain. • They write a letter from a Roman soldier in Britain, explaining why he is coming home.	• Can explain why the Romans abandoned Britain.
	2	• Children find out who the Scots and Anglo-Saxons were and why they came to Britain. • They take part in a debate to classify the newcomers as invaders or settlers.	• Can describe how and why the Scots and Anglo-Saxons came to Britain. • Can discuss whether they should be described as invaders or settlers.
2	1	• Children study images of Anglo-Saxons. • They design an Anglo-Saxon costume.	• Can describe the appearance of Anglo-Saxon men, women and children.
	2	• Children analyse Anglo-Saxon and Roman weaponry and armour. • They play a dice game simulating combat between Roman and an Anglo-Saxon soldier.	• Can draw comparisons between Anglo-Saxon weaponry and armour and those of the Romans. • Can use these comparisons to make a value judgement about fighting effectiveness.
3	1	• Children work in pairs to map areas where the Anglo-Saxons settled and some of the main Anglo-Saxon towns.	• Can identify the main areas of Britain where the Anglo-Saxons settled.
	2	• Children refer to a wordbank to identify place names that are of Anglo-Saxon origin, and to explain what some of them mean. • They discuss what these meanings tell us about Anglo-Saxon life.	• Can identify some place names of Anglo-Saxon origin, explain what some of them mean, and discuss what these meanings tell us about Anglo-Saxon life.
4	1	• Children read how Britain was ruled in Anglo-Saxon times and answer quiz questions. • They draw a diagram showing Anglo-Saxon social order.	• Can describe in general terms how Britain was ruled in Anglo-Saxon times.
	2	• Children study Anglo-Saxon law and order. • They play a game matching crimes to punishments. • They discuss whether laws were fair and whether punishments fitted the crimes.	• Can describe some laws in Anglo-Saxon Britain and express judgement about whether those laws were fair.
5	1	• Children work in groups to investigate homes of people in different social classes in Anglo-Saxon Britain. • They present their findings to the class.	• Can describe a typical home in Anglo-Saxon Britain.
	2	• Children compare an Anglo-Saxon village with a Roman town. • They discuss which they would rather live in, and explain why.	• Can draw comparisons between Anglo-Saxon villages and Roman towns, explaining which they would rather live in, and why.
6	1	• Children list categories of historical source. • They categorise examples of sources about the Anglo-Saxons and evaluate their reliability.	• Can identify and classify some of the evidence we have for what life was like in Anglo-Saxon Britain, and suggest what these sources tell us.
	2	• Children examine artefacts from the Sutton Hoo ship burial.	• Can explain what the Sutton Hoo ship burial tells us about the person buried there and about life in Anglo-Saxon Britain.
Assess and review		• To review the half-term's work.	

Expected prior learning
● This chapter can be taught without prior knowledge of the Anglo-Saxons.
● Children should have a thorough knowledge of Roman Britain in order to draw comparisons with the Anglo-Saxons. In particular they will need to be familiar with the Roman army, and the typical features of a town in Roman Britain.

Overview of progression
● Children will build on their enquiry skills, using a variety of different methods to research what life was like in Anglo-Saxon Britain. They will respond to written, pictorial and video accounts of Anglo-Saxon life, and learn about the way archaeological evidence from Sutton Hoo has contributed to our historical knowledge of the Anglo-Saxon period.
● Children will develop their ability to draw comparisons, as they consider similarities and differences between Anglo-Saxon and Roman warfare and settlements.
● Children will demonstrate their knowledge of the past in different ways, including debate, discussion, diagrams, design, games, practical activities and written work.

Creative context
● The content of this chapter has strong links with the English curriculum, with children engaging in various activities across the domains of spoken language, reading and writing. These include discussing, debating, presenting, reading for information and letter writing.
● Children develop their geographical skills as they explore maps showing the extent of Anglo-Saxon settlement in Britain and locate towns that were important during the Anglo-Saxon period.
● Children undertake historical research online, which addresses several requirements of the computing curriculum, including using the internet safely and responsibly, using search engines effectively, and evaluating online content.
● Lesson 1 in Week 2 has strong links to design and technology, with children designing, and possibly making, an Anglo-Saxon costume.
● Lesson 2 in Week 2, in which children play a battle-simulation game based on rolling dice, has strong links with mathematics, and could build on or lead into work on probability.

Background knowledge
● **Anglo-Saxon sources:** very few buildings survive from Anglo-Saxon times, as most were constructed of wood, with wattle and daub walls. The only stone buildings were monasteries and churches, and relatively few of these still survive today. The main evidence historians have for what life was like in Anglo-Saxon Britain comes from written sources and artefacts. Written sources include law codes, charters, stories, poetry and historical accounts written at the time or in later centuries. The single most important written source is *The Anglo-Saxon Chronicle*, a collection of historical and contemporary annals that chronicle the history of Anglo-Saxon Britain. There are many sources of artefacts from the Anglo-Saxon period, but the richest single source is at Sutton Hoo in Suffolk, the site of two Anglo-Saxon cemeteries. The most magnificent find at the site is the ship burial, presumed to be that of King Raedwald, the ruler of the East Angles.

Week I lesson plans

In this week's lessons the children are introduced to the Anglo-Saxon period and locate it on a timeline of British history. They explore the reasons for the Roman withdrawal from Britain and consider whether the peoples who came to Britain after the Romans left are best described as invaders or settlers. The children use and apply skills they will have learned in English lessons, including writing letters and holding a debate.

Lesson objectives
● To develop a chronologically secure knowledge and understanding of British, local and world history, establishing clear narratives within and across the periods they study.
● To regularly address and sometimes devise historically valid questions about change, cause, similarity and difference, and significance.

Expected outcomes
● All children can explain in simple terms why the Romans left Britain.
● Most children can explain in more detail why the Romans left Britain.
● Some children can explain why the Romans left Britain and can describe some of the consequences of Roman withdrawal.

Resources
Interactive activity 'Timeline maker' on the CD-ROM

I: Why did the Romans leave Britain?

Introduction
● Introduce the chapter, explaining that it looks at the period in British history after the Romans – the age of the Anglo-Saxons. Ask children to locate the Anglo-Saxon period on the interactive activity 'Timeline maker' on the CD-ROM.
● Explain that the Romans left Britain in AD410. Introduce this lesson's focus question: *Why did the Romans leave Britain?* Ask the children to suggest possible answers.

Group work
● Divide the class into groups of three or four. Ask each group to discuss why the Romans might have left Britain.
● Encourage groups to share their ideas. Establish that the Roman Empire was under threat from uprisings within its borders and from attacks from outside. The troops stationed in Britain were needed to defend more important territory on the continent. Although the Roman army and government left Britain, and Britain was no longer part of the Roman Empire, most Romano-British people stayed in Britain and did their best to carry on their lives as before.

Whole-class work
● Ask the children to describe the text and layout features of a letter (for example, address of sender and date on top right; forms of address; ways of signing off). Act as a scribe for the class, noting the features of a letter on the whiteboard.
● Present the class with the scenario in which a Roman soldier stationed in Britain in AD410 writes a letter to a friend or a relative explaining why he is leaving Britain and coming home. Discuss and note possible Roman names and a possible address for the Roman soldier.

Independent work
● Ask children to write a letter home from a Roman soldier stationed in Britain explaining why he is coming home.

Differentiation
● Support: provide children a template and/or wordbank for the letter.
● Challenge: let children use books or the internet to research some of the consequences of the Roman withdrawal.

Review
● At the end of the lesson, ask selected children to share their letters with the class.
● Ask the following additional questions: *Do you think the Romans were right to leave Britain? Why?*

2: The Scots and the Anglo-Saxons: invaders or settlers?

Lesson objectives
● To develop a chronologically secure knowledge and understanding of British, local and world history, establishing clear narratives within and across the periods they study.
● To develop the appropriate use of historical terms.

Expected outcomes
● All children can explain the difference between invaders and settlers.
● Most children can describe how and why the Scots and Anglo-Saxons came to Britain, and can discuss whether they should be described as invaders or settlers.
● Some children can put forward a compelling argument in support of their point of view.

Resources
History books and/or internet access

Introduction
● Introduce this lesson's focus question: *The Scots and the Anglo-Saxons: invaders or settlers?*
● Explain that the Scots and the Anglo-Saxons were two groups of people who came to live in Britain after the Romans left. Ask the children to discuss the terms *invader* and *settler* with a partner.
● Reach class consensus on the meanings of the terms *invader* and *settler* and the differences between them.

Paired work
● Put children into pairs, asking each pair to find out (using books or the internet) *who* the Scots and Anglo-Saxons were, and *how* and *why* they came to Britain. Ask pairs to discuss what they find out and decide whether they think the newcomers are best described as invaders or settlers.

Group work
● Divide the class into two groups, according to whether they think the newcomers should be classed as settlers or invaders. Oversee one of the groups, asking a teaching assistant to oversee the other.
● The adult working with each group should help the group to brainstorm arguments to support their position. The adult then asks the group to divide up into smaller groups, with each group preparing a short presentation based on one of the arguments.

Whole-class work
● Conduct a class debate, with groups on either side presenting their arguments.
● Explain to the children how you expect them to behave during the debate, perhaps displaying a list of rules, or working together to draw one up.
● Choose a moderator to lead the debate. You could do this yourself, or select a child for the role. The moderator needs to be able to speak clearly, communicate assertively but respectfully, keep everyone on task, and ensure all participants get a fair say.
● The moderator introduces the topic of debate, and invites representatives from each side of the issue to present their arguments, alternating between the two sides.
● Once all the prepared arguments have been presented, give teams the opportunity to prepare and present rebuttals in response to the opposing side's arguments.

> **Differentiation**
> ● Support: children may benefit from being grouped together and working with the help of an adult.

Review
● Complete the debate by asking children to vote for the point of view that was supported by the most compelling arguments. Ask: *Which way did you vote? Did you find the decision about which way to vote difficult to make? Why? Why not?*

Week 2 lesson plans

This week's lessons have links to design technology. The first lesson introduces an engaging and challenging group activity (creating an Anglo-Saxon costume) that will take several hours to complete. If necessary, the lesson can be completed in a shorter time frame if the children only design the costume, and do not go on to make it. In the second lesson the children use pictorial evidence to compare the fighting effectiveness of Anglo-Saxon and Roman soldiers, based on the armour and weapons technologies they used.

1: What did the Anglo-Saxons look like?

Lesson objective
● To develop a chronologically secure knowledge and understanding of British, local and world history, establishing clear narratives within and across the periods they study.

Expected outcomes
● All children can describe some features of Anglo-Saxon clothing.
● Most children can describe the appearance of Anglo-Saxon men, women and children at various levels of society.
● Some children can describe how clothes were made in Anglo-Saxon times.

Resources
Photocopiable page 'Anglo-Saxon clothing' from the CD-ROM; sketching and colouring pencils; materials and equipment for making an Anglo-Saxon costume (optional)

Introduction
● Introduce this lesson's focus question: *What did the Anglo-Saxons look like?*
● On the whiteboard, write some headings related to appearance, for example *Hairstyles, Headwear, Jewellery, Clothes* and *Footwear.*
● Working with partners, give the children a few minutes to discuss what they think the Anglo-Saxons looked like, choosing one or more of the headings to focus on.
● Discuss the children's ideas.

Whole-class work
● Display photocopiable page 'Anglo-Saxon clothing' from the CD-ROM. Very briefly explain the differences between the four classes of people illustrated.
● Discuss the clothing illustrated on the photocopiable page, relating it to the children's preconceptions from the introductory activity.

Group work
● Divide the class up into four or more groups. Assign one or more groups to each class of person on the photocopiable sheet: royalty, thanes (nobles), churls (commoners), and slaves.
● Challenge each group to design a costume for one of their members to wear that is based on the clothing depicted in the relevant picture.
● For slaves the main (and often only) item of clothing was a woollen tunic for men and a woollen ankle-length gown for women.
● Male churls wore one or more woollen tunics, a linen under-tunic, and woollen trousers. Female churls wore one or more woollen gowns with a linen underdress. Both sexes wore leather shoes and a cloak held in place by a brooch. After the introduction of Christianity, women wore head coverings.
● Thanes' clothes were similar to churls', but were more brightly coloured and more richly decorated. Thanes also wore more jewellery. Very wealthy thanes wore silk garments.
● The clothing of royalty was similar to that of thanes, but even more sumptuous. Kings and queens wore a crown.
● If possible, allocate time over the course of the next few weeks for each group to make the outfit they have designed. You might like to invite a parent or carer with needlework skills into school to help with this.

Differentiation
● Challenge: children could research how clothes were made in Anglo-Saxon times.

Review
● Bring the class together, encouraging pairs and individuals to share their designs.
● If any children have researched how Anglo-Saxon clothes were made, ask them to share what they have found out with the rest of the class.

Lesson objectives
● To develop a chronologically secure knowledge and understanding of British, local and world history, establishing clear narratives within and across the periods they study.
● To note connections, contrasts and trends over time.
● To regularly address and sometimes devise historically valid questions about change, cause, similarity and difference, and significance.

Expected outcomes
● All children can describe some differences between Anglo-Saxon and Roman soldiers.
● Most children can draw comparisons between Anglo-Saxon weaponry and armour and those of the Romans, and use these comparisons to make a value judgment about fighting effectiveness.
● Some children can compare the military strategy of the Anglo-Saxons with that of the Romans.

Resources
Standard six-sided dice; images showing re-enactors dressed as Anglo-Saxon soldiers and Roman soldiers

2: Who would win a fight between an Anglo-Saxon and a Roman?

Introduction
● Introduce this lesson's focus question: *Who would win a fight between an Anglo-Saxon and a Roman?*
● Display pictures showing Anglo-Saxon soldiers and Roman soldiers.
● Ask the children to identify the differences between the two groups of soldiers. Discuss which differences represent a battle advantage for the Romans and which represent a battle advantage for the Anglo-Saxons.

Whole-class work
● On the board write the headings *Armour* and *Weapons*. Ask the children to compare Roman armour and Anglo-Saxon armour and give them each a score between three and five, with three being poor, four good, and five very good. Repeat for weapons.
● Explain the rules of a simple dice-based combat game for two players: One player is a Roman soldier and the other is an Anglo-Saxon. Each player rolls a die, with the higher number attacking first. The attacking player rolls the die again for the attack. If the number they roll is *less than* their weapons number, the attack is on target, and the other player must try to block the attack by rolling a number *less than their* armour number. If they block the attack, they win that round. If they do not block, the attacking player wins. The next round starts with the player who did not attack this round making an attack.

Paired work
● Ask the children to play the dice game in pairs, recording the result of each round of play (Roman win or Anglo-Saxon win). Halfway through the time, ask partners to swap roles.

Differentiation
● Support: children could be paired with a more confident partner.
● Challenge: for homework children could research and compare the military strategies of the Anglo-Saxons and the Romans and draw conclusions from this about their relative effectiveness.

Review
● At the end of the lesson, review the results of the dice game. Ask each table to find the total number of games won by each side, and then work together to calculate whole-class totals.
● Ask: *Who would win a fight between an Anglo-Saxon and a Roman? Why?* (The answers to these questions will depend on the values the children assigned to each side's armour and weapons at the beginning of whole-class work.)

Week 3 lesson plans

This week's lessons have a geographical focus. In the first lesson the children find out which areas of Britain were settled by the Anglo-Saxons, and identify some of the modern-day towns and cities that were important in Anglo-Saxon times. In the second lesson the children find place names that are Anglo-Saxon in origin, work out their meanings, and consider what clues these meanings give us about life in Anglo-Saxon times.

1: Where did the Anglo-Saxons settle in Britain?

Lesson objective
● To develop a chronologically secure knowledge and understanding of British, local and world history, establishing clear narratives within and across the periods they study.

Expected outcomes
● All children can identify some of the areas of Britain where the Anglo-Saxons settled.
● Most children can identify the main areas of Britain where the Anglo-Saxons settled.
● Some children can explain the significance of one or more Anglo-Saxon towns.

Resources
Outline map of Britain; photocopiable page 23 'Double map of Britain' (for each pair, cut into half before the lesson); photocopiable page 'The countries and counties of modern Britain' from the CD-ROM; pencils and colouring pencils, erasers

Introduction
● Introduce this lesson's focus question: *Where did the Anglo-Saxons settle in Britain?*
● Display an outline map of Britain.
● Ask the children to suggest where the Anglo-Saxons might have settled first. (Along the east coast, because they came from the east.)
● Explain that it took the Anglo-Saxons a long time to settle further inland. Ask the children to consider in pairs the reasons for this.
● Discuss the children's suggestions. (Reasons include: there were very few roads, the Roman roads that remained were in disrepair, the Anglo-Saxons' main form of transport was boats, land transport was slow, they met resistance from local tribes, and they were used to living by the sea.)

Paired work
● Organise the class into pairs and give out pencils, colouring pencils and erasers.
● Distribute halves of photocopiable page 23 'Double map of Britain' to each pair. Emphasise the importance of not letting your partner see your map. Also give each child a copy of photocopiable page 'The countries and counties of modern Britain' from the CD-ROM.
● Ask the partner with map A to describe where the Anglo-Saxons settled (using the modern countries and counties) so that their partner can shade in the appropriate areas on their copy of the map. For example, the partner with map A might tell their partner to shade in all of England apart from Cornwall in the south-west and Cumbria in the north-west, and to shade in a small area of south-east Scotland covering most of the Scottish Borders, together with Edinburgh, Midlothian and East Lothian.
● Ask the partner with map B to describe the positions of towns and cities that were important in Anglo-Saxon times so that the first partner can write in their names on their copy of the map. For example, the partner with map B might tell their partner that the city of Winchester is shown by the dot that is in the county of Hampshire.
● Ask partners to compare maps and correct any errors.

> **Differentiation**
> ● Support: put children into mixed-ability groups of four rather than pairs, so that they have someone to work with.
> ● Challenge: ask children to find out about the significance in Anglo-Saxon times of one of the towns marked on the photocopiable page.

Review
● Ask a volunteer to mark on the displayed outline map of Britain the areas where the Anglo-Saxons settled. Ask: *Why do you think the Anglo-Saxons did not settle in Scotland, Wales and Cornwall?*

Lesson objectives
● To develop a chronologically secure knowledge and understanding of British, local and world history, establishing clear narratives within and across the periods they study.
● To note connections, contrasts and trends over time.
● To understand how our knowledge of the past is constructed from a range of sources.

Expected outcomes
● All children can identify some place names of Anglo-Saxon origin.
● Most children can identify some place names of Anglo-Saxon origin, explain what some of them mean, and discuss what these meanings tell us about Anglo-Saxon life.
● Some children can conduct their own research to add extra words and meanings to a wordbank of Anglo-Saxon place names.

Resources
Photocopiable page 'Wordbank of Anglo-Saxon place names' from the CD-ROM; maps of Britain, maps of the local area (optional)

2: What clues do Anglo-Saxon place names give us?

Introduction
● Introduce this lesson's focus question: *What clues do Anglo-Saxon place names give us?*
● Display photocopiable page 'Wordbank of Anglo-Saxon place names' from the CD-ROM, explaining how to use it. Leave this on display for use later in the lesson.
● On the whiteboard, write a place name that is familiar to the children and that is of Anglo-Saxon origin.
● Ask the children to use the wordbank to help them work out the meaning of the place name. Ask: *What clues does the place name give us about life during Anglo-Saxon times?*

Paired work
● Divide the class into pairs, giving each pair a map of Britain (and a map of the local area if you are using it). Also give each pair a copy of the wordbank. Challenge pairs to find ten place names on the map that are of Anglo-Saxon origin. Can they find place names that are different from those other pairs on their table have found?
● Ask pairs to work out and write down full or partial meanings of as many of the place names as possible.

Whole-class work
● Ask pairs to share some of the place names they have found, particularly those whose full meanings they have worked out.
● Discuss what clues these place names give us about life in Anglo-Saxon times. For example, *Oxford* means 'a river crossing for oxen'. It tells us the Anglo-Saxons kept oxen. Ask children to suggest what they might have used oxen for. (Pulling heavy loads.) This place name also tells us that Anglo-Saxons built settlements next to shallow areas of rivers, where it was easy to cross. This implies bridges were relatively rare. Ask children to suggest why. (Bridges are expensive to build and maintain, and for most of the Anglo-Saxon period the country was made up of several small kingdoms, so a bridge-building programme would have been a drain on taxes.)
● Ask any children who have found extra Anglo-Saxon place name words (see *Differentiation*) to share these with the class. Add them to the class display copy of the wordbank.

Differentiation
● Support: put children by placing them with a more confident partner.
● Challenge: ask children to conduct an internet search to find more Anglo-Saxon place name words and add them to the wordbank.

Review
● At the end of the lesson, challenge children to find place names containing the extra place name words you have added to the wordbank, or some or all of the following words: *ing* (people of); *bury* (fortified place); *stow* (meeting place); *nor* (north); *sud, sut* (south), and *ness* (headland).

Week 4 lesson plans

In this week's lessons the children consider how Anglo-Saxon Britain was ruled. In the first lesson the children name and locate the seven Anglo-Saxon kingdoms and investigate aspects of social order and the system of government. In the second lesson they learn about crime, trial and punishment in Anglo-Saxon times and use what they learn to draw a conclusion about whether or not the Anglo-Saxon justice system was fair.

I: How was Britain ruled in Anglo-Saxon times?

Introduction

● Introduce this lesson's focus question: *How was Britain ruled in Anglo-Saxon times?*
● Give out individual copies of photocopiable page 'How Britain was ruled in Anglo-Saxon times' from the CD-ROM. Allow enough time for everyone to read the text on the photocopiable page. Ask anyone who finishes reading before the time is up to write a question based on the text and keep it secret.
● Ask everyone to place their copy of the text face down, and then divide the class into groups. Ask each group a question based on the text. Include any questions children have written. Group members may confer to decide on the answer. Award 2 points for a correct answer. If a group does not answer correctly, open the question up for I point.

Paired work

● Ask children to work with a partner to draw a diagram showing Anglo-Saxon social order. They could create their diagram on paper, in three dimensions using modelling materials, or on a computer using a program with diagramming capability.

Whole-class work

● Ask pairs to share and explain their diagrams, inviting the rest of the class to provide feedback. The most successful diagrams could be put on display.
● If any children have compared and contrasted the Anglo-Saxon period with modern times (see *Differentiation*), ask them to present what they have found out.

> **Differentiation**
> ● Challenge: ask children to compare and contrast how Britain was ruled in Anglo-Saxon times with how it is ruled today.

Review

● Play a game testing children's knowledge of the names of the Anglo-Saxon kingdoms. Display photocopiable page 'Outline map of Anglo-Saxon England circa AD600' from the CD-ROM. Ask children to match each numbered kingdom with the correct name. Children could work individually, in pairs, or in groups. Review the answers, awarding a point for each correct answer.

Lesson objectives
● To develop a chronologically secure knowledge and understanding of British, local and world history, establishing clear narratives within and across the periods they study.
● To develop the appropriate use of historical terms.

Expected outcomes
● All children can name and locate some of the Anglo-Saxon kingdoms.
● Most children can name and locate the Anglo-Saxon kingdoms and describe Anglo-Saxon social order and the system of government.
● Some children can compare and contrast how Britain was ruled in Anglo-Saxon times with how it is ruled today.

Resources
Photocopiable pages 'How Britain was ruled in Anglo-Saxon times' and 'Outline map of Anglo-Saxon England circa AD600' from the CD-ROM; plain paper and colouring pencils OR modelling materials (such as dough, clay or aluminium foil) OR computer software with diagramming capability

Lesson objectives
● To develop a chronologically secure knowledge and understanding of British, local and world history, establishing clear narratives within and across the periods they study.
● To construct informed responses that involve thoughtful selection and organisation of relevant historical information.

Expected outcomes
● All children can describe some laws in Anglo-Saxon Britain.
● Most children can describe some laws in Anglo-Saxon Britain and express their judgment about whether those laws were fair.
● Some children can justify their opinions about Anglo-Saxon laws.

Resources
Information on ordeals for example, *Horrible Histories* clip 'Anglo-Saxon ordeals' (source online); photocopiable page 24 'Crime and punishment cards'; scissors

2: Were Anglo-Saxon laws fair?

Introduction
● Introduce this lesson's focus question: *Were Anglo-Saxon laws fair?*
● Give the students information about Anglo-Saxon ordeals (see *Resources*).
● Draw out the following: *What were ordeals?* (An ordeal was an unpleasant and often dangerous 'test' that a person accused of a crime had to undergo if they pleaded innocent. The outcome of the ordeal determined whether or not they were guilty.) *What different types of ordeal are mentioned in the clip?* (Ordeal by ducking, burning and cake.) *Was an ordeal a good way of finding out whether someone was guilty?* (No, because it did not rely on gathering evidence or collecting statements from witnesses.) *Did an ordeal give the accused a fair chance of going free?* (No. Firstly, the outcome of the ordeal bore no relation to whether the accused was guilty or innocent. Secondly, being found innocent was highly unlikely in most ordeals, and for some, like burning, it was actually impossible! Thirdly, for some ordeals, like ducking, you could only prove your innocence by dying or risking death.)

Group work
● Introduce photocopiable page 24 'Crime and punishment cards', which shows various crimes and typical punishments given for those crimes in Anglo-Saxon times.
● Divide the class into groups of three or four, giving each group a set of cards and a pair of scissors. Give groups a set time in which to match each crime card to the typical punishment given for that crime in Anglo-Saxon times. Encourage group discussion.

Whole-class work
● Go through the card-matching exercise, giving the correct answers. The cards match as follows: 1G, 2D, 3F, 4H, 5A, 6C, 7B and 8E.

Independent work
● Ask the children to produce a short written piece (for example a blog post, learning diary entry, or notes for a future class assembly) explaining what they have found out about Anglo-Saxon crime and punishment.

> **Differentiation**
> ● Support: in the independent-work activity you could support children with a wordbank or a writing template.

Review
● Lead a discussion about whether laws in Anglo-Saxon Britain were fair, and whether punishments fitted the crime. Ask: *In what ways was the Anglo-Saxon justice system unfair?*

Week 5 lesson plans

In this week's lessons the children explore Anglo-Saxon homes and villages. In the first lesson they research homes belonging to people of a particular social class, present what they have found out to their classmates, and learn from others' presentations. In the second lesson the children compare and contrast an Anglo-Saxon village with a Roman town, explaining which they would prefer to live in, and why.

1: What were homes like in Anglo-Saxon Britain?

Lesson objectives
● To develop a chronologically secure knowledge and understanding of British, local and world history, establishing clear narratives within and across the periods they study.
● To regularly address and sometimes devise historically valid questions about change, cause, similarity and difference, and significance.

Expected outcomes
● All children can describe some of the features of Anglo-Saxon homes.
● Most children can describe differences between the homes of people from different levels of Anglo-Saxon society.
● Some children can explain what the features of Anglo-Saxon homes tell us about daily life in Anglo-Saxon Britain.

Resources
Information bank on Anglo-Saxon homes; internet access; suitable books

Introduction
● Introduce this lesson's focus question: *What were homes like in Anglo-Saxon Britain?*
● On the whiteboard write a selection of about half a dozen words or phrases to do with homes (for example, *roof, walls, windows and doors, floor, furniture and decoration* and *heating*). Target your choices to the information you have available for the research task.
● In pairs, ask the children to choose one of these aspects and tell each other what they already know about it in relation to Anglo-Saxon homes.
● Highlight each aspect in turn, asking pairs who discussed this aspect to share what they already know. Correct any misconceptions.
● Emphasise the fact that the homes of people at different levels in Anglo-Saxon society were different, just as the homes of ordinary people today are different from stately homes and palaces.

Group work
● Organise the class into three groups. Give each group the task of researching and preparing a short presentation about the homes of people in a particular social class in Anglo-Saxon Britain: royalty, thanes (nobles) and churls (commoners).
● If groups will be conducting internet research, revise effective internet search techniques, e-safety considerations, and how to evaluate the reliability of online sources of information.
● Encourage each group to split into subgroups, with each subgroup tackling a different aspect of the home (possibly, but not necessarily, those written on the whiteboard).
● Give groups time (possibly outside history lessons) to finish their research and practise their presentations.

Whole-class work
● Ask groups to give their presentations to the rest of the class or to a wider audience (for example in a year group/key stage assembly).

Differentiation
● Support: in the group-work activity, children requiring more support could be given tasks that involve a smaller amount of writing (for example, creating a labelled diagram).
● Challenge: ask children not just to describe the features of Anglo-Saxon homes, but also to explain what these features tell us about daily life in Anglo-Saxon Britain.

Review
● Work together to draw up a list of differences between the homes of commoners and royalty in Anglo-Saxon times. Ask: *Compared to Anglo-Saxon times, do you think there are more or fewer differences between the homes of commoners and royalty today?*

Lesson objectives

● To develop a chronologically secure knowledge and understanding of British, local and world history, establishing clear narratives within and across the periods they study.
● To note connections, contrasts and trends over time and develop the appropriate use of historical terms.
● To regularly address and sometimes devise historically valid questions about change, cause, similarity and difference, and significance.

Expected outcomes

● All children can draw comparisons between Anglo-Saxon villages and Roman towns.
● Most children can draw comparisons between Anglo-Saxon villages and Roman towns, explaining which they would rather live in, and why.
● Some children can draw further comparisons between Anglo-Saxon villages and Roman towns.

Resources

Information bank on Anglo-Saxon village life; video clip of an Anglo-Saxon village: www.bbc.co.uk or interactive Anglo-Saxon village: www.pastexplorers.org.uk (optional)

2: Where would you rather live: an Anglo-Saxon village or a Roman town?

Introduction

● Introduce this lesson's focus question: *Where would you rather live: An Anglo-Saxon village or a Roman town?*
● Ask the children what they remember about towns in Roman Britain, for example, towns neatly laid out, cobbled roads, buildings made of stone, brick and tiles, and lots of public spaces and buildings (such as a forum, public baths, a basilica, temples, an amphitheatre and a theatre).

Whole-class work

● Give the children information about Anglo-Saxon villages. (For example, see the video clip and online interactive resource listed in *Resources*).
● Ensure discussion of the following. Anglo-Saxon villages were small, with even the largest having no more than a few hundred inhabitants. Homes served double duty as workshops where villagers made all the items they needed for day-to-day life. Villagers grew crops and kept animals inside the village. Many villages were surrounded by a high fence, to protect the livestock from wild animals.
● Draw a table on the whiteboard with four rows and three columns. Label the columns *Roman towns, Anglo-Saxon villages* and *Which I would prefer and why*. Label the rows with aspects of town design, for example, *Roads, Layout, Building materials, Types of buildings*. Ask the children to help you fill in one of the rows of the table.

Paired work

● Ask pairs to complete their own version of the table you have drawn on the board.
● Ask pairs to discuss with each other which they would rather live in – a Roman town or an Anglo-Saxon village – and explain why.

> ### Differentiation
> ● Support: pair children with a more confident partner.
> ● Challenge: encourage some pairs to extend their table by adding one or more extra aspects of town or village life, such as population size, water supply or waste management.

Review

● Ask: *If Roman towns seem to us to be more attractive places to live, why did the Anglo-Saxons choose not to live in them?* (They were not familiar with living in towns, and preferred to follow their existing lifestyle.) Almost all Anglo-Saxon buildings are long gone, but some features of Anglo-Saxon villages can still be found in villages in Britain today. *What are they?* (Timber-framed buildings and thatched roofs.)

Week 6 lesson plans

In this week's lessons the focus is on using historical sources to reconstruct the past. In the first lesson the children identify some of the sources of evidence we have for what life was like in Anglo-Saxon Britain, suggest what they tell us, and consider their reliability. In the second lesson the children examine the artefacts found at Sutton Hoo. They act as archaeologists, drawing and explaining their own conclusions about what the finds might tell us about life in Anglo-Saxon Britain. Finally, they find out what conclusions the experts have drawn from the evidence.

1: How do we know about Anglo-Saxon Britain?

Lesson objectives
● To develop a chronologically secure knowledge and understanding of British, local and world history, establishing clear narratives within and across the periods they study.
● To develop the appropriate use of historical terms.
● To understand how our knowledge of the past is constructed from a range of sources.

Expected outcomes
● All children can identify and classify some of the sources of evidence we have for what life was like in Anglo-Saxon Britain.
● Most children can identify and classify some of the sources of evidence we have for what life was like in Anglo-Saxon Britain, and can suggest what they tell us.
● Some children can evaluate the reliability of those sources.

Resources
A selection of Anglo-Saxon sources (artefacts, images and documents on loan from a local museum or library, and/or from books and the internet)

Introduction
● Introduce this lesson's focus question: *How do we know about Anglo-Saxon Britain?*
● On the board write: *How do we know about the past?* Ask the children, working in pairs or small groups, to brainstorm the question, noting down as many answers as they can think of.

Whole-class work
● Discuss the results of the brainstorming exercise, revising the term *historical source* and asking the children to explain the difference between a primary and secondary source.
● List on the board the major categories of historical sources – documents, buildings, images, artefacts (made objects) and oral testimony (eyewitness accounts). Ask the children which of these categories is not relevant to the study of the Anglo-Saxons, and why. (Oral testimony, as there is no one still alive from that period to interview, and no recordings were made at the time!)

Group work
● Organise the class into groups. Give each group a selection of Anglo-Saxon sources.
● Ask the children to examine the sources, writing notes for each source that assign it to the appropriate category from the board, identify it as a primary or secondary source, suggest what it tells us about life in Anglo-Saxon Britain, and evaluate its reliability as a source of evidence. Encourage pairs to discuss all aspects of the exercise.
● Ask pairs when they have finished to discuss their ideas with other pairs, amending or adding to their original notes afterwards, if they wish.

Differentiation
● Support: children requiring support should not be asked to evaluate the reliability of the sources of evidence.

Review
● Ask each group to choose one historical source and elect one or two members to present it to the class, explaining what category it belongs to, whether it is a primary or secondary source, what it tells us about life in Anglo-Saxon Britain, and how reliable it might be as a source of evidence.

Lesson objectives
● To develop a chronologically secure knowledge and understanding of British, local and world history, establishing clear narratives within and across the periods they study.
● To develop the appropriate use of historical terms.
● To understand how our knowledge of the past is constructed from a range of sources.

Expected outcomes
● All children can describe some of the objects found at Sutton Hoo.
● Most children can explain what the Sutton Hoo ship burial tells us about the person buried there and about life in Anglo-Saxon Britain.
● Some children can use their existing historical knowledge to inform their conclusions about the Sutton Hoo discovery.

Resources
Media resource 'Photos from Sutton Hoo' on the CD-ROM

2: The Sutton Hoo discovery: what does it tell us about Anglo-Saxon life?

Introduction
● Introduce this lesson's focus question: *The Sutton Hoo discovery : what does it tell us about Anglo-Saxon life?*
● Tell the children the background to the story of the Sutton Hoo discovery: Near the River Deben in Suffolk, at a place called Sutton Hoo, there is a field covered with grassy mounds. Show a photograph of the Sutton Hoo site. In 1939 an amateur archeologist named Basil Brown explored the largest mound and discovered a ship buried in it. Inside the ship were a coffin and a collection of artefacts.
● Tell the children to imagine it is 1939 and they are archaeologists helping Basil Brown to examine the objects he has found.

Group work
● Organise the class into groups. Give each group access to media resource 'Photos from Sutton Hoo' on the CD-ROM. Ask pairs within the groups to examine and discuss each object, making notes about what they think the object might be, what clues it gives us about the person who owned it, and what else it might tell us about life in Anglo-Saxon times.
● Spend time with each group, discussing their observations and ideas.

Differentiation
● Challenge: ask children to use their existing historical knowledge to inform their conclusions about the Sutton Hoo discovery, by, for example, drawing comparisons with Ancient Egyptian burial practices, or using their knowledge of early Christian symbolism from their study of the Roman period.

Review
● Ask the children: *Why do you think historians think it is a king who is buried in the ship at Sutton Hoo? Why do you think the king was buried in a ship and surround by his possessions?*

Curriculum objective

● To develop a chronologically secure knowledge and understanding of British, local and world history, establishing clear narratives within and across the periods they study.

Resources

Photocopiable page 25 'The Anglo-Saxons: what have you learned?'; teaching assistant (optional); sound recording equipment (optional); book-making materials (optional)

The Anglo-Saxons: what have you learned?

Revise

● Divide the class into mixed-ability teams for a quiz about the Anglo-Saxons. The quiz on the CD-ROM is not suitable yet, as it tests material not covered until Chapter 2. Use the questions supplied on photocopiable page 25 'The Anglo-Saxons: what have you learned?', or write your own.
● Quiz answers: 1c, 2b, 3c, 4a, 5b, 6c, 7a, 8c, 9b, 10a

Assess

● On the board write the following questions:
   1. How do we know about the Anglo-Saxons?
   2. What do you know about Anglo-Saxon society?
   3. What do you know about Anglo-Saxon laws?
   4. What do you know about Anglo-Saxon homes and settlements?
   5. What else do you know about Anglo-Saxons?
● Give children a set length of time (for example, 20 minutes) to answer these questions. Emphasise the importance of working independently.
● To encourage children to attempt all five questions, either remind them when it's time to move on to the next question, or display the questions one at a time.
● If any children struggle with reading or writing you could give them an alternative way of recording their answers (perhaps working with an adult and giving verbal responses which are recorded in an audio file).

Further practice

● Ask the children to incorporate what they know about the Anglo-Saxons into a picture book to give to a Key Stage 1 class.

Curriculum objective

● To understand how our knowledge of the past is constructed from a range of sources.

Resources

Six to eight replicas of Anglo-Saxon artefacts; laptops or tablets (optional)

Anglo-Saxon artefacts

Revise

● Review children's work on Anglo-Saxon sources of information from Week 6. Mix up the artefacts, images or documents and ask children in groups to examine, discuss or write about at least one source they have not previously covered.

Assess

● Place each replica artefact on a separate table, giving each a unique identifying number. Do not provide any information about the artefacts.
● Give children a set length of time (such as 20 minutes) to examine a given number of artefacts (for example, three). Children should move around the tables independently, so you may want to set a maximum number of people allowed at each table at any one time.
● Ask individuals to examine each object, list its *number*, write a *description* of it, and then write their *interpretation* of it – for example, what they think the object might be, what clues it gives about the person who owned it, and what else it might suggest about life in Anglo-Saxon times.

Further practice

● Ask the children to prepare a similar activity for their classmates, using photographs of Anglo-Saxon artefacts. They should bookmark their sources, so that children's interpretations of the artefacts can be compared with those of experts.

Name: _____

Date: _____

Double map of Britain

Anglo-Saxon Britain: map B

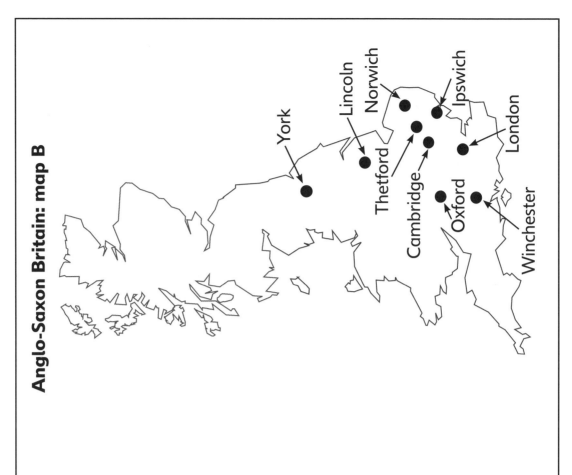

York
Lincoln
Norwich
Ipswich
London
Thetford
Cambridge
Oxford
Winchester

Anglo-Saxon Britain: map A

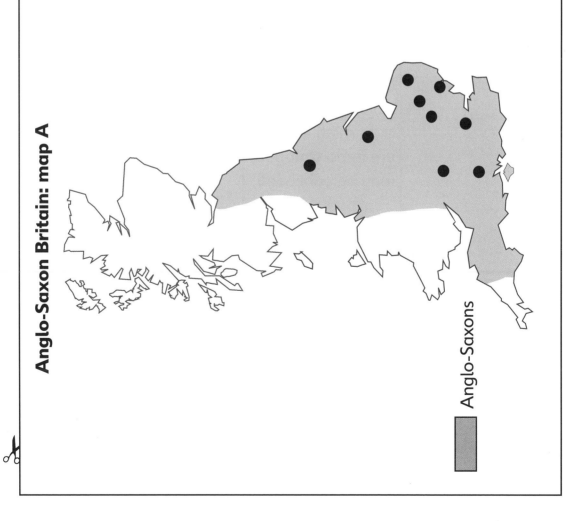

Anglo-Saxons

Name: _____   Date: _____

Crime and punishment cards

Crime 1: Killing a thane	**Punishment A:** Paying a fine of 30 shillings	**Crime 2:** Cutting off a nose	**Punishment B:** Paying a fine of 2 Shillings
Crime 3: Stealing	**Punishment C:** Paying a fine of 200 Shillings	**Crime 4:** Not having enough money to pay a fine	**Punishment D:** Paying a fine of 60 shillings
Crime 5: Cutting off an ear	**Punishment E:** Death by hanging, stoning, drowning or burning. If you are important you may be beheaded	**Crime 6:** Killing a churl	**Punishment F:** Having your hands cut off
Crime 7: Killing a slave	**Punishment G:** Paying a fine of 1200 shillings	**Crime 8:** Pleading not-guilty to a crime and then failing the ordeal	**Punishment H:** Being made a slave; if you are already a slave, being beaten and put in the stocks

PHOTOCOPIABLE

■SCHOLASTIC
www.scholastic.co.uk

Name: _____   Date: _____

The Anglo-Saxons: what have you learned?

■ Read the question and circle the correct answer.

1. Why did the Romans leave Britain?
a) They were defeated by the Picts.
b) The weather was too cold.
c) They needed to defend their homeland from attack.

2. Where did the Anglo-Saxons come from?
a) North-eastern Europe
b) North-western Europe
c) South-eastern Europe

3. Why did the Anglo-Saxons come to Britain?
a) They were invited.
b) They were looking for a better life.
c) Both a) and b).

4. What shape were Anglo-Saxon shields?
a) Round
b) Square
c) Rectangular

5. What does this Anglo-Saxon place name mean: Oxford?
a) A farmstead on a hill.
b) A place where cattle are driven across the river.
c) A village in a forest clearing.

6. Which of these social classes was the highest?
a) Churls
b) Slaves
c) Thanes

7. What was the punishment for stealing?
a) Having your hands cut off.
b) Paying a fine of 20 shillings.
c) Being ducked.

8. Which of these things would you find in an Anglo-Saxon village?
a) A forum
b) A theatre
c) Neither a) nor b)

9. Which are the two richest sources of evidence we have about the Saxons?
a) Buildings and artefacts
b) Artefacts and documents
c) Documents and buildings

10. Who was buried in the ship at Sutton Hoo?
a) King Raedwald
b) King Vortigern
c) King Ethelred

I can work independently to answer detailed questions on Anglo-Saxon life.

How did you do?

PHOTOCOPIABLE

The Anglo-Saxons (2)

In this chapter, the children explore further Anglo-Saxon culture, including daily life, childhood, food, art, language, literature and religion. After investigating Anglo-Saxon paganism, they learn how the Anglo-Saxons converted to Christianity. In the final week they construct a timeline of the Anglo-Saxon period, considering what the Anglo-Saxons left behind, and debating which aspect of their legacy is most significant.

Chapter at a glance

Curriculum objective

• Britain's settlement by Anglo-Saxons and Scots.

Week	Lesson	Summary of activities	Expected outcomes
1	1	• Children research daily life in Anglo-Saxon Britain and note differences between daily life then and daily life today. • They express and justify their opinions relating to these differences.	• Can identify differences between daily life in Anglo-Saxon times and daily life today. • Can express and justify their opinions about these differences.
	2	• Children discuss Anglo-Saxon childhood. • They play a board game popular with Anglo-Saxon children.	• Can describe some important features of Anglo-Saxon childhood and distinguish between the lives of boys and girls.
2	1	• Children sort foods into those that the Anglo-Saxons ate and those that they did not eat. • They follow a recipe to make, taste and evaluate an Anglo-Saxon dish.	• Can describe Anglo-Saxon food and express their opinions about it.
	2	• Children examine examples of Anglo-Saxon art, identifying common motifs. • They create their own design in Anglo-Saxon style, and then use this design to create an Anglo-Saxon-style artefact.	• Can create an original design in an Anglo-Saxon style.
3	1	• Children learn the names of some animals in Old English, comparing their present-day form with their original form. • They create a picture dictionary of Old English.	• Can name some modern English words of Anglo-Saxon origin and compare their present-day form with their original form.
	2	• Children investigate the development of Anglo-Saxon writing, writing their names in runes. • They print designs featuring runes.	• Can write their names in Anglo-Saxon runes.
4	1	• Children are introduced to Beowulf. They read part of the story written in modern English. • They act out scenes, and discuss what the story tells us about the Anglo-Saxons.	• Can retell part of the legend of Beowulf and discuss what the story tells us about the Anglo-Saxons.
	2	• Children research an Anglo-Saxon god or goddess and make a poster. • They identify which Anglo-Saxon deities give their names to days of the week.	• Can name the principle deities worshipped by the Anglo-Saxons. • Can explain the link between Anglo-Saxon gods and the days of the week.
5	1	• Children read an account of how Anglo-Saxon England was converted to Christianity. • They retell the story as a TV news report.	• Can describe how the Anglo-Saxons were converted to Christianity.
	2	• Children examine a page from the Lindisfarne Gospels. They learn about the creation of the manuscript and discuss its significance. • They create illuminated lettering in Anglo-Saxon style.	• Can explain the significance of the Lindisfarne Gospels.
6	1	• Children identify significant events in Anglo-Saxon Britain and put them on a timeline.	• Can create a timeline of Anglo-Saxon Britain.
	2	• Children list things the Anglo-Saxons left behind. • They debate which aspect of the Anglo-Saxons' legacy is the most significant.	• Can debate the importance of various aspects of the Anglo-Saxons' legacy.
Assess and review		• To review the half-term's work.	

Expected prior learning

● It is assumed that children have already studied Year 5 Autumn 1: The Anglo Saxons (1).
● Children will need a thorough knowledge of Roman Britain before studying this unit. In the assessment activity at the end of the chapter, children are required to demonstrate their knowledge about the Anglo-Saxons by comparing life in Anglo-Saxon Britain to life in Roman Britain.

Overview of progression

● Children will build on their enquiry skills, using a variety of different methods to research what life was like in Anglo-Saxon Britain. They will respond to written, pictorial and video accounts of Anglo-Saxon life, and learn how various sources, particularly written sources (such as the legend of Beowulf and the Lindisfarne Gospels), have contributed to our historical knowledge of the Anglo-Saxon period.
● Children will develop their ability to draw comparisons, as they consider similarities and differences between daily life in Anglo-Saxon times and daily life today.
● Children will demonstrate their knowledge of the past in different ways, including debate, discussion, design, games, practical activities and written work.

Creative context

● The content of this chapter has strong links with the English curriculum, with children engaging in various activities across the domains of spoken language, reading and writing. These include applying research skills, learning about etymology (word origins), acting out scenes from a story, writing a playscript, and taking part in debates and presentations.
● Children undertake historical research online, which addresses several requirements of the computing curriculum, including using the internet safely, using search engines effectively, and evaluating online content.
● There are links to mathematics, with children exploring game strategy in Week 1 Lesson 2 and symmetry in Week 2 Lesson 2.
● There are links to art and design throughout the chapter. Children draw a design based on Anglo-Saxon motifs, create a model of an Anglo-Saxon style object, and explore printmaking and calligraphy.
● The lessons in Week 5, which explore the conversion of the Anglo-Saxons to Christianity and the significance of the Lindisfarne Gospels, have links to RE.

Background knowledge

● The Anglo-Saxons who came to Britain worshipped a range of gods and goddesses very closely related to those of Norse mythology. Tiw was the god of war and gave his name to Tuesday. Woden was the king of the gods, and gave his name to Wednesday. Thunor was the god of storms, lightning and thunder, and was Woden's son. He gave his name to Thursday. Frige, who was married to Woden, was the goddess of marriage, childbirth, the home, Earth and the harvest. She gave her name to Friday. The other days of the week are named after heavenly bodies (the Sun, the Moon and Saturn) and originate from even earlier times. The modern English words for these days are derived from the Anglo-Saxon translations of their Latin names.
● The Lindisfarne Gospels are a single manuscript containing the gospels of Matthew, Mark, Luke and John, which recount the life and teachings of Jesus Christ. It was written some time between AD680 and 720 at the monastery at Lindisfarne in Northumbria. The Lindisfarne Gospels are significant because they are considered to be one of the greatest masterpieces of Anglo-Saxon art. They also contain the oldest translation of the gospels into English. Unusually for the time, when a manuscript was normally created by a team of people, the Lindisfarne Gospels are believed to be the work of just one person – possibly Bishop Eadfrith, the leader of the monastery. It is estimated the manuscript would have taken at least five years to complete.

Week 1 lesson plans

In this week's lessons children find out more about what life was like for ordinary people in Anglo-Saxon Britain. In Lesson 1 they apply research skills to investigate several aspects of daily life, and compare and contrast them with the same aspects of daily life in Britain today. They express their opinions about these contrasts, and provide evidence to support their claims. In Lesson 2 the children investigate what it was like to be a child in Anglo-Saxon Britain, complete a reading comprehension exercise about Anglo-Saxon childhood, and play a board game played by Anglo-Saxon children.

1: Was daily life in Anglo-Saxon Britain better or worse than daily life in Britain today?

Lesson objectives
● To develop a chronologically secure knowledge and understanding of British, local and world history, establishing clear narratives within and across the periods they study.
● To note connections, contrasts and trends over time.
● To regularly address and sometimes devise historically valid questions about change, cause, similarity and difference, and significance.

Expected outcomes
● All children can relate some facts about daily life in Anglo-Saxon Britain.
● Most children can compare daily life in Anglo-Saxon Britain with daily life in Britain today, say which they think is better, and explain why.
● Some children can make comparisons between daily life in Anglo-Saxon Britain and daily life in Roman Britain.

Resources
Books about the Anglo-Saxons and/or internet access

Introduction
● Introduce this lesson's focus question: *Was daily life in Anglo-Saxon Britain better or worse than daily life in Britain today?*
● Ask: *Based on what you know already about how the Anglo-Saxons lived, do you think daily life in Anglo-Saxon Britain was better or worse than daily life in Britain today? What evidence do you have to support your opinion?*

Whole-class work
● On the board write a few headings relating to aspects of daily life, for example, *Work, Leisure, Health* and *Transport*. Tell the children you want them to research information about these aspects of daily life in Anglo-Saxon times.
● Provide children with the necessary books and/or allow them to use - internet safe - search to find online sources of information.

Group work
● Divide the class into groups for the research work. Ask each group to create a table with two columns, the first column listing facts about daily life in Anglo-Saxon times and the second column listing matching facts about daily life today. The table could be on paper or in electronic format.

Whole-class work
● Ask groups to share what they have found out. For selected facts, perhaps those where the contrast between Anglo-Saxon times and modern times is the greatest, ask the children to say which is better – the historical or modern-day situation – and explain their reasoning.

Differentiation
● Support: you could specify the websites children use to do their research, making sure the text is at an appropriate reading level.
● Challenge: ask some children to compare daily life in Anglo-Saxon Britain with daily life in Roman Britain.

Review
● Ask the children whether their opinion about Anglo-Saxon daily life has changed at all after doing their research in this lesson and if so, how it has changed, and why.

Lesson objective
● To develop a chronologically secure knowledge and understanding of British, local and world history, establishing clear narratives within and across the periods they study.

Expected outcomes
● All children can describe some important features of Anglo-Saxon childhood.
● Most children can describe some important features of Anglo-Saxon childhood and distinguish between the lives of boys and girls.
● Some children can explain the differences in the lives of children at different levels of society.

Resources
Information on Anglo-Saxon childhood; photocopiable page 41 'Taefl: an Anglo-Saxon board game'; coloured counters; chess pieces (optional)

2: What was it like being a child in Anglo-Saxon Britain?

Introduction
● Introduce this lesson's focus question: *What was it like being a child in Anglo-Saxon Britain?*
● If possible, watch and discuss 'Ordinary families in Anglo-Saxon times' from the BBC Primary History website (see *Resources*).

Whole-class work
● Distribute or display information about Anglo-Saxon childhood. Ask: *What differences were there between the lives of boys and girls in Anglo-Saxon times?* (Girls learned housekeeping skills such as weaving, cooking and brewing beer. Boys learned their father's trade, how to fight, and outdoor skills such as farming, fishing and hunting.) *How were toys and games different from those today? How were they the same?* (Anglo-Saxon toys were usually home-made. Many are familiar to children today, including dolls, toy swords and board games.)
● Tell the children that they are going to have a go at playing the popular Anglo-Saxon board game, Taefl.
● Display photocopiable page 41 'Taefl: an Anglo-Saxon board game', and read through the rules of the game together, demonstrating how to play.

Paired work
● Organise the class into pairs, giving each pair a copy of the photocopiable page and coloured counters in three colours. Each pair will need sixteen white counters, eight black counters and a single counter in different colour (or you could give children a chess piece – a king if one is available).
● Give pairs time to play the game using the board on the photocopiable page. (A chessboard cannot be used for the game, as it doesn't have enough squares). If possible, allow enough time for each player to play black at least once.
● If you have time at the end of the game you could discuss game strategies with the class.

> **Differentiation**
> ● Challenge: children to research the differences in the lives of children at different levels of society.

Review
● Give children a quick quiz. For example:
1. True or false? Most Anglo-Saxon children learned to read and write. (Answer: false.)
2. Which of these jobs did both girls and boys do?
a) weave b) fetch water c) hunt wild boar d) cook
(Answer: fetch water.)
3. At what age could an Anglo-Saxon be tried for a crime?
a) 10 b) 12 c) 14 d) 16
(Answer: 10.)
4. What were dolls made of?
a) plastic b) china, c) stone d) wood and rags
(Answer: wood and rags.)
5. Who ran the only schools?
a) the king b) the government c) the church d) thanes
(Answer: the church.)

Week 2 lesson plans

In this week's lessons the children take a closer look at Anglo-Saxon culture. In Lesson 1 they investigate what the Anglo-Saxons ate, and follow recipes to make Anglo-Saxon dishes. They evaluate Anglo-Saxon food in general, and the dishes they make and sample in particular. In Lesson 2 the children apply their knowledge and skills in art and design. They identify some of the features of Anglo-Saxon art, copy Anglo-Saxon motifs, create their own original design in an Anglo-Saxon style, and then use their design to create an Anglo-Saxon style artefact.

Lesson objective
● To develop a chronologically secure knowledge and understanding of British, local and world history, establishing clear narratives within and across the periods they study.

Expected outcomes
● All children can name some foods eaten by the Anglo-Saxons.
● Most children can describe Anglo-Saxon food in general and express their opinions about it.
● Some children can suggest how healthy the typical Anglo-Saxon diet was.

Resources
Photocopiable page 'Anglo-Saxon recipes' from the CD-ROM, or other Anglo-Saxon recipes; cooking equipment and ingredients needed to make the recipe(s)

1: Anglo-Saxon food: delicious or disgusting?

Introduction
● Introduce this lesson's focus question: *Anglo-Saxon food: delicious or disgusting?*
● On the board write the following list of foods: sugar, honey, bread, potatoes, bananas, apples, peas, sweetcorn, eggs, cheese, tomatoes, pineapples, pork, oranges, fish. Ask the children to sort the foods into two groups: foods they think the Anglo-Saxons *did* eat and foods they think the Anglo-Saxons *did not* eat.
● Share the answers to the activity: the Anglo-Saxons did eat: honey, bread, peas, eggs, cheese, pork, fish; they did not eat: sugar, potatoes, bananas, sweetcorn, tomatoes, pineapples and oranges.
● Explain why the Anglo-Saxons did not eat certain foods (for example, because they were unknown to the Anglo-Saxons as they came from another part of the world).
● Ask the children for their initial thoughts on whether Anglo-Saxon food sounds like it was delicious or disgusting.
● Share the Anglo-Saxon recipes from photocopiable page 'Anglo-Saxon recipes' from the CD-ROM with the class and explain that they will be making and then sampling the dishes, so that they can get a better idea of what Anglo-Saxon food tasted like.

Group work
● Allocate time for groups of children to make the dishes in the recipes. You may want to include a teaching assistant for this activity. Be aware of any food allergies or other dietary restrictions, and ensure health and safety guidelines are followed.
● Give the children the opportunity to taste and evaluate the dishes.

Differentiation
● Support: organise the children into mixed-ability groupings for the cooking activity.
● Challenge: children to find out further information about the typical Anglo-Saxon diet and evaluate how healthy it was.

Review
● Ask the children to explain what the Anglo-Saxons ate.
● Ask any children who have evaluated the healthiness of the Anglo-Saxon diet (see *Differentiation*), to share what they have found out and explain their conclusions.
● Revisit the focus question, *Anglo-Saxon food: delicious or disgusting?* and put it to a class vote.

Lesson objective
● To develop a chronologically secure knowledge and understanding of British, local and world history, establishing clear narratives within and across the periods they study.

Expected outcomes
● All children can copy motifs found in Anglo-Saxon art.
● Most children can describe the main features of Anglo-Saxon art.
● Some children can create an original design in an Anglo-Saxon style artefact.

Resources
Images showing examples of Anglo-Saxon art and design including several round forms (such as brooches, shields, plates, bowls); art sketchbooks; art pencils; colouring pencils; erasers; drawing compasses; modelling materials (such as modelling clay, potter's clay, corrugated cardboard); modelling equipment; scissors; double-sided sticky tape or glue (optional)

2: What was Anglo-Saxon art like?

Introduction

● Introduce this lesson's focus question: *What was Anglo-Saxon art like?* Discuss what the term *motif* means in this context: a recurring shape, form or subject.
● Display the images you have collected showing examples of Anglo-Saxon art and design. Ask the children to look for any recurring themes, forms, patterns or colours, and discuss these with a partner. The particular features children identify will depend on the selection of images you have chosen, but Anglo-Saxon art typically has some of the following features: interlacing patterns, abstract geometric design elements, animal shapes, and bright colours.
● Discuss ideas together as a class.

Independent work

● Children will need the images close at hand for the rest of the lesson.
● Ask the children to copy one or more Anglo-Saxon motifs of their choice into their sketchbooks.

Whole-class work

● Draw the children's attention to the round forms in the images, and discuss what objects they might or could be (for example, shield, brooch, pendant, plate or bowl).
● Discuss the types and orders of symmetry used in the round designs.
● Ask the children to create their own design for a round object based on one or more of the Anglo-Saxon motifs in the images.

Independent work

● Give children time to create their own round design in their sketchbooks and colour it in.

Differentiation
● Challenge: children can make the artefact they have designed (such as a brooch or pendant in modelling clay, a plate or bowl in potter's clay, or a shield in corrugated cardboard); the detail of their design could be engraved or built up in layers; in a later session, give the children an opportunity to add colour to their artefacts.

Review

● Ask children to evaluate their own completed artefacts, as well as artefacts made by other members of the class. Criteria for evaluation could include: authenticity of style, originality of design, visual appeal, sturdiness, and attention to detail.

Week 3 lesson plans

This week's lessons have a focus on continuity and change, and contain a strong creative element. In the first lesson the children compare and contrast some modern English words of Anglo-Saxon origin with their original Old English form, and collaborate to create a picture dictionary in order to teach Old English words to younger children. In the second lesson the children investigate the development of Anglo-Saxon writing, learn how to write their names in runes, and create printed designs featuring Anglo-Saxon runes.

1: Which Anglo-Saxon words have made it into modern English?

Introduction

● Introduce this lesson's focus question: *Which Anglo-Saxon words have made it into modern English?* Explain that *Old English* is the name we use for the language spoken by the Anglo-Saxons.

Whole-class work

● Give the children photocopiable page 'Old English word list' from the CD-ROM. Discuss similarities and differences between the Old English and modern English forms of the words.
● Tell the children they are going to work together to create a picture dictionary of Old English words and then use it to teach some Old English words to a class of children in Key Stage 1. Explain the form the picture dictionary will take (for example, paper or digital), or let the children decide.

Paired work

● Ask the children to work in pairs to choose words from the photocopiable page to include in the picture dictionary, creating a separate illustrated dictionary page for each word. Explain that you do not want any pages duplicated, so children will need to devise a system for keeping track of which words are already covered.

Differentiation
● Support: pair children with a more confident partner.
● Challenge: ask children to learn more about the pronunciation of Old English, to practise saying each word, and to memorise it.

Review

● Ask: *In what way is the Old English word like the modern English word? In what way is it different?*

Lesson objectives
● To develop a chronologically secure knowledge and understanding of British, local and world history, establishing clear narratives within and across the periods they study.
● To note connections, contrasts and trends over time.
● To regularly address and sometimes devise historically valid questions about change, cause, similarity and difference, and significance.

Expected outcomes
● All children can name some modern English words of Anglo-Saxon origin.
● Most children can name some modern English words of Anglo-Saxon origin and compare their present-day form with their original form.
● Some children can also memorise some of the Old English words.

Resources
Photocopiable page 'Old English word list' from the CD-ROM

Lesson objectives
● To develop a chronologically secure knowledge and understanding of British, local and world history, establishing clear narratives within and across the periods they study.
● To note connections, contrasts and trends over time.

Expected outcomes
● All children can identify runes used by the early Anglo-Saxons.
● Most children can write their names in Anglo-Saxon runes.
● Some children can read and interpret Anglo-Saxon runes.

Resources
Media resource 'Anglo-Saxon documents and artefacts displaying writing' on the CD-ROM; photocopiable page 42 'Anglo-Saxon runes'; paper and pencils; print making materials and equipment (such as, paper, printing inks, ink trays, rollers, polystyrene printing tiles, tile-scoring implements, and drying racks); tracing paper

2: How did the Anglo-Saxons write?

Introduction
● Introduce this lesson's focus question: *How did the Anglo-Saxons write?*
● Display the media resource 'Anglo-Saxon documents and artefacts displaying writing' on the CD-ROM. Ask: *What do you notice about the writing?* Give the children a few minutes to discuss this with a partner.
● Encourage the children to share what they have discussed. Bring out the fact that these images don't show just one type of writing.

Whole-class work
● Give a very brief overview of the development of the written forms of Old English. Explain that the language was first written using a type of writing called runes. Runes have angular letter shapes and are well suited to carving in stone. From around the 9th century onwards runes were replaced by a version of the Latin alphabet, introduced by Christian missionaries (who we will learn about in Week 5). This Latin script went through several different forms over the course of the next couple of centuries.
● Display photocopiable page 42 'Anglo-Saxon runes'. Explain that the runes were named after everyday words in Old English and that each rune represents a sound from the word (often, but not always the initial letter). For example, the rune that looks like a capital M is called *eh*, which means 'horse'. The rune represents the initial sound of *eh* (e). The rune that looks like a straight-sided, tipped-over S is called *sigel*, which means 'sun'. The rune represents the initial sound of *sigel* (s).
● Work together to write a name phonetically using the runes.

Independent work
● Give the children time to practise writing their names in runes.
● Show the children how to carve their name in runes into a printing block (they will need to do this back to front, so they might want to write their name the right way round on a piece of tracing paper and then turn it over).
● Give the children an opportunity to use their printing block to create pieces of printed artwork (for example, multiple greetings cards or bookmarks in different colours, or wrapping paper with a repeating pattern).

Review
● Give the children an informal test by asking them to write their name in runes without looking at a visual reference.

Week 4 lesson plans

In this week's lessons the children continue to explore Anglo-Saxon culture. In the first lesson they are introduced to the epic poem *Beowulf*, listening to the prologue in the original Old English, reading a retelling in modern English of part of the legend, and acting out scenes from the story. They consider what *Beowulf* tells us about the Anglo-Saxons. In the second lesson the children find and record information about some of the Anglo-Saxon deities, create a poster featuring each deity, and discover which Anglo-Saxon deities give their names to modern days of the week.

1: The legend of Beowulf: what does it tell us about the Anglo-Saxons?

Lesson objectives
● To develop a chronologically secure knowledge and understanding of British, local and world history, establishing clear narratives within and across the periods they study.
● To regularly address and sometimes devise historically valid questions about change, cause, similarity and difference, and significance.
● To understand how our knowledge of the past is constructed from a range of sources.

Expected outcomes
● All children can explain what Beowulf is.
● Most children can retell the legend of Beowulf and discuss what the story tells us about the Anglo-Saxons.
● Some children can write a playscript retelling the legend of Beowulf.

Resources
A version of the Beowulf prologue, such as photocopiable page 'The prologue from *Beowulf*' from the CD-ROM (for the teacher to perform) or a video clip showing the prologue from in the original Old English; photocopiable page 'Beowulf and Grendel' from the CD-ROM

Introduction
● Introduce this lesson's focus question: *The legend of Beowulf: what does it tell us about the Anglo-Saxons?*
● Explain that Beowulf is an epic poem, more than three thousand lines long, written in Old English. The poem, which is set in Scandinavia, the lands of the poet's ancestors, tells the story of three battles fought by the legendary hero Beowulf: the first against the monster Grendel, the second against Grendel's mother, and the third against a dragon.

Whole-class work
● Explain that, as most people in Anglo-Saxon times couldn't read or write, poems were not read, but performed. Draw parallels with the epic poetry of Greece.
● If possible, show a video clip of the prologue of *Beowulf* performed in the original language. Ask the children if any Old English words sounded similar to modern English words (for example, *him, that, God, send, Beowulf, king*). If watching a video clip is not possible, perform a dramatic reading of photocopiable page 'The prologue from *Beowulf*' from the CD-ROM.

Group work
● Display a copy of photocopiable page 'Beowulf and Grendel' from the CD-ROM, which summarises part of the story of Beowulf in modern English.
● Work with the class to divide the story into scenes. Divide the class into the same number of groups as scenes, assigning one scene to each group.
● Ask each group to prepare a dramatisation to tell their part of the story to the rest of the class at the end of the lesson.

Whole-class work
● Ask groups to act out their scenes from the story and give each other feedback about the effectiveness of their dramatisations.

> **Differentiation**
> ● Challenge: ask children to write a playscript telling part of the legend of Beowulf. The playscripts could be kept for use in an end of term assembly on the Anglo-Saxons.

Review
● Ask: *What does the legend of Beowulf tell us about the Anglo-Saxons?* (They wrote poems that told stories, they enjoyed scary stories, their Scandinavian heritage was important to them, and they valued the ability to fight and outwit opponents, because their heroes were warriors.)

2: What gods did the Anglo-Saxons worship?

Introduction

Lesson objectives
- To develop a chronologically secure knowledge and understanding of British, local and world history, establishing clear narratives within and across the periods they study.
- To regularly address and sometimes devise historically valid questions about change, cause, similarity and difference, and significance.
- To note connections, contrasts and trends over time.

Expected outcomes
- All children can say which days of the week are named after Anglo-Saxon gods and goddesses.
- Most children can name and describe the principle gods and goddesses worshipped by the Anglo-Saxons. They can explain the link between Anglo-Saxon gods and the modern days of the week.
- Some children can describe some of the religious practices and festivals of the Anglo-Saxons.

Resources
Information about Anglo-Saxon gods (try www.earlybritishkingdoms.com and follow the links to Kids – Religion – Saxon gods), particularly Woden, Thunor, Tiw, Frige and Eostre; poster paper'; coloured pens

- Introduce this lesson's focus question: *What gods did the Anglo-Saxons worship?*
- Explain that the Anglo-Saxons who came to Britain were pagan (they had many gods, like the Greeks and the Romans).
- Tell the children that some days of the week are named after Anglo-Saxon gods. Ask them if they know which days these are, and who each day is named after. Make a note of any suggestions, so that children can check them later.

Whole-class work

- Organise the class into five mixed-ability groups. Assign each group one of five Anglo-Saxon gods: Woden, Thunor, Tiw, Frige or Eostre.
- Ask the children to research information about their given god, and then to use the information to create a poster about their god.
- Discuss and note the information the children could include on their poster, for example, Name, God or goddess of _____, Associated with _____, Sacred animal(s) and/or objects, Special abilities, Special day/month, Other information.
  - *Tiw was the god of war and gave his name to Tuesday.*
  - *Woden was the king of the gods, and gave his name to Wednesday.*
  - *Thunor was the god of storms, lightning and thunder, and was Woden's son. He gave his name to Thursday.*
  - *Frige, who was married to Woden, was the goddess of marriage, childbirth, the home, Earth and the harvest. She gave her name to Friday.*
  - *The other days of the week are named after heavenly bodies (the Sun, the Moon and Saturn) and originate from even earlier times.*

Group work

- Give the children time to research the information they need, and to start work on designing and creating their posters.
- At the end of the lesson, ask a representative from each group to share the information they have collected with the rest of the class. Establish the correct answers relating to the names of the days of the week.

Differentiation
- Support: make sure the groups are mixed-ability.
- Challenge: set some children to research Anglo-Saxons' religious practices and festivals.

Review

- Ask: *Does anything you have found out about this god or goddess remind you of any modern Christian practices or festivals?*

Week 5 lesson plans

In this week's lessons the focus is on religion. In the first lesson the children study a text relating the series of events that led to Anglo-Saxon Britain becoming a Christian nation. They then retell this narrative in the form of a script for a television report. In the second lesson the children investigate the significance of the Lindisfarne Gospels. They look at a page from the manuscript, read a cartoon strip describing how it was created, and create their own illuminated lettering.

1: How were the Anglo-Saxons converted to Christianity?

Introduction
- Begin the class in newsreader persona, giving a news report of an Anglo-Saxon story from your desk. Alternatively, show the video clip 'The Anglo-Saxon Report' (see *Resources*).
- Introduce this lesson's focus question: *How were the Anglo-Saxons converted to Christianity?*
- Tell the children they will be reading a text about how the Anglo-Saxons were converted to Christianity and then writing a script for presenting the information in the text as a television news report.

Whole-class work
- Display and/or distribute printouts of photocopiable page 'The conversion of the Anglo-Saxons to Christianity' from the CD-ROM, giving children time to read through the text.
- Discuss the text and ask questions to test children's comprehension.
- Revise the main features of a playscript, and discuss any specific requirements for the script they are about to write.

Paired work or Independent work
- Working in pairs or independently, ask the children to write a script for a television news report on how the Anglo-Saxons were converted to Christianity. Explain that the best scripts will be chosen to be 'produced'.

Group work
- Once the best scripts have been chosen (by you or as voted on by the children), organise the class into groups to prepare for and rehearse the television-style reports.
- Arrange a time for groups to present their reports to the rest of the class. You could also arrange for the reports to be filmed (ideally by children).

Differentiation
- Support: children could work in a small group with an adult to help when writing their scripts.

Review
- Ask the children to provide each other with feedback on their reports.
- You could upload the video of the most successful report to the school learning site or blog.

Lesson objectives
- To develop a chronologically secure knowledge and understanding of British, local and world history, establishing clear narratives within and across the periods they study.
- To develop the appropriate use of historical terms.
- To regularly address and sometimes devise historically valid questions about change, cause, similarity and difference, and significance.

Expected outcomes
- All children know that the Anglo-Saxons were converted to Christianity.
- Most children can describe how the Anglo-Saxons were converted to Christianity.
- Some children can relate specific events in the Anglo-Saxons' conversion to Christianity.

Resources
Video clip *Horrible Histories* 'The Anglo-Saxon Report' (source online); photocopiable page 'The conversion of the Anglo-Saxons to Christianity' from the CD-ROM; filming recording equipment (optional)

Lesson objectives
● To develop a chronologically secure knowledge and understanding of British, local and world history, establishing clear narratives within and across the periods they study.
● To regularly address and sometimes devise historically valid questions about change, cause, similarity and difference, and significance.

Expected outcomes
● All children can explain what the Lindisfarne Gospels are.
● Most children can explain the significance of the Lindisfarne Gospels.
● Some children can describe the various stages that would have been involved in creating the Lindisfarne Gospels.

Resources
A display page from the Lindisfarne Gospels, such as from The British Library website; photocopiable page 43 'Illuminated letters'; art pencils; erasers; crayons or pencils in various colours, including gold; black display paper or book-making paper (optional)

2: Why are the Lindisfarne Gospels so important?

Introduction
● Introduce this lesson's focus question: *Why are the Lindisfarne Gospels so important?*
● Ask: *What do you already know about Lindisfarne? What is a gospel? What do you think the Lindisfarne Gospels might be?*
● Display the page from the Lindisfarne Gospels sourced online from the British Library website. Discuss its features and ask the children how they think the Lindisfarne Gospels might have been made. (Key features from the first page of St Matthew's gospel are: illuminated letters, most notably the large initial letters decorated with interlacing and spiral patterns influenced by Anglo-Saxon jewellery and enamel work; decoration around the letters in the form of patterned backgrounds and an ornate border; inks in various colours have been used, as well as text in various styles and sizes.)
● Introduce the terms *manuscript* for a book written by hand and *illuminated manuscript* for a manuscript that is decorated (usually using gold leaf and/or coloured inks).

Whole-class work
● Briefly tell the story of the Lindisfarne Gospels (see *Background knowledge* on page 27) and explain why they were significant at the time and why they are still significant today.
● Further information is available via the British Library online pages.

Independent work
● Give out copies of photocopiable page 43 'Illuminated letters', and the art materials listed in *Resources*.
● Ask the children to use the photocopiable page to help them create their own illuminated lettering in the style of the Lindisfarne Gospels.
● When the children have finished their illuminated lettering they could mount it on black paper and create a display, or stick it into a handmade book to create their own Anglo-Saxon 'manuscript'.

Differentiation
● Challenge: children could find out more about the various stages of creating a manuscript in Anglo-Saxon times, and write a report to add to the class display or 'manuscript'.

Review
● Ask: *Why do you think someone would have been willing to give up years of their life to work on the manuscript?* (To show their religious devotion.) *Why was the manuscript so heavily decorated?* (To show how important the text was.) *What do you think the finished book would have been used for?* (It would have been used as an object of veneration; a way of honouring 'the word of God'.)

Week 6 lesson plans

During this final week of the topic the children have an opportunity to look back at what they have learned over the course of the past two chapters. In Lesson 1 the children research dates of events to create a timeline of Anglo-Saxon Britain, and in Lesson 2 they consider the legacy of the Anglo-Saxons, and take part in a debate to decide which of the things they left behind is the most significant.

1: What does a timeline of Anglo-Saxon Britain look like?

Lesson objectives
● To develop a chronologically secure knowledge and understanding of British, local and world history, establishing clear narratives within and across the periods they study.
● To note connections, contrasts and trends over time and develop the appropriate use of historical terms.

Expected outcomes
● All children can use research skills to find the dates of key events in Anglo-Saxon Britain.
● Most children can create a timeline of Anglo-Saxon Britain.
● Some children can write summaries of timeline events.

Resources
Interactive activity 'Timeline maker' on the CD-ROM (and group access); information bank on the Anglo-Saxons, such as books and/or internet access

Introduction
● Introduce this lesson's focus question: *What does a timeline of Anglo-Saxon Britain look like?*
● Working in pairs, ask the children to list all the events they have learned about over the course of Chapters 1 and 2. Create a collated list of events on the board.
● Ask the children to order the events from earliest to latest; but do not give answers yet.

Group work
● In each group assign one individual or pair to work with the interactive activity 'Timeline maker' on the CD-ROM to create a timeline of Anglo-Saxon Britain.
● Ask the rest of the group to work in pairs or individually to write a sentence or two describing an event from the list on the board, use books and/or the internet to find out the date of the event, and then pass on their notes to the pair using the timeline tool.
● Once a group has entered all the listed events on their timeline, ask them to find more events from the Anglo-Saxon period (AD410 to 1066) to add to the timeline.
● Encourage group members to swap roles at intervals so that everyone gets a chance to use the timeliner maker.

Whole-class work
● Ask the children to share the dates they have found out for the events listed on the board, and check to see if their original order was correct.
● Ask the children to report back on any additional events they added to the timeline. Discuss the significance of the first Viking raids in 793, and the fact that they will be looking at events from then and up to 1066 in more detail next year, in a study of the Vikings.

Differentiation
● Support: mixed-ability groupings may be useful for the group work, with children paired with a more confident partner.
● Challenge: ask some children to write summaries of timeline events and add these to the timeline.

Review
● Review the timelines and choose the most complete one to print out for display and/or for use in Year 6, during the chapters on the Vikings.

Lesson objectives
● To develop a chronologically secure knowledge and understanding of British, local and world history, establishing clear narratives within and across the periods they study.
● To note connections, contrasts and trends over time and develop the appropriate use of historical terms.
● To regularly address and sometimes devise historically valid questions about change, cause, similarity and difference, and significance.
● To construct informed responses that involve thoughtful selection and organisation of relevant historical information.

Expected outcomes
● All children can explain what the Anglo-Saxons left behind.
● Most children can debate the importance of various aspects of the Anglo-Saxons' legacy.
● Some children can put forward a compelling argument in support of their point of view.

Resources
Teaching assistants

2: Of all the things the Anglo-Saxons left behind, which is the most significant?

Introduction
● Introduce this lesson's focus question: *Of all the things the Anglo-Saxons left behind, which is the most significant?*
● Ask the children, working in pairs, to brainstorm categories of things under the heading *Things the Anglo-Saxons left behind.* Add anything they have left out (for example, artefacts, buildings, religious practices, place names, names for the days of the week, language in general).
● Discuss the meaning of the word *significant.*
● Ask pairs to discuss which of the things the Anglo-Saxons left behind they think is the most significant, and why.

Group work
● Divide the class into groups, according to which aspect of the Anglo-Saxons' legacy they think is the most significant. If possible, assign an adult to each group.
● The adult working with each group should help the group to brainstorm arguments to support their position. The adult then asks the group to divide up into smaller groups, with each group preparing a short presentation based on one of the arguments.

Whole-class work
● Conduct a class debate, with each group presenting their arguments.
● Explain to the children how you expect them to behave during the debate, perhaps displaying a list of rules, or working together to draw one up.
● Choose a moderator to lead the debate. You could do this yourself, or select a child for the role. The moderator needs to be able to speak clearly, communicate assertively but respectfully, keep everyone on task and ensure all participants get a fair say.
● The moderator introduces the topic of debate, and invites representatives from each side of the issue to present their arguments, alternating between the two sides.
● Once all the prepared arguments have been presented, give teams the opportunity to prepare and present rebuttals in response to the opposing side's arguments.

Differentiation
● Support: children may benefit from working with an adult.

Review
● Complete the debate by asking children to vote for the point of view that was supported by the most compelling arguments. Then ask: *Which way did you vote? Did you find the decision about which way to vote difficult to make? Why? Why not?*

Curriculum objective
● To regularly address and sometimes devise historically valid questions about change, cause, similarity and difference, and significance.

Resources
Interactive activity 'Anglo-Saxons quiz' on the CD-ROM; computer access; example of a mind map; video recording equipment (optional)

Anglo-Saxon mind map

Revise

● Introduce the interactive activity 'Anglo-Saxons quiz' on the CD-ROM.
● Organise the class into pairs, giving each pair computer access to the quiz, and give children time to answer the questions.
● Alternatively, complete the quiz questions as a whole class, using the whiteboard.

Assess

● Revise the term *mind map* and show an example. Ideally, the mind map should be one drawn by members of the class.
● Tell the children they will be creating a mind map. On the centre of the board write: *How was life in Anglo-Saxon Britain different from life in Roman Britain?*
● Give the children a set length of time (such as 20 minutes) to complete the task. Emphasise the importance of working independently for this task. Encourage the children to work fast and to include as much breadth *and* depth of information as they can.
● Ask any children who struggle with writing to write the main headings only (go for breadth rather than depth). They could communicate details to you verbally later.

Further practice

● Ask children to incorporate what they have learned about the Anglo-Saxons into one of the following:
    ● a short video presentation to upload to the school learning platform
    ● an assembly for the rest of the school, parents and carers.

Curriculum objective
● To develop the appropriate use of historical terms.

Resources
Multiple sets of historical term cards; scissors

Anglo-Saxon terminology

Revise

● Organise the class into groups, giving each group a set of historical term cards. Each card should feature an historical term from the Anglo-Saxons study (for example, invader, settler, thane, churl, freeman, slave, kingdom, Northumbria, Mercia, East Anglia, Essex, Kent, Sussex, Wessex, wergild, ordeal, thatch, wattle and daub, oral testimony, artefact, Taefl, runes, pagan, conversion, missionary, manuscript, illuminated, and legacy)
● Ask each group of children to work together collaboratively to sort the cards into groups.
● Discuss with children the criteria they have used for sorting the cards.

Assess

● Introduce the assessment task: choose four of the words from the cards. Each word must belong to a different group from the sorting activity. For each word write a definition and then use the word in context, in a sentence or short paragraph.
● Demonstrate the task, choosing one of the words from the cards. Encourage children to help you write the definition and suggest a sentence or short paragraph in which to put the word in context. Tell children this word is now 'off limits'.
● Give the children a set length of time (such as 20 minutes) to complete the task. Emphasise the importance of working independently.

Further practice

● Challenge children to create a card game that involves matching historical terms with their definitions.

Name: _____   Date: _____

Taefl: an Anglo-Saxon board game

■ Board games were a popular Anglo-Saxon pastime. The diagram below shows the board layout for a two-player game called Taefl.

How to play

I. Set the white counters, black counters and the king on the Taefl board as indicated. The king is the main black counter. (You could use a chess piece for the king.)

2. Players should take it in turns to move one of their pieces backwards, forwards or sideways. Counters cannot be moved diagonally. A piece can be moved any number of squares but it has to stop if another counter blocks the way.

3. Opponent's counters may be removed if they become surrounded by your own counters, for example:

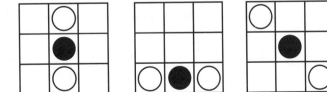

4. Black wins the game if the king reaches Home ('H' squares in the four corners). White wins the game by taking the king, surrounding the black counters or by blocking the way to all four Home corners. White is NOT ALLOWED in the shaded squares.

SCHOLASTIC www.scholastic.co.uk   **PHOTOCOPIABLE**   100 HISTORY LESSONS ■ 41

Anglo-Saxon runes

■ Write your name phonetically using the runes.

f	u	th	o	r
k	g	w	h	n
i	j	p	x	s
t	b	e	m	l
ng	d	a	y	ea
ia	k	g	st	

Name: _____ Date: _____

Illuminated letters

■ Below are some examples of the decorated letters found on Anglo-Saxon manuscripts. Can you tell what letters they are?

1.  2.  3.

4.  5.  6.

■ Make up your own letters in the space below. You could use the initials of your name.

The Maya (1)

This chapter is the first half of a study on the ancient Maya civilisation of Central America. Children begin by locating the Maya civilisation on a map and a timeline. They examine various primary sources left behind by the Maya, including buildings and monuments. They investigate social order and the system of justice in the Maya civilisation and learn about Maya homes and cities. Finally, they explore two aspects of Maya culture: the games they played and the stories they told.

Chapter at a glance

Curriculum objectives

• Examine a non-European society that provides contrasts with British history: Mayan civilisation *circa* AD900.

Week	Lesson	Summary of activities	Expected outcomes
1	1	• Children read about the ancient Maya civilisation. • They use the information to locate and record the civilisation on a map and on a timeline.	• Can locate the ancient Maya civilisation on a map of the world and on a timeline.
	2	• Children examine examples of primary sources left behind by the Maya. • They categorise the sources, and suggest what each source might be evidence of. • They write a detailed description and interpretation of one of the sources.	• Can describe some of the evidence left behind by the ancient Maya civilisation.
2	1	• Children read a text about the palace at Palenque. • They use internet research skills to find out more about it. • They discuss what the palace tells us about ancient Maya civilisation.	• Can explain what the palace at Palenque tells us about the ancient Maya civilisation.
	2	• Children compare Maya pyramids with Egyptian pyramids. • They build a model of a Maya pyramid.	• Can draw comparisons between the Maya pyramids and the pyramids of ancient Egypt.
3	1	• Children investigate examples of Maya *stelae*. • They design and make a *stela*-style poster that gives pictorial information about the locality, the school and the class.	• Can explain what *stelae* are and explain some of the things they tell us about the ancient Maya.
	2	• Children examine and discuss illustrations showing ancient Maya clothing. • They design a royal costume for King Pacal.	• Can design authentic-looking Maya costumes.
4	1	• Children compare and contrast an ancient Maya home with an Anglo-Saxon home. • They discuss which they would rather live in and explain why.	• Can draw comparisons between ancient Maya homes and Anglo-Saxon homes. • Can express and justify their preferences.
	2	• Children compare the Maya city of Chichén Itzà with ancient Rome. • They write a recount of a trip to Chichén Itzà from the point of view of an ancient Roman.	• Can draw comparisons between Chichén Itzà and ancient Rome. • Can suggest what an ancient Roman might have thought of Chichén Itzà.
5	1	• Children read about Maya social structure and play a game based on it.	• Can describe how the Maya were ruled.
	2	• Children read about Maya laws and compare them with laws in Anglo-Saxon Britain. • They devise a game based on Maya laws.	• Can describe some ancient Maya laws, and compare and contrast them with laws in Anglo-Saxon Britain.
6	1	• Children explore the Mesoamerican Ballgame. • They devise and play their own ball games.	• Can describe the ball game played by the Maya. • Can devise and play a similar ball game.
	2	• Children explore the Maya creation myth, then retell the story in the form of a cartoon strip.	• Can retell the Maya creation myth.
Assess and review		• To review the half-term's work.	

Expected prior learning

- Children do not need any prior knowledge of the ancient Maya civilisation.
- It is assumed that children have studied Anglo-Saxon Britain and are also familiar with the ancient city of Rome and with ancient Egypt.

Overview of progression

- Children will build on their enquiry skills, using a variety of methods to research what life was like in the ancient Maya civilisation. They will respond to written, pictorial and video accounts of Maya life, and learn how various sources, particularly architectural sources (such as the palace at Palenque and various pyramids and *stelae*), have contributed to our historical knowledge of the ancient Maya civilisation.
- Children will also develop their ability to draw comparisons, as they consider similarities and differences between the Maya and the Anglo-Saxons, Romans and Egyptians.
- Children will demonstrate their knowledge of the past in different ways, including discussions, models, costumes, posters and games, and writing texts.

Creative context

- The content of this chapter has strong links with the English curriculum. Children take part in discussions, apply research skills, answer comprehension questions, write a detailed description and interpretation of an historical source, and write a recount.
- Children undertake historical research online, which addresses several requirements of the computing curriculum, including using the internet safely, using search engines effectively, and evaluating online content.
- Several activities in this chapter have links to design and technology: comparing the design of Maya and Egyptian pyramids, building a model of a Maya pyramid, designing a costume for King Pacal, and designing a board or card game based on Maya laws.
- There are links to geography, with children locating the ancient Maya civilisation on a globe or a map of the world and, optionally, also on a map of central America.
- Two activities in this chapter have links to art and design: creating a *stela*-style poster, and drawing a cartoon strip to retell the Popol Vuh story.
- One activity has links to PE: the children devise and play a game based on the Mesoamerican Ballgame.

Background knowledge

- The Maya were an ancient civilisation of Mesoamerica (a region covering all of Central America and parts of North and South America). The Maya are unique among pre-Columbian Native American cultures in having the only known fully developed written language. They are also known for their art and architecture, for their knowledge of mathematics and astronomy, and their sophisticated system of calendars.
- At its height, during the Classic Period between 250AD and 900AD, the Maya civilisation extended across a huge area covering the modern-day countries of Guatemala and Belize, and parts of Mexico, El Salvador and Honduras.
- The Maya were not a single people living in a single nation – they were a group of peoples whose cultures were very closely related. They spoke a range of languages and lived in many separate city-states.
- The Maya civilisation underwent a major collapse at the end of the Classic Period, but Maya culture survived. The Maya people also survived the arrival of the conquistadors and Spanish colonisation. Today, Maya people form a sizeable proportion of the population in many countries in Mesoamerica, and millions of people still speak a Mayan language.

Week I lesson plans

Lesson I begins by providing an opportunity to assess children's prior knowledge about the ancient Maya civilisation. The children then read an introductory text about the Maya and use the information it contains to mark the position of the Maya on a map of the world and on a timeline. During the lesson they collect questions about the Maya, and choose one of these to research and answer for homework. In Lesson 2 the children examine and interpret examples of primary sources left behind by the Maya, writing a detailed description and interpretation of one of them.

I: The Maya: when and where did they live?

Lesson objective
● To develop a chronologically secure knowledge and understanding of British, local and world history, establishing clear narratives within and across the periods they study.

Expected outcomes
● All children can describe when and where the ancient Maya civilisation took place.
● Most children can locate the ancient Maya civilisation on a map of the world and on a timeline.
● Some children can use what they know about where and when the ancient Maya civilisation took place to suggest features they would expect the civilisation to have.

Resources
Outline maps of the world; blank timelines; photocopiable page 'Who were the Maya? from the CD-ROM; globes, atlases or online map of the world; coloured pencils or pens

Introduction
● Explain to the children that this term they will be studying the ancient civilisation of the Maya.
● Introduce this lesson's focus question: *The Maya: when and where did they live?*
● Organise the class into groups, giving each group a copy of an outline world map and a blank timeline. Ask children to mark the Maya civilisation on the world map and on the timeline.
● Ask groups to share their ideas about when and where the Maya civilisation took place. Do not correct any misconceptions at this stage.

Paired work
● Organise the class into pairs, giving each pair access to a globe, atlas or online map of the world, a copy of photocopiable page 'Who were the Maya?' from the CD-ROM (or display this at the front of the class), a fresh outline map of the world, and a fresh timeline. Ask pairs to read the text on the photocopiable page and use the information it provides to mark the Maya civilisation on the map and the timeline.
● Ask any pairs who finish their map and timeline to write three questions about the Maya they would like to find out the answers to.

Whole-class work
● Review the correct answers to the focus question.
● Ask any children who have written about features they would expect the ancient Maya civilisation to have (see *Differentiation*) to share their ideas, explaining their reasoning.
● Ask any pairs who wrote questions about the Maya to share them. Write selected questions on the board.
● Ask children to choose one of the questions on the board to research for homework.

Differentiation
● Challenge: ask some children to use what they know about where and when the ancient Maya civilisation took place to write down features they would expect the ancient Maya civilisation to have.

Review
● Compare the completed timelines and maps from the paired work with those produced in the introductory activity. Ask: *What have you learned about the Maya during this lesson?*

2: What evidence have the Maya left behind?

Introduction
● Introduce this lesson's focus question: *What evidence have the Maya left behind?*
● On the board write two headings: *Probably* and *Probably not*. Ask the children, working in pairs, to brainstorm all the types of historical evidence they can think of, categorising each type of evidence as either *Probably* (left behind by the Maya) or *Probably not* (left behind by the Maya).
● Sources of historical evidence can include: documents (e.g. books, letters, diaries, stories and poems), buildings, human and animal remains, made objects (historians call these artefacts), images (paintings, drawings and photographs), and oral testimony (eyewitness accounts). Children should realise that, because the Maya lived such a long time ago, there are some types of evidence they probably did not leave behind (such as photographs and oral testimony).
● Discuss children's ideas.

Group work
● Organise the class into groups, giving each group access to the media resource '*Photos of evidence left behind by the Maya*' on the CD-ROM.
● Ask groups to discuss and make a note of what they think each pictured object might be.

Whole-class work
● Discuss children's ideas about what each object might be and then disclose the correct answers.
  ● Calendar round from the Maya period
  ● Maya temple at Copan
  ● Pre-Columbian painted vase
  ● Pyramid known as El Castillo has become the towering icon of Chichén Itzà
  ● Piece of jewellery from the Maya period
  ● Chak Mul sacrificial statue of the Mayan at Chichén Itzà
● Choose one of the objects to study more closely. Firstly, work together with the children to build up a detailed verbal description of it.
● Next, help the children to interpret the object by asking some or all of the following questions:
  ● *Who might have built/made it?*
  ● *What was it used for?*
  ● *Who might have used it?*
  ● *How was it used?*
  ● *When was it used?*
  ● *Was it a special object/place or an everyday one?*
  ● *How might it have looked different when it was new?*
● Finally, ask: *What does it tell us about the Maya?*

Independent work
● Ask children to choose one of the objects in the photos, go through the same process of describing and interpreting as you went through as a class, and record their description and interpretation in writing. You may want to give children a prompt sheet to help them, listing the questions above.

Review
● Ask several children who wrote about the same piece of evidence to share their interpretations. Compare and contrast the various interpretations, asking the rest of the class to give their opinions. Ask: *Do you think all historians agree about the past? Why not?*

Week 2 lesson plans

In this week's lessons the children look at some examples of Maya architecture. In Lesson 1 they investigate the palace and other buildings at Palenque, and suggest what they tell us about the ancient Maya. In Lesson 2 the children research specific examples of Maya pyramids, compare and contrast them with the pyramids of ancient Egypt, and build a model of a Maya pyramid. This lesson may take several sessions to complete, and could possibly be linked with work in design and technology.

1: What can we learn about the Maya from the palace at Palenque?

Introduction

● Introduce this lesson's focus question: *What can we learn about the Maya from the palace at Palenque?*
● Display photocopiable page 'The palace of Palenque' from the CD-ROM, drawing attention to the map showing the location of Palenque. Explain that Palenque is an important Maya site because it contains some of the finest examples we have of Maya architecture, sculpture and carving.

Paired work

● Organise children into pairs, giving each pair a copy of the photocopiable page. Give children time to read the text, and then discuss it together as a class.
● Ensure each pair has access to the internet. Ask children to find out more about the city of Palenque, and make notes about what they discover. You could give children a list of topics to choose from, such as the Temple of Inscriptions, the Temple of the Cross, the Temple of the Sun, and the Temple of the Foliated Cross. Some children could find out more about Pacal the Great.

Whole-class work

● Ask children to describe one thing they have found out about Palenque, and explain what this tells us about the ancient Maya civilisation.
● Revise the features of a report. (You could use a page from a non-fiction book about the Maya as an example.)

Independent work

● Ask individuals to write a report based on the notes they took. They will need to complete this for homework or in subsequent sessions.

Differentiation
● Support: establish mixed-ability pairings, and during independent work provide children with appropriate scaffolding and/or adult support.
● Challenge: ask children to explain what the relationship between Palenque's palace and the rest of the city tells us about the ancient Maya civilisation.

Review

● Ask the children to review each other's reports (whether or not they are finished), and to give constructive feedback on how to improve them. You could ask children to use the 'two stars and a wish' format.

Lesson objectives
● To develop a chronologically secure knowledge and understanding of British, local and world history, establishing clear narratives within and across the periods they study.
● To construct informed responses that involve thoughtful selection and organisation of relevant historical information.
● To understand how our knowledge of the past is constructed from a range of sources.

Expected outcomes
● All children can describe some of the features of the palace at Palenque.
● Most children can explain the relationship between Palenque's palace and the rest of the city.
● Some children can explain what the relationship between Palenque's palace and the rest of the city tells us about the ancient Maya civilisation.

Resources
Photocopiable page 'The palace of Palenque' from the CD-ROM; computers with internet access (for pairs); one or more non-fiction books about the ancient Maya; teaching assistant (optional)

2: Are the Maya pyramids like the Egyptian pyramids?

Lesson objectives
● To develop a chronologically secure knowledge and understanding of British, local and world history, establishing clear narratives within and across the periods they study.
● To understand how our knowledge of the past is constructed from a range of sources.

Expected outcomes
● All children can describe a typical Maya pyramid.
● Most children can draw comparisons between the Maya pyramids and the pyramids of ancient Egypt.
● Some children can build a scale model of a Maya pyramid.

Resources
Information on Mesoamerican pyramids (shape, building, materials, locations, purpose), from books and/or the internet; model-building materials and equipment (such as corrugated card, clay, building blocks, wire mesh and plaster bandage, papier mâché)

Introduction

● Introduce this lesson's focus question: *Are the Maya pyramids like the Egyptian pyramids?*
● Write the following headings on the board: *Shape, Building materials, Purpose,* and *Other features.* Give groups a few minutes to list as much as they can remember about the Egyptian pyramids under each of these headings. (Shape: square-based true pyramids; Building materials: mainly limestone; Purpose: Tombs; Other features: the four walls at the base of each pyramid are aligned to the four points of the compass; the Great Pyramid was the tallest man-made structure in the world for over 3800 years.)
● Review what the children have written, correcting any misconceptions.

Paired work

● Share the information about Mesoamerican pyramids. Wikipedia, for example, has individual entries on El Castillo, The Great Pyramid of Cholula, Temple of the Cross, Temple of the Inscriptions, and the Pyramid of the Magician. Whatever source of information you provide the children with, it needs to include a photograph of each pyramid, together with information about building materials, purpose and other features.
● Ask the children to read about one (or more) of these Maya pyramids and compare and contrast them with Egyptian pyramids. Ask them to record their observations in a table listing differences in one column and similarities in another.
● Discuss pairs' observations.
● Similarities: both Egyptian pyramids and Maya pyramids were built of limestone; both had square or rectangular bases; both were aligned in a special way.
● Differences: all the Maya pyramids are step pyramids, whereas the most famous Egyptian pyramids (those at Giza) are true pyramids with smooth sides; Maya pyramids were mainly used as temples and Egyptian pyramids were mainly used as tombs; Egyptian pyramids had a point at the top and Maya pyramids did not.

Group work

● Organise the class into groups, asking each group to start work on planning and building a model of a specific Maya pyramid. Provide a variety of model-building materials and equipment for children to choose from. This part of the lesson may take several sessions to complete.

> ### Differentiation
> ● Challenge: encourage children to build their model to scale.

Review

● Ask groups to share their plans for their model pyramid. Discuss proposed construction materials and techniques as a class, asking children to consider the possible advantages and disadvantages of each material and/or technique.

SPRING 1

WEEK 3

Week 3 lesson plans

This week's lessons have strong links to design. In Lesson 1 the children investigate some examples of Maya *stelae* (stone monuments). They design and make a *stela*-style poster that commemorates a recent or upcoming event in the locality, the school or the class. In Lesson 2 the children discuss what they already know about what the Maya looked like. They read an illustrated text describing Maya clothing, answering comprehension questions on the text and writing some of their own. They use what they have learned to help them design a costume for King Pacal of Palenque. Some children may go on to make a wearable costume based on their design.

1: What are *stelae* and what can they tell us about the Maya?

Introduction
● Introduce this lesson's focus question: *What are* stelae *and what can they tell us about the ancient Maya?*
● Ask the children if they can remember what *stelae* are from their work on ancient Greece, Rome and/or Egypt. (A *stela* is a slab of wood or – most often – stone, erected as a monument. The word has several forms: *stele* (plural *steles*) from Greek and *stela* (plural *stelas* or *stelae*) from Latin.)
● Discuss the sorts of things *stelae* in ancient Greece, Rome or Egypt were erected to commemorate.

Whole-class work
● Display the interactive activity 'Gallery of Maya *stelae*' on the CD-ROM. Ask: *What features seem to be typical of Maya stelae?* Give the children a few minutes to discuss this question with a partner, and then discuss ideas as a class.
● Choose (or ask the children to choose) one of the *stelae* to look at in greater detail. Click on the picture of the *stela* to access a larger view.
● Ask: *What do you think this* stela *shows?* Give the children a few minutes to discuss this question with a partner, and then discuss ideas as a class.
● Click on the large image of the *stela* to access some explanatory text. Either ask volunteers to read this out to the class, or ask children to read it for themselves. Ask follow-up questions to test their comprehension.
● Discuss what recent or upcoming events in the locality, school or class might be suitable for commemoration.

Group work, Paired work or Independent work
● Organise the children to work in groups, pairs or independently.
● Challenge each group, pair or individual to design and make a *stela*-style poster that commemorates an important recent or upcoming event in the locality, the school or the class.

Differentiation
● Support: pair children requiring support with a more confident partner.
● Challenge: some children to find out about *stelae* from other ancient cultures (such as China or Africa) for homework.

Review
● Ask: *Who do you think might have ordered the creation of the Maya stelae? What reasons might they have had to commemorate certain events? Who do you think their intended audience was?*

Lesson objectives
● To develop a chronologically secure knowledge and understanding of British, local and world history, establishing clear narratives within and across the periods they study.
● To develop the appropriate use of historical terms.
● To understand how our knowledge of the past is constructed from a range of sources.

Expected outcomes
● All children can explain what *stelae* are.
● Most children can explain what *stelae* are and explain some of the things they tell us about the ancient Maya.
● Some children can describe *stelae* from a range of cultures and explain their significance to historians.

Resources
Interactive activity 'Gallery of Maya *stelae*' on the CD-ROM; poster-making materials

Lesson objective
● To develop a chronologically secure knowledge and understanding of British, local and world history, establishing clear narratives within and across the periods they study.

Expected outcomes
● All children can describe the clothes the Maya wore.
● Most children can design an authentic-looking Maya costume.
● Some children can explain the differences in clothing between different levels of Maya society.

Resources
Media resource 'What did the Maya look like?' on the CD-ROM; art materials suitable for drawing a costume design (paper-based or digital); internet access (optional); materials and equipment for making a wearable costume

2: What did the Maya look like?

Introduction
● Introduce this lesson's focus question: *What did the Maya look like?*
● Ask: *What do you know already about what the Maya looked like?* Give the children a few minutes to discuss this question with a partner, and then ask them to share their ideas with the rest of the class.

Whole-class work
● Organise the children into pairs. Display the media resource 'What did the Maya look like?' on the CD-ROM.
● Discuss the pictures in the resource together.
    ● Top picture: Maya Noble and commander – two dignitaries in full regalia.
    ● Middle picture: Maya woman
    ● Bottom picture: Maya man stone relief detail in Chichén Itzà
● Ask, for example:
    ● *What differences were there between the way men dressed and the way women dressed?*
    ● *Which pictures show nobles and which show commoners?*
    ● *How can you tell? Apart from clothing, what else did the Maya wear?* (for example, jewellery and tattoos.)
    ● *How do you think the place where the Maya lived affected how they dressed?*
● Give the children the task of designing an original costume for King Pacal of Palenque to wear to an important event. The costume must be in keeping with what Maya men wore, and must be appropriate for someone of royal birth.

Independent work
● Give the children time to design their costumes. You may want to give those who would like to search the internet for images of King Pacal the opportunity to do so.
● When the children have finished their designs you could ask them to annotate them and mount them for a classroom or corridor display. If they have created their designs digitally you could ask them to upload them to the class blog or the school learning platform.

Differentiation
● Support: children can be supported by working in a group with an adult during the paired activity.
● Challenge: some children could create a wearable costume based on their design.

Review
● Ask the children to share and discuss their designs. Give them feedback on their designs based on both authenticity and creativity.
● If any children create a wearable costume based on their design, you could arrange for them to show their work in a short, informal fashion show.

Week 4 lesson plans

In this week's lessons the children explore Maya homes and cities. In Lesson 1 they research the homes of ordinary people in the ancient Maya civilisation, comparing them with the homes of ordinary people in Anglo-Saxon Britain. In Lesson 2 the children compare and contrast the Maya city of Chichén Itzà with the ancient city of Rome. They suggest what a citizen of ancient Rome might have thought of Chichén Itzà, and they use their ideas to create a recount of a visit to Chichén Itzà written from the point of view of an ancient Roman.

1: Which would you rather live in: a Maya home or an Anglo-Saxon home?

Lesson objectives
• To develop a chronologically secure knowledge and understanding of British, local and world history, establishing clear narratives within and across the periods they study.
• To note connections, contrasts and trends over time.
• To regularly address and sometimes devise historically valid questions about change, cause, similarity and difference, and significance.

Expected outcomes
• All children can describe an ancient Maya home.
• Most children can draw comparisons between ancient Maya homes and Anglo-Saxon homes. They can express and justify their preferences.
• Some children can compare the homes of Maya and Anglo-Saxon royalty as well as commoners.

Resources
Information bank on Maya homes, such as books and/or internet access

Introduction
• Introduce this lesson's focus question: *Which would you rather live in: a Maya home or an Anglo-Saxon home?*
• Ask the children what they remember about Anglo-Saxon homes at various levels of society. Focus in particular on the homes of commoners (churls).
• Explain that, even though Maya royalty lived in grand palaces built of stone, most people in Maya society lived in much simpler homes, and during this lesson they will be finding out about the homes of ordinary people, and comparing them with the homes of ordinary people in Anglo-Saxon society.
• From work covered in computing lessons, revise effective internet search techniques, e-safety considerations, and how to evaluate the reliability of online sources of information.
• Make children aware that the Maya people still exist today, so they will need to check that the information they collect is about the ancient Maya civilisation.

Paired work
• Organise the class into pairs, asking each pair to use books and the internet to research information about the homes of ordinary people in the ancient Maya civilisation, and make notes about what they find out.

Whole-class work
• Draw a table on the board with the title *Maya homes and Anglo-Saxon homes* and two columns: *Similarities* and *Differences*. Similarities might include: made of materials that rot (including wood), just one room, thatched roof, few or no windows; differences might include: Maya homes built facing east and built on top of a mound or base, walls of Maya houses covered in mud and often rounded.
• Ask children to copy and complete the table using the information collected.

Group work
• Ask each pair to join with another pair to make a group of four, and share what they have found out.
• Ask: groups to discuss the focus question: *Which would you rather live in: a Maya home or an Anglo-Saxon home?*

Differentiation
• Challenge: encourage confident pairs to compare the homes of kings as well as commoners.

Review
• Ask children to say whether they would rather live in a Maya home or an Anglo-Saxon home, explaining their reasoning.
• Take a class vote on the lesson's focus question.

Lesson objectives

● To develop a chronologically secure knowledge and understanding of British, local and world history, establishing clear narratives within and across the periods they study.
● To note connections, contrasts and trends over time.
● To regularly address and sometimes devise historically valid questions about change, cause, similarity and difference, and significance.

Expected outcomes

● All children can describe some of the features of Chichén Itzà.
● Most children can draw comparisons between Chichén Itzà and ancient Rome. They can suggest what an ancient Roman might have thought of Chichén Itzà.
● Some children can say which of the two cities they think was more advanced, explaining their reasoning.

Resources

Information bank on Chichén Itzà, such as photographs, a map and written information

2: What might a Roman have thought of a Maya city?

Introduction

● Introduce this lesson's focus question: *What might a Roman have thought of a Maya city?* Explain that an ancient Roman never actually visited a Maya city, as Europeans did not discover the Americas until the fifteenth century.
● Give the children a few minutes to brainstorm with a partner what they remember about the city of ancient Rome. Encourage them to take notes.

Whole-class work

● Discuss the children's ideas from the brainstorming activity, such as streets laid out on a grid system; cobbled roads; sophisticated water supply and drainage systems; buildings made of stone, brick and tiles; lots of public spaces and buildings (such as a forum, public baths, a basilica, temples, amphitheatres – like the Colosseum – and theatres).
● Explain that Chichén Itzà was the largest city of the ancient Maya civilisation, and in many ways the ancient Maya equivalent of ancient Rome.

Group work

● Organise the pairs from the introductory activity into groups of four or six and give out information about Chichén Itzà.
● Ask groups to discuss and note the similarities and differences between Chichén Itzà and ancient Rome, referring to their notes from the introductory brainstorming activity. Similarities include the use of stone as a building material and the presence of temples. Differences that a Roman would have noticed at Chichén Itzà include the way the city is laid out (not in a grid), the architectural style of the buildings, the absence of some familiar features such as public baths and amphitheatres, and the presence of unfamiliar features such as pyramids and a ball court.

Whole-class work

● Revise the features of a recount text, for example, past tense, introductory paragraph, sequence of events, and concluding paragraph.
● Set the children the task of writing a recount of a visit to Chichén Itzà from the point of view of an ancient Roman. Explain that the concluding paragraph should sum up the visitor's opinion of the city.

Independent work

● Give the children time, working independently, to write their recounts.

Differentiation

● Support: during independent could be provided with appropriate scaffolding and/or adult support to help them write their recounts.
● Challenge: invite some children to say which of the two civilisations they think was more advanced, and to explain their reasoning.

Review

● Ask the children who have considered the comparative civilisation level of ancient Rome and the ancient Maya (see *Differentiation*) to share their ideas with the rest of the class, using what they say as the starting point for a whole-class discussion.

Week 5 lesson plans

This week the children learn something about ancient Maya society – how it was ruled and structured, and how its legal system worked. In Lesson 1 they read about how the Maya were ruled, answer quiz questions on what they have read, and then play a card game that reinforces their knowledge of some of the important divisions in ancient Maya society. In Lesson 2 the children investigate the Maya justice system, compare and contrast it with the system in Anglo-Saxon Britain, and make a judgement about which civilisation's laws were tougher. They devise and create a game that tests players' knowledge of ancient Maya law.

1: How were the Maya ruled?

Lesson objective
● To develop a chronologically secure knowledge and understanding of British, local and world history, establishing clear narratives within and across the periods they study.

Expected outcomes
● All children can read about how the Maya were ruled.
● Most children can describe how the Maya were ruled.
● Some children can draw comparisons between how the Maya were ruled and how other civilisations they have studied were ruled.

Resources
Photocopiable page 59 'How were the Maya ruled?'; questions you have prepared about the photocopiable text; photocopiable page 60 'Maya card game' (four copies per group of students); scissors

Introduction
● Introduce this lesson's focus question: *How were the Maya ruled?*
● Give out individual copies of photocopiable page 59 'How were the Maya ruled?'. Allow enough time for everyone to read the text.
● Ask everyone to place their copy of the text face down, and then divide the class into groups. Give the children a quiz based on the text.

Whole-class work
● Display photocopiable page 60 'Maya card game' and explain how to play the game, as follows:
  ● The deck of cards is made up of four copies of the photocopiable page. The first player shuffles the deck and deals nine cards to each player. The person to the right of the dealer plays the first card. The players continue in order, each playing a card. The highest card wins the trick. The won trick is placed in front of the trick winner and that person starts the next trick by playing a card. Play continues like this until all nine tricks have been won. The player with the most tricks wins the 'hand'. The player to the dealer's left deals the next hand. Whoever wins the most hands wins the game.
  ● If there is a tie for the highest card, the trick is set aside, and the winner of the next trick collects both tricks. If the last trick of a hand is tied, it goes to the player who won the first trick.

Group work
● Organise the class into groups of between three and five children, giving each group four card copies of photocopiable page 60 'Maya card game', and a few pairs of scissors. Ask children to cut out the cards and play several hands of the game.

> **Differentiation**
> ● Challenge: children can be set a homework activity to draw comparisons between how the Maya were ruled and how other civilisations they have studied were ruled, asking them to present their conclusions to the class in a later lesson.

Review
● Give children a quick test on the characters featured in the card game and their relative positions in Maya society. For example, you could give children a set of cards with the numbers cut off, and ask them to order the characters from highest to lowest social standing.

Lesson objectives

● To develop a chronologically secure knowledge and understanding of British, local and world history, establishing clear narratives within and across the periods they study.
● To note connections, contrasts and trends over time.
● To regularly address and sometimes devise historically valid questions about change, cause, similarity and difference, and significance.

Expected outcomes

● All children can describe some ancient Maya laws.
● Most children can describe some ancient Maya laws, and compare them with laws in Anglo-Saxon Britain.
● Some children can evaluate which system of justice was fairer and explain their reasoning.

Resources

Photocopiable page 61 'What were Maya laws like?'; materials for making games (such as card games or board games)

2: Were ancient Maya laws tougher than Anglo-Saxon laws?

Introduction

● Introduce this lesson's focus question: *Were ancient Maya laws tougher than Anglo-Saxon laws?*
● Ask the children to discuss with a partner what they can remember about Anglo-Saxon laws. Share ideas as a class.
● Establish some of the main features of the Anglo-Saxon justice system: no courts or prisons; no weighing up of evidence for or against; punishments included fines, being beaten and put in the stocks, enslavement, removal of body parts or being put to death; those who pleaded innocent were given ordeals, which often resulted in their death.

Paired work

● Give out copies of photocopiable page 61 'What were Maya laws like?'. Ask children to read the text on the photocopiable page and discuss the questions with their partner.
● Ask pairs to make notes comparing and contrasting Maya laws and Anglo-Saxon laws.

Whole-class work

● Briefly review the discussion questions on the photocopiable page.
● Lead a discussion comparing and contrasting Maya laws with laws in Anglo-Saxon Britain. Ask: *What was similar about the two systems of justice? What was different about them?*
● Ask children to think of board games and card games they enjoy playing, and in particular those games that test a player's knowledge in some way. Take children's suggestions.
● Choose a game that is likely to be familiar to the children, and briefly revise how it works. Ask children to suggest how they might adapt this game mechanism to create a game that tests players' knowledge of Maya laws.
● If you have time, repeat the process for another familiar game.

Paired work

● Ask children to work in pairs to devise and make a game based on Maya laws.
● Set aside time for children to finish their games and to play each other's finished games.

Differentiation

● Support: during the first paired activity, children requiring support should be grouped together and given adult support.
● Challenge: during the second paired activity, discuss with children how they can ensure the game they develop effectively tests players' knowledge of the Maya legal system.

Review

● Ask: *If you had been accused of a crime, which system of justice would you prefer to be tried under? Why?*
● Revisit the lesson's focus question by asking: *Do you think ancient Maya laws were tougher than Anglo-Saxon laws? Why? Why not?*

Week 6 lesson plans

This week's lessons explore two aspects of Maya culture: the games they played and the stories they told. In Lesson 1 the children investigate the Mesoamerican Ballgame (a hugely important cultural phenomenon throughout Mesoamerica, a version of which was played by the Maya). After studying the game, the children devise and play their own ball game loosely based on it. In Lesson 2 the children explore the Maya creation myth, Popol Vuh, in which the Ballgame plays a central role. They retell the story in the form of a cartoon strip.

1: What games did the Maya play?

Introduction
● Introduce this lesson's focus question: *What games did the Maya play?*

Paired work
● Give children a copy of photocopiable page 'The Mesoamerican Ballgame' from the CD-ROM. Ask them to note any facts they find particularly interesting, challenging them to write down at least five.
● Reconvene as a whole class, asking each pair to share one or two of the most interesting facts they discovered.
● Ask the children which features of the game could be incorporated into a ball game they could play in school.

Group work
● Organise the class into groups, asking each group to devise and play a ball game based on the Mesoamerican Ballgame.
● You may decide to have an initial planning session in the classroom followed by an active session in the hall or playground, or you may decide to go straight into the active session.
● When the children have decided on the rules of their game and tested it out within the group, ask them to teach the rules to another group and test the game together. Encourage groups to tweak the rules in response to the results of the testing.
● Ask each group to write up the rules of their game.
● Make multiple copies of each set of game rules and arrange for an active session in which children get the chance to play as many of the games as possible.

> **Differentiation**
> ● Challenge: let some children test and develop their ball game further (maybe outside school hours) in order to make it as good as possible.

Review
● Ask the children questions to help them evaluate their own and others' games; for example: *What difficulties did you encounter when playtesting your game? How did you resolve them? Which game created by another group did you enjoy playing the most? What was it about this game that made it particularly enjoyable to play?*

Lesson objective
● To develop a chronologically secure knowledge and understanding of British, local and world history, establishing clear narratives within and across the periods they study.

Expected outcomes
● All children can describe the ball game played by the Maya.
● Most children can devise and play a game that is similar to the ball game played by the Maya.
● Some children can test, develop and improve their ball game.

Resources
Photocopiable page 'The Mesoamerican Ballgame' from the CD-ROM; PE equipment; access to the hall or playground

2: What stories did the Maya tell?

Lesson objective
● To develop a chronologically secure knowledge and understanding of British, local and world history, establishing clear narratives within and across the periods they study.

Expected outcomes
● All children can read a Maya myth.
● Most children can retell a Maya myth in outline.
● Some children can retell a Maya myth in greater detail.

Resources
Photocopiable page 'The Maya creation story' from the CD-ROM; example of a cartoon strip; cartoon strip materials and equipment (paper-based or digital); teaching assistant (optional)

Introduction
● Introduce this lesson's focus question: *What stories did the Maya tell?*
● Ask: *What is a myth?* Ask children to give examples of myths they know.
● Explain that one important myth told by the Maya was their creation story, known as the Popol Vuh. Tell the children they will be reading story and then retelling it in the form of a cartoon strip.

Paired work
● Organise the children into pairs, giving each pair a copy of the photocopiable page 'The Maya creation story' from the CD-ROM.
● Look at the first section of the story together as a class, reading the text, and then locating this part of the story on the diagram.
● Ask pairs to read the rest of the story independently, locating each part of the story on the diagram.

Whole-class work
● Ask questions about the story; for example:
  ● *Who were the first humans created by the gods?*
  ● *What was special about them?*
  ● *How did they anger the gods of the underworld, the Lords of Xibalba?*
  ● *Why do you think the Lords of Xibalba displayed the head of Hun Hunahpu in a tree?*
  ● *Who were Hunahpu and Xbalanque?*
  ● *What happened in the end of the story to the first humans, Vucub Hunahpu and Hun Hunahpu?*
  ● *Why do you think the Maya gods and heroes are depicted as ballplayers?*
● Revise the features of a cartoon strip, referring to an example.

Paired work or Independent work
● Ask children, working in pairs or individually, to retell the Popol Vuh story in the form of a cartoon strip. They could create their cartoon using paper-based materials or digital tools. You may need to give children extra time to finish their cartoons, or ask them to complete them for homework.

Differentiation
● Support: in the paired activities, you may want to provide children with the help of an adult.

Review
● Make the finished cartoons available for the rest of the class to read. Encourage children to give each other feedback on how effectively each cartoon retells the myth. You could ask children to rate each other's retellings against various criteria (for example, clarity, completeness, quality of language and quality of artwork).

Curriculum objective
● To note connections, contrasts and trends over time.

Resources
Photocopiable pages 'Ancient Maya quiz' from the CD-ROM

Mayans versus Anglo-Saxons

Revise
● On the whiteboard, display photocopiable pages 'Ancient Maya quiz' from the CD-ROM.
● Divide the class into teams for the quiz, allowing team members to confer before giving their answer.
● The answers are: 1b, 2c, 3d, 4d, 5a, 6b, 7b, 8d, 9a, 10c.

Assess
● On the board draw a table with two columns. Give the table the title *The Maya and the Anglo-Saxons: a comparison*. Label one column *Similarities* and the other *Differences*.
● Give the children a set length of time (such as 20 minutes) to copy and complete the table, listing as many similarities and differences as they can between the Anglo-Saxons and the Maya.
● Tell the children that it is important that they work independently for this task, because you need a record of what they know, not what someone else knows.
● If you have any children who really struggle with writing you might want to assess what they know through a one-to-one conversation conducted with a teaching assistant, or which you conduct yourself later.

Further practice
● Ask teams or pairs to write additional questions for the quiz, providing multiple-choice answers to choose from. The rest of the class could then have a go at answering the questions.

Curriculum objective
● To develop a chronologically secure knowledge and understanding of British, local and world history, establishing clear narratives within and across the periods they study.

Resources
Writing materials; paper

A Maya report

Revise
● Working in groups, ask children to make a list of the aspects of the ancient Maya civilisation they have investigated so far.
● Discuss ideas together as a class and draw up a complete list on the board (for example, where and when the Maya lived, the evidence they left behind, the palace at Palenque, pyramids, *stelae*, clothing, homes, cities, social structure, laws, games and stories).

Assess
● Ask the children to choose one of the aspects of the Maya civilisation they have studied during this chapter and write a report on it. In their report they should explain as much as possible about what they know. Tell the children it is important they work independently.
● If you did the report-writing activity in Week 2 Lesson 1, the children will already have written a report about the palace at Palenque, so make this subject off-limits.
● You might want to revise the features of a report, especially if you did not complete the report-writing activity in Week 2 Lesson 1.
● If you have any children who struggle with writing you might want to assess what they know through a one-to-one conversation conducted with a teaching assistant, or which you conduct yourself later.

Further practice
● Ask children to choose another aspect of the ancient Maya civilisation and write a different type of text based on it (for example, a story, poem, advert, or cartoon strip).

How were the Maya ruled?

The Maya people never formed
a single nation. They lived in
separate states. Some of these
were independent city-states, and
some states were made up of
several cities.

Mayan king at court

Kings

Most of the Maya states were ruled by a king. The kings justified their claim
to power by declaring they were descended from the gods. They had huge
monuments built to prove how powerful they were. Maya kings were military
leaders, and were expected to carry out raids against rival city-states. Sometimes
a Maya state was ruled by a queen, but this usually only happened if there was
no male heir.

Nobles

Nobles lived in the central areas of Maya cities. They were wealthy and literate.
Each noble family specialised in a particular occupation, passing knowledge from
generation to generation. Nobles served as government officials, tribute collectors
(tribute was a type of tax), military leaders, high priests, plantation managers, and
trade expedition leaders.

Commoners

Commoners lived on the outskirts of Maya cities. They worked as farmers,
labourers, soldiers, artisans and merchants. Commoners were not allowed to wear
the same types of clothing as nobles wore, and could not buy or use luxury goods.
Commoners had to pay tribute to the king, the local ruling nobles, and to the gods
in the form of labour, goods and a portion of their harvests.

Slaves

People might become slaves as a punishment
for committing a crime or for failing to pay
their debts. Prisoners of war who were
not sacrificed were usually enslaved. Very
poor people sometimes sold themselves or
members of their family into slavery. Slaves
were usually sacrificed when their owners
died, in the belief that they would continue to
serve them in the afterworld.

Mayan slaves

Name: _____ Date: _____

Maya card game

King **12**	High priest **11**	Government official **10**	Military leader **9**
Tribute collector **8**	Cocoa plantation manager **7**	Merchant **6**	Artisan **5**
Soldier **4**	Farmer **3**	Labourer **2**	Slave **1**

What were Maya laws like?

The king and his council issued the laws of a Maya state, and officials known as batabs were responsible for carrying them out.

Trials were usually held in public meeting houses. Witnesses testified under oath, and the batab weighed up the evidence, before ordering an appropriate punishment. There was no right of appeal; the batab's decision was final.

If the crime was accidental, the batab would give a less severe punishment than if it was deliberate. The victim of a crime or their family could pardon the person who committed the crime, which also made the punishment less severe. Punishments were usually carried out immediately.

The Maya did not have prisons and many crimes were punishable by death. These included murder, treason (plotting against the king), arson (setting fire to property) and burglary. The other main punishments the Maya used were restitution (compensating the victim's family) and enslavement (being ordered into slavery).

Sentences of enslavement and restitution did not always apply just to the person who committed the crime, but were also sometimes given to members of the criminal's family.

Any nobles who were found guilty of a crime were punished severely. Those who escaped the death penalty were forced to have their faces tattooed as a permanent record of what they had done.

Questions for discussion

1. Witnesses testified under oath. What does this mean?
2. Why do you think punishments were usually carried out immediately?
3. Why do you think nobles found guilty of a crime were punished more severely than other people?
4. Which aspects of Maya law do you think were fair?
5. Which aspects of Maya law do you think were unfair?

Written task: Make notes comparing and contrasting Maya laws with Anglo-Saxon laws.

The Maya (2)

In this chapter, the children explore Maya culture, including food, art, writing, trade, the calendar system, mathematics, science, and religious rituals. They consider how civilised the ancient Maya were compared with the Anglo-Saxons. They investigate the mystery behind the collapse of the ancient Maya civilisation, evaluating the evidence in support of theories that attempt to explain it. They research a question of their choice about the Maya. Finally, they present what they have learned.

Chapter at a glance

Curriculum objectives

• A non-European society that provides contrasts with British history: Mayan civilisation *circa* AD900.

Week	Lesson	Summary of activities	Expected outcomes
1	1	• Children explore foods the ancient Maya ate. • They follow a recipe to make a Maya-style chocolate drink and devise a simple modern-day menu based on Mayan-ingredients.	• Can describe the diet of the ancient Maya.
	2	• Children examine examples of Maya art, comparing it with the art of the Anglo-Saxons. • They create a T-shirt design in a Maya style.	• Can compare the art of the ancient Maya with the art of the Anglo-Saxons.
2	1	• Children look at the glyphs used by the Maya and discuss their characteristics. • They investigate syllable glyphs and use them to write their name.	• Can recognise Maya glyphs and use syllable glyphs to write their names.
	2	• Children research the goods the Maya traded with their neighbours, discussing the likely effect of this trade on the ancient Maya civilisation.	• Can explain the impact that trade had on the ancient Maya civilisation.
3	1	• Children read and discuss a text on the Maya calendar system. • They explore the Maya Long Count calendar, and use it to find the day they were born.	• Can give a simple explanation of how the ancient Maya calendar worked.
	2	• Children answer questions about maths and science in the ancient Maya civilisation. • They learn to read and write Maya numbers • They play bingo using Maya numbers.	• Can describe some of the Maya's scientific and mathematical achievements. • Can read and write numbers in the Maya number system.
4	1	• Children research an aspect of the ancient Maya religion and write a report. • The class discusses the importance of religion to the Maya.	• Can describe some ancient Maya religious beliefs and practices. • Can evaluate how important religion was in the lives of the ancient Maya.
	2	• Children research Maya burials and draw up a list of similarities and differences. • They create a model of a Maya burial.	• Can compare the burial rites of the ancient Maya with those of the Anglo-Saxons.
5	1	• Children compare different aspects of Anglo-Saxon and Maya culture. • They make a judgement about which culture was more civilised.	• Can discuss the comparative levels of civilisation of the ancient Maya and the Anglo-Saxons.
	2	• Children research theories about the causes of the collapse of the ancient Maya civilisation and the evidence supporting each theory. • They take part in a debate to decide which theory is most convincing.	• Can evaluate the evidence in support of several theories about the causes of the collapse of the ancient Maya civilisation. • Can say which theory they think is the most convincing, and explain why.
6	1	• Children note what else they would like to find out about the Maya. • They research answers to their questions, evaluating their sources for reliability.	• Can devise historically valid questions about the ancient Maya civilisation. • Can research answers to their questions, evaluating the sources they use for reliability.
	2	• Children choose a method of sharing what they have found out about the Maya, and an audience to share it with. • They prepare and give group presentations.	• Can choose an appropriate method of presenting what they have found out. • Can prepare and give a presentation of their findings.
Assess and review		• To review the half-term's work.	

Expected prior learning

- It is assumed that children have already studied: The Maya (1).
- Children will need a thorough knowledge of Anglo-Saxon Britain before studying this unit (for example, by covering the first two units in this book).

Overview of progression

- This chapter, in conjunction with the previous chapter, provides children with knowledge and understanding of a non-European society that provides contrasts with British history.
- In this chapter the children continue to address historically valid questions about change, cause, similarity and difference, and significance. They have the opportunity to note connections, contrasts and trends over time and develop the appropriate use of historical terms. They use a range of sources to construct informed responses that involve thoughtful selection and organisation of relevant historical information.
- Children demonstrate their knowledge of the past in different ways, including taking part in discussions and debates, creating designs, playing games, writing a variety of texts, and devising and giving presentations.

Creative context

- This chapter has strong links with the English curriculum. Children take part in discussions and debates, apply research skills, answer comprehension questions, follow a recipe, investigate and use an ancient writing system based on syllables, write a menu, write historically valid questions, and prepare a presentation.
- Children undertake research online, which addresses several requirements of the computing curriculum, including using the internet safely and responsibly, using search engines effectively, and evaluating online content.
- Some lessons link to design and technology – children devise a menu based on ingredients the Maya used, and they create a model of a Maya burial.
- There are links to geography, with children investigating the impact of international trade both historically and in the present day.
- The second lesson in Week 1 has links to art and design, with the children studying Maya art and creating their own original design in the Maya style.
- Two aspects of Maya culture covered in this chapter have links to mathematics; specifically to place value: reading and writing numbers using the Maya number system, and investigating the complex Maya calendar.

Background knowledge

- The Maya people once occupied a vast geographical area, and belonged to one of the most advanced civilisations in the Americas. They developed a written language, and invented the mathematical concept of zero. They used their knowledge of astronomy and mathematics to develop a complex and highly accurate calendar system. This calendar system informed the agricultural year and religious observances, which were closely interlinked.
- No one knows for sure why the Maya civilisation collapsed and why the Maya people abandoned their cities to live in small, scattered villages. In fact, some historians have described it as the biggest mystery in archaeology. Many different theories have been put forward to explain why the Maya civilisation went into decline. Some of the major theories are foreign invasion, epidemic diseases, collapse of trade routes, drought, and ecological collapse. Of course, it is possible that the decline of the classic Maya civilisation was due to a combination of several of these factors.

Week 1 lesson plans

In this week's lessons the children take a closer look at Maya culture. You will need to follow your school's food safety guidelines in Lesson 1 as children will investigate what the Maya ate, follow a recipe to make a Maya-style chocolate drink, and sample it (if they are brave enough!). They then devise a modern-day menu using ingredients known to the Maya. In Lesson 2 the children apply their knowledge and skills in art and design. They identify some of the features of Maya art, and compare and contrast it with Anglo-Saxon art. They copy Maya motifs, and then create their own original Maya-style T-shirt design.

1: What did the Maya eat and drink?

Lesson objective
● To develop a chronologically secure knowledge and understanding of British, local and world history, establishing clear narratives within and across the periods they study.

Expected outcomes
● All children can name some foods eaten by the Maya.
● Most children can describe the diet of the Maya.
● Some children can explain the influence of Maya food on the food eaten in Mesoamerica and the rest of the world today.

Resources
Interactive activity 'What did the Maya eat and drink?' on the CD-ROM; photocopiable page 77 'Maya-style chocolate drink'; cocoa powder; ground cinnamon; chilli powder; teaspoons; water; paper or plastic cups; paper towels; example menu; internet access (for extension activity only)

Preparation
● Ensure you follow your school's guidelines regarding food safety, in regard both to hygiene procedures and to minimising the risk of allergic reactions.

Introduction
● Introduce this lesson's focus question: *What did the Maya eat and drink?*
● Display interactive activity 'What did the Maya eat and drink?' on the CD-ROM, ensuring the children understand what to do.
● Work through the activity together, or allow children to work in pairs if computers are available. Recap which foods the Maya did and did not eat.
● Ask the children to suggest why the Maya did not eat certain foods (because they were unknown to them, as they came from another part of the world).

Group work
● Organise the class into small groups and give each group a copy of photocopiable page 77 'Maya-style chocolate drink'.
● Together read and discuss the introductory text *Eight fascinating facts about chocolate.*
● Give each group the necessary ingredients and equipment, and ask them to follow the recipe on photocopiable to make a Maya-style chocolate drink.
● Encourage children to sample the drink and write a description of what it tastes like.

Paired work
● Tell children they will be devising a menu for a meal based on ingredients the Maya would have used.
● Revise the features of a menu, displaying and discussing an example.
● Give the children time to devise and present their menus using Maya ingredients.

> **Differentiation**
> ● Support: use mixed ability groupings for the group work and paired work.
> ● Challenge: encourage some children to research the influence of ancient Maya food on the food eaten in Mesoamerica and the rest of the world today.

Review
● Ask pairs to assess each other's menus against the criteria you give them, such as taste appeal, nutritional balance, inclusivity (options for vegetarians and those with food allergies) and presentation.

2: Maya art: how does it compare to Anglo-Saxon art?

Introduction

● Introduce this lesson's focus question: *Maya art: how does it compare to Anglo-Saxon art?*
● Display the media resource 'Examples of Maya art' on the CD-ROM. Ask the children to look for any recurring themes, forms, patterns or colours, and discuss these with a partner, then discuss ideas together as a class.
  ● Picture 1: Mayan ruins, Honduras
  ● Picture 2: Mayan ruins at Kabah, Palace of the Masks, Yucatan, Mexico
  ● Picture 3: Mayan ruins at Chichén Itzà, Scoring ring in the Great ball game field, Yucatan, Mexico
  ● Picture 4: Vessel fragment
  ● Picture 5: Cylindrical vessel decorated with date glyphs and a Mayan ball player wearing black body paint and heavy padding for competition
  ● Picture 6: Picture of Maya man - stone relief detail in Chichén Itzà

Independent work

● If possible, use class computers to allow the children to view the images of Maya art close at hand.
● Ask the children to copy one or more Maya motifs of their choice into their sketchbooks.
● Ask the children to look at the Anglo-Saxon-style art they produced during the autumn term (for example, by turning back in their sketchbooks).

Group work

● Organise the class into groups, asking each group to discuss and record the similarities and differences between the art of the two cultures not just in terms of motifs, but also in terms of techniques and materials.
● Ask a volunteer from each group to talk to the class about what the group noticed.

Independent work

● Ask the children to create their own design for a Maya-style image that they could use to decorate a T-shirt.
● If you have enough time and appropriate resources, you could give children the opportunity to print their design onto a T-shirt in class (maybe during an art and design lesson). Otherwise, printing the T-shirt could be an optional homework activity.

> **Differentiation**
> ● Challenge: you could challenge children to research both ancient and contemporary Maya styles in a particular area of design (such as clothing or ceramics).

Review

● Ask individuals to show their T-shirt designs to the rest of the class. Encourage children to give each other constructive feedback on their designs, explaining which aspects they think work well and why, and which aspects might be improved.
● Ask any children who have researched an area of Maya design to share what they have found out.

Week 2 lesson plans

Lesson 1 has links with English and with other areas of study in history. Children look at examples of characters from various writing systems. From these they identify the glyphs used by the ancient Maya and discuss their characteristics. They examine a set of syllable glyphs and use them to write their names. Lesson 2 has links with geography. The children consider the huge impact of international trade on life in Britain today. They conduct research into the types of goods the Maya traded with neighbouring cultures, and consider the impact this trade might have had on the ancient Maya civilisation.

1: How did the Maya writing system work?

Lesson objective
● To develop a chronologically secure knowledge and understanding of British, local and world history, establishing clear narratives within and across the periods they study.

Expected outcomes
● All children can recognise Maya glyphs.
● Most children can write their name using Maya glyphs.
● Some children can combine 'idea glyphs' to create new words.

Resources
Media resource 'Examples of characters from different writing systems' on the CD-ROM; photocopiable page 'What did the Maya use writing for?' from the CD-ROM; photocopiable pages 'Maya glyphs for syllables' from the CD-ROM; squares of art paper

Introduction
● Introduce this lesson's focus question: *How did the Maya writing system work?*
● Give children a short amount of time to brainstorm with a partner the different things we use writing for today. Challenge them to get a minimum number within a set time limit. Discuss ideas.
● Display the media resource 'Examples of characters from different writing systems' from the CD-ROM. Challenge children to identify which culture each set of characters comes from.
● Discuss the characteristics of the glyphs used by the Maya.

Paired work
● Organise the children into pairs, giving each pair a copy of photocopiable page 'What did the Maya use writing for?' from the CD-ROM.
● Ask pairs to read and discuss the text and then write down three questions about it for another pair to answer.
● Organise pairs to pair up to form groups of four, swap questions and then ask and answer each other's questions verbally.

Whole-class work
● Ask children questions about the text they read during the paired activity. You could use your own questions or use questions children have written.
● Display the photocopiable pages 'Maya glyphs for syllables' from the CD-ROM. Explain how the syllable glyphs work, working together to write an example name on the board.

Independent work
● Ask children to practise writing their name using Maya syllable glyphs. Ask them to write the syllables of their name so that they form as close to a square shape as possible.
● When children are confident in writing their name in Maya syllable glyphs, give them a pre-cut square of art paper and ask them to produce a large version of their name for display.

> #### Differentiation
> ● Challenge: ask children to research Maya 'idea glyphs' and experiment with combining them to create new words.

Review
● Ask groups (or the whole class) to put their name glyphs together to form a single piece of 'writing'. Put the finished piece on display. Challenge children to look at the completed piece(s) and try to decipher the individual names that make it up.

2: How did trade affect the way the Maya lived?

Lesson objectives
● To develop a chronologically secure knowledge and understanding of British, local and world history, establishing clear narratives within and across the periods they study.
● To regularly address and sometimes devise historically valid questions about change, cause, similarity and difference, and significance.

Expected outcomes
● All children can name some of the goods the ancient Maya traded with their neighbours.
● Most children can suggest the impact of this trade on the ancient Maya civilisation.
● Some children can describe how trade with the Maya impacted other Mesoamerican cultures.

Resources
Information bank on Maya trade, for example, books and/or internet access

Introduction
● Introduce this lesson's focus question: *How did trade affect the way the Maya lived?*
● Ask: *How does trade affect the way we live today?* Give the children, working in pairs, a few minutes to make a list of all the food they have eaten today, all the clothes they are wearing today, all the objects they have used today. Ask: *How many items are there on your list?*
● Discuss with the children where the food, clothes and objects come from. Ask: *If Britain did not trade with other countries, how many of these would you have to cross off your list? What impact would it have on your life if you did not have access to these items?*
● Discuss another impact of international trade: the wealth brought into the country from selling British goods overseas.

Paired work
● Organise the class into pairs, giving each pair access to the information you have found and/or access to the internet. Ask pairs to research some or all of the following questions:
  ● *What goods did the Maya trade?* They traded a wide variety of items including food (such as fish, squash and corn), raw materials (such as limestone, wood and obsidian) and manufactured goods (such as paper, furniture and clothing).
  ● *What currency did they use?* The Maya did not use money as we understand it today. For trading everyday items they used barter, cocoa beans or stone beads. Luxury goods were traded for gold, jade or copper.
  ● *How did Maya trade develop over time?* Over time, cities grew, and craftsmen in each city began to specialise, both of which increased the importance of trade.

Whole-class work
● Discuss the results of children's research as a class.

Independent work
● Ask individuals to write a report that answers the lesson's focus question: *How did trade affect the way the Maya lived?* If you are short on time, writing the report could be a homework activity.

Differentiation
● Support: additional adult support may be required to encourage and help children during the independent work.
● Challenge: ask children to find out more about the cultures the Maya traded with and suggest what impact trade with the Maya might have had on them.

Review
● Select several important features or aspects of Maya trade identified during the paired work and the subsequent whole-class discussion.
● For each of these aspects, ask the children, working in groups, to brainstorm the impact it might have had on the ancient Maya civilisation. Discuss their ideas.

Week 3 lesson plans

In Lesson 1 the children investigate the Maya calendar system. They watch a video clip introducing the calendar, and then read and discuss a text describing in more detail. They explore an interactive version of the Maya Long Count calendar, use it to find the day they were born, and then copy the glyphs for their birth date. In Lesson 2 the children consider what evidence they already have about the Maya's achievements in maths and science. They answer questions on a text about maths and science in the ancient Maya civilisation. They learn to read and write Maya numbers, and play a game of bingo using them.

1: How did the Maya calendar work?

Lesson objective
● To develop a chronologically secure knowledge and understanding of British, local and world history, establishing clear narratives within and across the periods they study.

Expected outcomes
● All children can describe the Maya calendar in general terms.
● Most children can give a simple explanation of how the ancient Maya calendar worked.
● Some children can convert dates from the Maya long count calendar into the Gregorian calendar.

Resources
Photocopiable page 78 'How does the Maya calendar work?'; internet access (for pairs) (optional); online interactive Long Count Maya calendar, such as www.nytimes.com and search for 'the Long Count'

Introduction
● Introduce this lesson's focus question: *How did the Maya calendar work?*
● Briefly explain to the children that the ancient Maya invented a complex and accurate calendar system that allowed them to order their society. They used the calendar for practical purposes, such as working out the best times for planting crops, as well as religious purposes, such as timing sacrifices to the gods. Only the ruling classes had full knowledge of how the calendar worked, and they held on to this secret in order to secure their power over the rest of society.

Whole-class work
● Display or give out copies of photocopiable page 78 'How does the Maya calendar system work?'. Together read and discuss the text.
● Display an interactive Long Count calendar (see *Resources*). Discuss the meaning of the icons (on the *New York Times* calendar, these are shown in the key at the top of the page) and how they are each made up of a name part (cycle glyph) and a number part (number glyph). The *New York Times* calendar automatically shows today's date in the Maya calendar, but it can be changed to show any date by clicking on the arrows above and below the icons. Ask the children to predict what Gregorian date will be displayed if you move one of the icons one place up or down. Start by changing the K'in icon, and then make the questions harder by changing the Uinal or Tun icons. For a real challenge you could change more than one icon.

Paired work
● Organise the class into pairs, giving each pair access to the internet. If computer access for pairs is not available, display the interactive on the whiteboard and invite individuals to the front of the class to work on it
● Challenge children to change the online calendar so that it displays their birth date, and then take a screenshot of the part of the screen showing the Maya date.
● When both partners have saved their birth dates as screenshots, ask them to copy them onto paper.
● Children could add their birth date glyphs to the display of name glyphs.

Differentiation
● Support: the Maya calendar is challenging, so it is advisable to use mixed-ability pairs throughout the lesson.
● Challenge: children to memorise their birth date in the Maya Long Count calendar (for example, a birthday of 28 February 2006 would be 12 Bak'tuns, 19 K'atuns, 13 Tuns, 1 Uinal, 12 K'ins).

Review
● Display the interactive Long Count calendar on the whiteboard, challenging children to predict what Gregorian date will be represented when you rotate one of the Maya glyphs a certain number of steps in a certain direction.

Lesson objective
● To develop a chronologically secure knowledge and understanding of British, local and world history, establishing clear narratives within and across the periods they study.

Expected outcomes
● All children can describe some of the scientific and mathematical achievements of the Maya.
● Most children can read and write numbers in the Maya number system.
● Some children can use the Maya system of multiplying numbers.

Resources
Photocopiable page 'Maya scientific achievements' from the CD-ROM; photocopiable page 79 'The Maya number system'; cards with Maya numbers written on them (from 0 to 29)

2: How much did the Maya know about maths and science?

Introduction
● Introduce this lesson's focus question: *How much did the Maya know about maths and science?*
● Ask: *Do you think the Maya knew a lot about maths and science? What evidence do you have so far to support your theory?* Ask children to brainstorm ideas with a partner.
● Discuss the children's ideas.

Paired work
● Organise the class into pairs and give each pair a copy of the photocopiable page 'Maya scientific achievements' from the CD-ROM.
● Give pairs time to read through the text and discuss the following questions (which you could write on the board):
    ● *Which scientific achievements of the Maya does the article mention?*
    ● *What aspects of Maya technology were surprisingly advanced?*
    ● *Is there anything else surprising about Maya technology?*
    ● *Which of the Maya's scientific achievements would have required knowledge of mathematics?* (Astronomy, architecture and calendar systems.)

Whole-class work
● Discuss children's answers to the paired activity.
● Display photocopiable page 79 'The Maya number system'. Ask: *Can you work out how the Maya number system works?* Give pairs a few minutes to discuss this and then share their ideas with the class.
● Hold up one Maya number card at a time, asking the children to say the number aloud. You could make this into a team game.
● Give the children some numbers above 29 to write and decipher.
● Play a game of Maya number bingo. Ask each child to draw a 3 by 3 grid, writing a different Maya number between 0 and 29 in each cell of the grid. Ask a volunteer to draw a Maya number card and say the number on it aloud, without showing the card to the rest of the class. Play progresses in the usual manner.

Differentiation
● Support: it may be appropriate to group less confident children together for the paired activity and give them adult assistance.
● Challenge: children to research and try out the multiplication method used by the Maya.

Review
● Give children a short, informal quiz to test their knowledge of Maya scientific achievements and their recall of the Maya number system.

Week 4 lesson plans

In Lesson 1 the children consider the significance of religion in the ancient Maya civilisation. They begin by working in groups to research a particular aspect of the ancient Maya religion, and then write a report based on their research. Groups share their findings, and then the class discusses the importance of religion in the lives of the ancient Maya. Lesson 2 focuses on burial customs. Children revise what they know about Anglo-Saxon burials. They research Maya burial customs and draw up a list of similarities and differences. Finally, children design and make a model of a Maya burial.

1: How important was religion to the ancient Maya?

Lesson objectives
● To develop a chronologically secure knowledge and understanding of British, local and world history, establishing clear narratives within and across the periods they study.
● To regularly address and sometimes devise historically valid questions about change, cause, similarity and difference, and significance.

Expected outcomes
● All children can describe an aspect of the ancient Maya religion.
● Most children can evaluate how important religion was to the ancient Maya.
● Some children can compare the religion of the ancient Maya with that of the modern Maya.

Resources
Photocopiable page 'An introduction to ancient Maya religion' from the CD-ROM; internet access (for groups)

Introduction
● Introduce this lesson's focus question: *How important was religion to the ancient Maya?*

Whole-class work
● Write the following four headings on the board: *Deities, Priests, Rituals* and *Sacred places*, and discuss their meanings.
● Display the photocopiable page 'An Introduction to ancient Maya religion' from the CD-ROM and read it together.
● Tell the children they will be researching one of the four aspects of the ancient Maya religion. Stress that the Maya still live in Mesoamerica today, and although their religious practices are related to those of their ancient ancestors, they are not the same. Children need to take care that the information they collect relates to ancient, rather than modern practices.

Group work
● Divide the class into four groups, assigning each group one of the four aspects of religion.
● Give each group time to research information about the aspect of religion they are investigating. If internet access is not available in class, this part of the lesson could be completed for homework.
● You might like to give each group one or two questions to help focus their research. For example:
  ● Deities:
    ● *Who were the most important gods, and why?*
    ● *What links were there between religion and agriculture?*
  ● Priests:
    ● *What were the most important parts of a priest's job?*
    ● *Could anyone become a priest?*
  ● Rituals:
    ● *Why did the ancient Maya believe rituals were necessary?*
    ● *What was the purpose of blood letting and sacrifice?*
  ● Sacred places:
    ● *What part did pyramids play in the ancient Maya religion?*
    ● *What natural landscape features were sacred to the ancient Maya?*

Independent work
● Ask children to write a short report on ancient Maya religion based on the research they have done.

Review
● Ask each group to report back on what they have found out.
● Discuss the focus question. Conclude that religion was of central importance in the ancient Maya culture, influencing many aspects of life.

Lesson objectives
● To develop a chronologically secure knowledge and understanding of British, local and world history, establishing clear narratives within and across the periods they study.
● To note connections, contrasts and trends over time.
● To regularly address and sometimes devise historically valid questions about change, cause, similarity and difference, and significance.

Expected outcomes
● All children can describe the burial rites of the ancient Maya.
● Most children can compare the burial rites of the ancient Maya with those of the Anglo-Saxons.
● Some children can explain what the ancient Maya's burial practices tell us about their culture.

Resources
Photocopiable page 'Maya burial customs' from the CD-ROM; modelling materials (such as junk, clay, plaster bandage, balsa wood, polystyrene, or a 3D modelling program on a computer)

Introduction
● Introduce this lesson's focus question: *How did a Maya burial compare with an Anglo-Saxon burial?*
● Ask the children to discuss with a partner what they can remember about Anglo-Saxon burial customs (for example, from their study of the ship burial at Sutton Hoo). Share ideas as a class.
● Establish some of the main features of Anglo-Saxon burial. Burials typically included grave goods such as weapons and jewellery, many burials were in burial mounds, and some important people, like kings, had ship burials.

Paired work
● Organise the class into pairs, giving each pair a copy of the photocopiable page 'Maya burial customs' from the CD-ROM.
● Give children time to read the photocopiable page and make notes about how a Maya burial compares with an Anglo-Saxon burial.

Whole-class work
● Work together as a class to draw up a list of similarities and differences between Maya and Anglo-Saxon burial practices.

Independent work or Paired work
● Set individuals and/or pairs the task of creating a model of a Maya burial. Encourage them to make the model interactive in some way (for example, with moving or removable parts) and to include some sort of written information so that people who view the model can understand what all the elements are.
● Give children a list of materials and/or equipment they can choose from to make their model. Alternatively you could specify the material(s) you want them to use, or give them completely free rein over their choice of materials.
● Give children time to design and make their model.

Differentiation
● Challenge: ask some children to explain what the ancient Maya's burial practices tell us about their culture.

Review
● Give children an opportunity to examine, evaluate and feed back on each other's models. You could give children a list of criteria against which to judge each other's models, such as historical authenticity, interactivity, aesthetic appeal and sturdiness.

Week 5 lesson plans

This week the children begin to wrap up their study of the Maya. In Lesson 1 they consider whether the Maya were more or less civilised than the Anglo-Saxons. They compare and contrast different aspects of Anglo-Saxon and Maya culture, discussing which culture is the more civilised in each aspect. Taking an overview, they make a judgement about which culture is more civilised overall. In Lesson 2, the children research theories about why the Maya civilisation collapsed and the evidence supporting each theory. They take part in a debate about which theory is the most convincing.

1: Were the Maya more or less civilised than the Anglo-Saxons?

Lesson objectives
● To develop a chronologically secure knowledge and understanding of British, local and world history, establishing clear narratives within and across the periods they study.
● To develop the appropriate use of historical terms.
● To regularly address and sometimes devise historically valid questions about change, cause, similarity and difference, and significance.
● To construct informed responses that involve thoughtful selection and organisation of relevant historical information.

Expected outcomes
● All children can compare and contrast aspects of Maya culture with aspects of Anglo-Saxon culture.
● Most children can discuss the comparative levels of civilisation of the ancient Maya and the Anglo-Saxons.
● Some children can explain and justify their judgement.

Resources
A3 paper; blank cards; glue (optional); digital cameras (optional)

Introduction
● Introduce this lesson's focus question: *Were the Maya more or less civilised than the Anglo-Saxons?*
● Ask: *What do we mean by civilised?* Give children a few minutes to discuss this question with a partner, and then share their ideas with the class. Reach agreement about the meaning of the word, perhaps writing a definition on the board.
● Help the class to make a list of all the cultural features they have studied in both cultures. (for example, clothing, social organisation, laws, homes, settlements, burial, food, art, writing, stories, and religion).

Group work
● Give each group a sheet of A3 paper and some blank cards. Ask each group to write one cultural feature from the board on each card.
● On the board sketch a horizontal line with an arrow at either end. Label the left half of the line *Maya LESS civilised than Anglo-Saxons* and label the right half of the line *Maya MORE civilised than Anglo-Saxons*. In the centre of the line draw a short vertical line, labelling it *about the same/no evidence*. Ask groups to copy this diagram onto their A3 paper.
● Ask groups to discuss each cultural feature and place it in the appropriate place on the diagram. Next, ask them to record what they have done, for example by sticking the cards down and/or by taking a digital photo.

Differentiation
● Challenge: expect confident learners to explain their reasoning, both of their overall judgement, and of specific judgements they have made regarding particular cultural features; ask: *do you think each aspect of culture is equally is important? If not, which aspects do you think are more important than others? Why?*

Review
● Ask each group to show their diagram and say whether it suggests the Maya were, overall, more civilised or less civilised than the Anglo-Saxons.
● Ask the class to take a vote on the answer to the focus question: *Were the Maya were more or less civilised than the Anglo-Saxons?* Ask children to explain how they used the diagram to help them make their final judgement.

Lesson objectives

● To develop a chronologically secure knowledge and understanding of British, local and world history, establishing clear narratives within and across the periods they study.
● To regularly address and sometimes devise historically valid questions about change, cause, similarity and difference, and significance.
● To construct informed responses that involve thoughtful selection and organisation of relevant historical information.
● To understand how our knowledge of the past is constructed from a range of sources.

Expected outcomes

● All children can evaluate the evidence in support of several theories about the causes of the collapse of the ancient Maya civilisation.
● Most children can say which theory they think is the most convincing, and explain why.
● Some children can put forward a compelling argument in support of their point of view.

Resources

Books about the Maya and/or internet access; teaching assistant (optional)

2: The Maya mystery: why did the Maya civilisation collapse?

Introduction

● Introduce this lesson's focus question: *Why did the Maya civilisation collapse?*
● Explain that some time around AD 1000 the Maya civilisation underwent a collapse. The Maya cities were abandoned. When Spanish explorers arrived 500 years later, the Maya people were living in small, scattered villages, and their ancestors' cities were in ruins.
● Explain that no one knows what happened to make the Maya civilisation collapse, but historians have suggested a range of possible explanations.

Paired work

● Organise the class into pairs, giving each pair access to information on the Maya.
● Ask pairs to research theories about the causes of the collapse of the ancient Maya civilisation and the evidence supporting each theory. You could provide them with useful search terms, such as *classic Maya collapse, Maya collapse, fall of the Mayan civilisation,* or *Mayan collapse theories.*
● There are many theories about what happened to the ancient Maya civilisation, but no one knows certain what happened. Possible explanations include warfare, civil strife, earthquakes, volcanic eruptions, an epidemic of a deadly disease, or famine brought about by drought, which may in turn have been caused by deforestation. Experts are still trying to gather the evidence they need in order to work out which of these theories is correct. The present consensus is that the Maya collapse was most likely caused by a combination of several of these factors, and that drought probably played a central role.

Whole-class work

● Collate a list of all the theories the children have discovered for the collapse of the Maya civilisation.

Group work

● Divide the class into groups, according to which theory of the collapse of the Maya civilisation they think is the most plausible.
● Ask each group to think of arguments to support their position, and then divide up into smaller groups, with each group preparing a short presentation based on one of the arguments.

Whole-class work

● Conduct a class debate, with each group presenting their arguments.

Differentiation
● Support: during group work you might want to provide adult assistance for individuals who may struggle with the activity.

Review

● Complete the debate by asking children to vote for the theory that was supported by the most compelling arguments. Explain that a combination of explanations could also be considered as a valid theory, so allow children to vote for that option, too.

Week 6 lesson plans

In Lesson 1 the children ask their own questions about the Maya that have not been answered during the study. They research answers to their questions, evaluating their sources for reliability, and share their findings with an audience in school. In Lesson 2 the children review the aspects of the Maya civilisation they have investigated over the course of the study. Working in groups they choose one aspect of the Maya civilisation to share with a wider audience. They choose a method of sharing what they have found out about this aspect of the Maya. Each group then plans, prepares and shares their presentation.

1: What other questions would we like to ask about the Maya?

Lesson objectives
● To develop a chronologically secure knowledge and understanding of British, local and world history, establishing clear narratives within and across the periods they study.
● To regularly address and sometimes devise historically valid questions about change, cause, similarity and difference, and significance.
● To construct informed responses that involve thoughtful selection and organisation of relevant historical information.

Expected outcomes
● All children can ask questions about the ancient Maya civilisation.
● Most children can research answers to their questions.
● Some children can evaluate the sources they use for reliability.

Resources
Books about the Maya and/or internet access, other resources will vary

Introduction
● Introduce this lesson's focus question: *What other questions would we like to ask about the Maya?*

Paired work
● Ask: *What questions would you like to ask about the Maya?* Organise the class into pairs and give children time to discuss and write down their questions.

Whole-class work
● Ask pairs to share their questions, creating a class list. Help children to adapt their questions if necessary so that they are specific, and cover one of the historical concepts of change, cause, similarity and difference, and significance. The questions in the list need to be distinct from one another, so encourage children to offer only questions that are not already covered by questions already on the board.
● If researching online, revise effective internet search techniques, e-safety considerations and how to evaluate the reliability of online sources of information.
● Discuss possible ways of presenting research results and agree on a common presentation approach that all pairs will use in order to create a whole-class outcome.

Paired work or Independent work
● Ask individuals or pairs to choose a question from the list to research, and make or collect appropriate notes that will help them answer their question.
● When they have found out the answer to their question they should present it using the agreed method.
● Ask selected pairs or individuals to collect research results together to create the whole-class outcome.
● Share the outcome with an audience within school (for example, another class).

Review
● Give the children, as a class ,a short, informal quiz on the questions they have researched.

Lesson objective
● To develop a chronologically secure knowledge and understanding of British, local and world history, establishing clear narratives within and across the periods they study.

Expected outcomes
● All children can choose an appropriate method of presenting what they have found out about the Maya.
● Most children can prepare and give a presentation of their findings.
● Some children can present their findings in an original or entertaining way.

Resources
Resources will vary

2: How could we present what we have found out?

Introduction
● Introduce this lesson's focus question: How could we present what we have found out?
● Ask: *Which aspects of the Maya civilisation have we found out about?* Give the children time, working in pairs or small groups, to brainstorm answers to this question. Discuss answers.

Whole-class work
● Explain to the children that the class will divide into groups and that each group will prepare a presentation about a different aspect of the Maya civilisation.
● Lead a discussion on possible forms the presentations could take (for example, poster, booklet, video, visual display, web page and so on). You may want to steer children towards or away from certain types of presentation, depending on the time and/or resources available, or depending on their learning needs.
● Lead a discussion on possible audiences to share the presentation with, such as the head teacher, another class, the rest of the school, a neighbouring or twinned school, parents and/or carers, or the general public (for example, by sharing it online).

Group work
● Poll children about which aspects of the Maya civilisation they would like to focus on in their presentation, and divide the class into groups accordingly.
● On the board write the following questions:
  ● *Which aspect of the Maya civilisation will your presentation be about?*
  ● *What form will your presentation take?*
  ● *Who will you share your presentation with?*
  ● *What things do you need to do in order to get your presentation ready?*
  ● *Which group member(s) will do each thing?*
● Give the children time, working in their groups, to discuss and answer these questions, making notes about what they decide.
● Discuss each group's ideas with them in terms of feasibility.
● Give children time to prepare, rehearse (if necessary) and give their presentations.

Differentiation
● Support: children may benefit from an adult working with them during some or all of the group work activities.
● Challenge: expect some children to present their findings in an original and/or entertaining way, for example as a song, or as a stop-motion animation.

Review
● Ask the children to evaluate each other's presentations, explaining aspects that worked well, as well as suggestions for improvement. Feedback could be collected and given on a group basis. In this way, everyone gets a chance to contribute their ideas, and suggestions for improvement may be easier to give and receive, as they lose the personal element.

Curriculum objective
● To note connections, contrasts and trends over time.

Resources
Pencils

Ancient Maya versus ancient Greece?

Revise

● On the board write just *two* of the following words: architecture, laws, games, stories, food, art, writing, trade, calendar, science, maths, religion, and burial.
● Explain to the children that these are two of the aspects of Maya civilisation they have been studying. Give children the task, working in pairs, to draw up a complete list.
● Discuss children's ideas, compiling a complete list on the board.
● Ask children to make a list on the board of the other civilisations they have learned about in history lessons since Year 3 (ancient Egypt, ancient Greece, ancient Rome, and Anglo-Saxon Britain).

Assess

● Ask the children to find and record as many similarities as they can between Maya civilisation and the other civilisations they have studied. They should think about each aspect of civilisation in turn, whether the same aspect of one of more of the other civilisations is similar in some way, and if it is, describe how it is similar.
● Explain that there are similarities, for example, between Maya and Egyptian architecture. One similarity is that both civilisations built pyramids. Another is that the stone they used for building was limestone.
● Give the children a set length of time for the task, emphasising the importance of working independently.
● If you have any children who struggle with writing you might want to assess what they know through a one-to-one conversation.

Further practice

● Ask children to draw a diagram showing the similarities as connections between the different civilisations.

Curriculum objectives
● To construct informed responses that involve thoughtful selection and organisation of relevant historical information.

Resources
Multiple sets of cards with facts about the ancient Maya (some negative, such as *The Maya practised human sacrifice*, some positive, such as *The Maya punished accidental crimes more leniently than deliberate ones*, and some neutral, such as *The Maya invented a system of writing*); good/bad lines in paper or card (see the *Revise* section)

The good, the bad, the Maya

Revise

● On the board write *Was the ancient Maya civilisation good or bad?*
● On the board draw a good/bad line: a horizontal line with arrows on either end, the left half labelled *Bad*, and the right half, *Good*.
● Display one of the Maya fact cards. Ask a volunteer to place the card in the 'correct' position on the good/bad line, explaining their decision. Open the placement of the card to discussion. Repeat for one more card.

Assess

● Organise the class into groups, giving each group a good/bad line and a set of Maya fact cards.
● Ask children to arrange the cards on the line, discussing the placement of each card. Visit each group, asking them to explain their decisions.
● Gather the class together and ask: *Which cards did you find the hardest to place? Why? Overall, do you think the ancient Maya civilisation was good or bad? Can you justify your answer?*

Further practice

● Ask children to write additional fact cards about the ancient Maya civilisation to add to the good/bad line.

Maya-style chocolate drink

Eight fascinating facts about chocolate
- Chocolate is made from cocoa beans, which are the seeds of the cocoa tree.
- To the Maya, cocoa pods (the fruit of the cocoa tree) symbolised life and fertility.
- Maya priests presented cocoa beans as offerings to the gods in religious ceremonies.
- The Maya used cocoa beans as currency.
- Maya literature refers to chocolate as 'the food of the gods'.
- The Maya did not eat chocolate; they drank it.
- The Maya made their chocolate drink with water, not milk, and they did not sweeten it. They also drank it cold.
- The Maya added spices to their chocolate drink, including chillies!

Recipe for a Maya-style chocolate drink
- Follow this recipe to make a Maya-style chocolate drink and then taste it.

Equipment:
1 jug, 1 teaspoon, 1 whisk, 1 cup per person

Ingredients:
3 teaspoons cocoa powder
1 teaspoon ground cinnamon
pinch of chilli powder
1 cup of water

Method:
1· Put the cocoa, cinnamon and chilli into a jug.
2· Fill a cup with water· Pour a small amount of the water onto the dry ingredients, while stirring with a spoon.
3· Keep adding a little more water and stirring until the mixture forms a paste.
4· Stir the paste until it is smooth.
5· Slowly pour the rest of the water onto the paste while beating with the whisk.
6· Keep whisking until the drink is frothy.
7· Pour a little chocolate drink into each cup.

How does the Maya calendar system work?

The Maya calendar system is made up of three different calendars. They are the Haab' (the civil calendar), the Tzolk'in (the divine calendar) and the Long Count calendar.

The Tzolk'in combines weeks of different lengths. There is a numbered week of 13 days and a named week of 20 days. They run alongside each other, to produce a 260-day cycle.

The Haab' consists of 18 months of 20 days each, followed by 5 extra days. This gives a year length of 365 days. The Tzolk'in and Haab' are combined to form what is known as the Calendar Round.

The Long Count calendar

The Long Count calendar counts the number of days since the beginning of the world, which the ancient Maya believed was in 3114BC.

The basic unit is the k'in (day). The other units are:

uinal	(1 uinal = 20 k'in = 20 days)
tun	(1 tun = 18 uinal = 360 days = about 1 year)
k'atun	(1 k'atun = 20 tun = 7,200 days = about 20 years)
bak'tun	(1 bak'tun = 20 k'atun = 144,000 days = about 394 years)

A date in the Long Count calendar is written as a series of five numbers with dots between like this: 13.0.3.1.14

This date reads: 13 bak'tuns, 0 k'atuns, 3 tuns, 1 uinal, 14 k'ins.

We would write this date as 9 January, 2016.

Logically, the first date in the Long Count calendar should be 0.0.0.0.0, but the bak'tuns are numbered from 1 to 13 rather than 0 to 12, so this first date is actually written 13.0.0.0.0. The Long Count calendar rolled over to 13.0.0.0.0 again on 21 December 2012. Some people thought this meant the ancient Maya had predicted this date would be the end of the world.

Name: _____   Date: _____

The Maya number system

0	1	2	3	4
(shell)	•	••	•••	••••

5	6	7	8	9
▬	• ▬	•• ▬	••• ▬	•••• ▬

10	11	12	13	14
▬ ▬	• ▬ ▬	•• ▬ ▬	••• ▬ ▬	•••• ▬ ▬

15	16	17	18	19
▬ ▬ ▬	• ▬ ▬ ▬	•• ▬ ▬ ▬	••• ▬ ▬ ▬	•••• ▬ ▬ ▬

20	21	22	23	24
• (shell)	• •	• ••	• •••	• ••••

25	26	27	28	29
• ▬	• • ▬	• •• ▬	• ••• ▬	• •••• ▬

A local history study (1)

In this child-centred, enquiry-led chapter, the children make the decisions about which aspect of local history to study, which historical questions to answer, and what the final outcome will be. Even though the chapter is child-led, it still requires thorough teacher preparation. First, you will need to choose three or four aspects of local history for the class to choose from. You might want to consider running Week 1's lessons (in which the children decide which historical questions to investigate) at the end of the spring term, to give yourself time to collect resources over the Easter holidays.

Chapter at a glance

Curriculum objective

• A local history study.

Week	Lesson	Summary of activities	Expected outcomes
1	1	• Children consider a range of topics for the local history study. • They debate which topic to study then take a vote.	• Can say which aspect of local history they would like to study, and explain why.
	2	• Children decide how they will share what they find out and who they will share it with.	• Can say how they would like to share what they find out, and explain why.
2	1	• Children discuss what they already know about the chosen topic, and make notes about what they would like to find out. • They turn these notes into historically relevant questions, and choose which ones to focus on.	• Can frame historically relevant questions about the aspect of local history they have chosen to study.
	2	• For each focus question, children identify a range of sources which they could use to find out the answer.	• Can identify a range of sources they could use to find out the answers to their questions.
3	1	• Children explore methods for evaluating the reliability of evidence from a range of sources.	• Can evaluate evidence from a range of sources.
	2	• Children design and carry out interviews with and/or surveys of local people to gather evidence their focus questions.	• Can use interviews and/or surveys to gather historical evidence.
4	1	• Children study building related to their chosen topic and use what they find out to answer one or more of their focus questions.	• Can use buildings to gather historical evidence.
	2	• Children visit an archaeological site and use what they find out as evidence to answer one or more of their focus questions.	• Can use a visit to an archaeological site to gather historical evidence.
5	1	• Children examine historical artefacts and use what they find out as evidence to answer one or more of their focus questions.	• Can use artefacts to gather historical evidence.
	2	• Children examine gravestones and use what they find out as evidence to answer one or more of their focus questions.	• Can use gravestones to gather historical evidence.
6	1	• Children visit a museum exhibit and use what they find out as evidence to answer one or more of their focus questions.	• Can use a visit to a local museum to gather historical evidence.
	2	• Children listen to a presentation by a local historian and ask follow-up questions. They use what they find out as evidence to answer one or more of their focus questions.	• Can use a visit by a local historian to gather historical evidence.
Assess and review		• To review the half-term's work.	

■ SCHOLASTIC
www.scholastic.co.uk

Expected prior learning

● Children do not need any prior knowledge of local history, but familiarity with the local area (from a local study in geography, for example) would be useful.
● It is assumed that children are familiar with the concept of historical evidence, and can name a range of sources from which historians gather evidence about the past.

Overview of progression

● This chapter and the next provide children with knowledge and understanding of an aspect of local history. At the start of the study, children devise historically valid questions about change, cause, similarity and difference, and significance. They have the opportunity to note connections, contrasts and trends over time and develop the appropriate use of historical terms. They use a range of sources to construct informed responses that involve thoughtful selection and organisation of relevant historical information.
● Depending on the nature of the focus questions the children choose, the local history study could be an overview study, in which children look at an aspect of local history over an extended period of time, or a depth study in which they examine a specific event, series of events, or short period of time in more detail.

Creative context

● The children will be working towards a final outcome that allows them to share what they have found out with a wider audience. It is in guiding the children towards this final outcome that you will be able to make the most of creative opportunities and cross-curricular links. Some possible final outcomes might be: turning the classroom into a museum, creating a documentary film, publishing an e-book, creating a website or putting on an assembly.

Background knowledge

● The first five lessons of this chapter are foundational – every class should cover them, in the order in which they are presented. The remaining lessons are optional. Choose the lessons that are appropriate for the local history topic the children are investigating, and for the range of evidence you have access to. Cover these lessons in whichever order suits you. As the local history study continues in the following chapter, you may want to choose some of this half term's lessons from the first four weeks of the next chapter.
● Although the children will be choosing the aspect of local history they will be studying, you will need to provide them with a list of three or four appropriate topics from which to choose. The programme of study for history gives non-statutory examples for the local history study, which make a good starting point for ideas.
● Whatever topics you choose they should all be locally significant, of potential interest to the children, and well supported by evidence. If you are not familiar with the history of the local area, you could ask for advice from a local history society (www.local-history.co.uk/Groups/) or the history department at a local secondary school.

Week I lesson plans

During this first week of the local history study the children make important decisions that will affect the course of history lessons for the rest of the term. In the first lesson they are presented with a choice of several possible subjects, and hold a debate to decide which aspect of local history they will study. In the second lesson, the children brainstorm different ways they could present the information they have found out at the end of the study, working together to evaluate each option and choose the most appropriate one. Given the subject of the study and the final outcome they have chosen, they also decide on their target audience.

I: Which aspect of local history shall we study?

Lesson objective
● To develop a chronologically secure knowledge and understanding of British, local and world history, establishing clear narratives within and across the periods they study.

Expected outcomes
● All children can say which aspect of local history they would like to study.
● Most children can say which aspect of local history they would like to study, and explain why.
● Some children can put forward a compelling argument in support of their choice.

Resources
A list of three or four possible topics for the local history study; the help of one or more teaching assistants or other adults (optional)

Introduction
● Tell the children that over the course of the term they will be investigating an aspect of local history.
● Introduce this lesson's focus question: *Which aspect of local history shall we study?*
● Present the children with several (perhaps three or four) local history topics from which to choose. See *Background knowledge* on page 81 for advice on choosing appropriate topics.

Paired work
● Give the children some time to discuss with a partner which of the topics they would most like to study, and why.

Group work
● Divide the class into groups, according to which topic they would prefer to study. If possible, assign an adult to each group.
● The adult working with each group should help the group to consider arguments to support their position. The adult then asks the group to divide up into smaller groups, with each group preparing a short presentation based on one of the arguments.

Whole-class work
● Conduct a class debate, with each group presenting their arguments.
● Remind the children how you expect them to behave during a debate.
● Choose a moderator to lead the debate. You could do this yourself, or select a child for the role. The moderator needs to be able to speak clearly, communicate assertively but respectfully, keep everyone on task, and ensure all participants get a fair say.
● The moderator introduces the topic of debate, and invites representatives from each group to present their arguments, perhaps using a timer to make sure each group is given a fair chance to put their point across.

Differentiation
● Support: mixed-ability pairings may be useful for the paired work; in the group work, children requiring support may benefit from being grouped together and working with an adult.

Review
● Before the children vote, emphasise the importance of the decision they make, as whichever topic gets the most votes will be the history topic for the rest of the term. After the vote, ask: *Did you find the decision about which way to vote difficult to make? Why? Why not?*

2: How could we share what we find out?

Introduction
● Introduce this lesson's focus question: *How could we share what we find out?*
● Explain to the children that before they start work on their study you want them to have an end product in mind. This end product will be something that lets them share what they have found out with other people.

Paired work
● Ask the children, working in pairs, to consider possible answers to the focus question *How could we share what we find out?* Some possible final outcomes might be: turning the classroom into a museum, creating a documentary film, publishing an e-book, creating a website, or putting on an assembly.
● Make a list on the board of all the suggestions that are practicable. Explain to the children that before they can make a final decision about what the end product will be, they will need to choose their audience, as this will affect the type of end product that will be appropriate.
● Ask the children, working with a different partner this time, to think about possible audiences for their end product. Suitable examples include: a particular class or year group in school, the whole school, a partner school (such as a feeder school), the local cluster of schools, the local community in general (perhaps via local radio), parents or carers, or the general public (for example, via the web).
● Take children's suggestions, discussing which methods of sharing their knowledge might be appropriate for which audience.

Group work
● Organise the class into groups, asking each group to discuss the suggestions on the board, expressing their opinions and preferences.
● Encourage children to evaluate each method of sharing knowledge in turn, identifying its advantages and disadvantages.
● You may wish to use the following additional questions: *What aspects do you need to consider when you are evaluating different ways of sharing your knowledge? In what ways will your choice of end product affect your choice of audience?*
● Finally, ask each group to arrange the methods in order of preference.

> **Differentiation**
> ● Challenge: invite some children to lead the discussion during group work.

Review
● Ask the children to help you devise a fair way of making the decision about which method of sharing knowledge the class will use, which takes into account the opinions of all the groups. For example, you could ask each group to list their top three methods, giving three points to their first choice, two points to their second choice, and one point for their third choice. Once you have devised a method, use it to make the final decision.
● Announce the audience for the final product, depending on the decision made.

Week 2 lesson plans

This week the children continue to make decisions about how they will approach the local history study. In the first lesson they decide which historical questions they will be answering and in the second lesson they consider where they might find the answers to these questions. They begin by listing a range of sources historians use to answer historical questions and then identify which sources (both generally and specifically) they might be able to use to find out the answers to the questions they have chosen.

1: Which questions do we want to answer?

Lesson objectives
● To develop a chronologically secure knowledge and understanding of British, local and world history, establishing clear narratives within and across the periods they study.
● To regularly address and sometimes devise historically valid questions about change, cause, similarity and difference, and significance.

Expected outcomes
● All children can make notes about what they would like to find out about during the local history study.
● Most children can use their notes to pose historically relevant questions.
● Some children can suggest what they think the answers to their questions might be, explaining their reasoning.

Resources
Photocopiable page 95 'What is a good question for a historical investigation?'

Introduction
● Introduce the focus question: *Which questions do we want to answer?*
● Ask the children what they already know about the chosen topic. Create a list entitled *What we know* and keep it to refer to during the last lesson in the next chapter.

Independent work
● Ask: *What would you like to find out about the topic?* Give the children time to make notes about what they would like to find out over the course of the local history study.

Whole-class work
● Tell the children they will be using their notes to come up with several historically relevant questions that they will investigate over the course of the study.
● Display photocopiable page 95 'What is a good question for a historical investigation?', and discuss it with the class.

Paired work
● Ask the children to work with a partner to turn the notes they have made into questions suitable for an historical investigation, using the information on the photocopiable page to help them.

Group work
● Ask pairs to form groups of four, share the questions they have written and choose one question to share with the class.

Whole-class work
● Ask a volunteer from each group of four to share their chosen question with the class, and write it on the board. If any group suggests a question that is similar to one already on the board, ask them to choose an alternative.

Differentiation
● Support: you could group them together for the independent activity and work with them.
● Challenge: during the paired activity encourage children to suggest what the answers to their questions might be, and to explain their reasoning.

Review
● Ask the children to choose which questions they will answer during the study, helping them to decide how they will make the choice. Depending on the subject of the topic and the nature of the questions, ask the class to choose between three and six questions with which to start their investigation.

Lesson objectives
● To develop a chronologically secure knowledge and understanding of British, local and world history, establishing clear narratives within and across the periods they study.
● To understand how our knowledge of the past is constructed from a range of sources.

Expected outcomes
● All children can name a range of sources historians use to answer historical questions.
● Most children can identify which sources they might be able to use to find out the answers to their questions.
● Some children can suggest which sources they might investigate first and explain why.

Resources
Video clip 'How to research the past' from the BBC hands on history website (optional); photocopiable page 96 'Where could we find answers to our questions?'

2: Where might we find the answers to our questions?

Introduction

● Introduce this lesson's focus question: *Where might we find the answers to our questions?*
● You could watch a video clip giving an overview of the variety of sources historians use to help them answer historical questions. See *Resources* for a suggestion.
● Alternatively, you could ask the following questions:
  ● *How might talking to people help to answer your questions?* (Depending on the topic, you might be able to talk to people with direct experience, or people who have studied the subject, such as members of a local history society – or both.)
  ● *How might visiting places in the locality help to answer your questions?* (All sorts of places in the locality can be rich sources of historical information: libraries, archives, museums, newspaper offices, and street features such as architecture, dates on buildings, old street signs, statues, plaques.)
  ● *How might going online help to answer your questions?* (You can use a search engine to search the web for pages on the topic you are investigating – taking care to assess the information you find for reliability – and you can search online historical archives, such as the National Archives).

Paired work

● Ask the children, working with a partner, to list all the types of historical sources they know.

Whole-class work

● Discuss the lists of historical sources children drew up during the paired work activity. Establish that historical sources can be documents (such as books, letters, diaries, stories and poems), buildings, human and animal remains, made objects (artefacts), images (paintings, drawings and photographs), or oral testimony (eyewitness accounts).
● Revise the list of focus questions for the local history study that the children chose in the previous lesson.

Group work

● Organise the class into pairs or small groups. For each focus question, ask the children to identify a range of sources (in both general and specific terms), which they could use to find out the answer. Ask the children to record their ideas on a copy of photocopiable page 96 'Where could we find answers to our questions?'.
● In discussion with each group, identify opportunities for the children to collect information for themselves using the sources they have identified.

Differentiation
● Support: used mixed-ability groupings for group work.
● Challenge: during the group work, challenge children to suggest which sources they might investigate first and explain why.

Review

● Discuss children's ideas from the group-work activity. Work together to collate a class list of sources of historical information that are not accessible in school. Discuss which of these could be accessed for homework, and which could be accessed during one or more class visits.

Week 3 lesson plans

In Lesson 1 the children consider the need to evaluate their sources when collecting historical evidence. They practise evaluating a range of evidence relating to their chosen local history topic. Whether or not Lesson 2 is appropriate for your class will depend on the local history topic they have chosen to study. In Lesson 2 the children write and conduct interviews and/ or surveys to collect evidence from local people on an aspect of local history within living memory. They then analyse and interpret the information they have collected. This lesson will take three sessions to complete.

1: How can we evaluate evidence?

Lesson objectives
• To develop a chronologically secure knowledge and understanding of British, local and world history, establishing clear narratives within and across the periods they study.
• To construct informed responses that involve thoughtful selection and organisation of relevant historical information.
• To understand how our knowledge of the past is constructed from a range of sources.

Expected outcomes
• All children can select which sources to use to answer historical questions.
• Most children can evaluate evidence from a range of sources.
• Some children can rank historical sources in order of usefulness, explaining their reasoning.

Resources
A range of historical sources related to the topic of the local history, only some of which are relevant to the focus questions; photocopiable page 97 'Evaluating evidence flowchart'

Introduction
• Introduce this lesson's focus question: *How can we evaluate evidence?* Discuss what is meant by *evaluate*.
• Display the range of sources you have collected. Tell the children that they will be evaluating these as sources of evidence.
• Display and recap the focus questions the children chose in Week 2.

Group work
• Tell children that the first thing to do when evaluating sources is to decide which sources to use. Suggest they do this by asking: *Will this source help us answer one of our questions?*
• Divide the class into as many groups as there are historical sources, giving each group a few minutes to examine each source and discuss whether they think it will help them to answer one of the focus questions, before moving on to the next source.

Whole-class work
• Ask each group to give feedback on the group activity, establishing which of the sources are relevant.
• Display photocopiable page 97 'Evaluating evidence flowchart'. Choose one of the sources the children have already identified as being relevant, and work through the flowchart questions together for that source.

Paired work
• Give out copies of the photocopiable page, asking pairs to choose two of the historical sources (one language-based source and one non-language-based source). For each source ask them to work through the flowchart and write down the answers to the questions.

> **Differentiation**
> • Challenge: ask children to evaluate all the historical sources and then rank them in order of usefulness.

Review
• Ask children to share their evaluations. Establish that some sources are more useful than others, because they are more informative and/or more reliable.
• Ask any children who have evaluated all the sources and ranked them in order of usefulness to share their results and explain their reasoning.

Lesson objectives

● To develop a chronologically secure knowledge and understanding of British, local and world history, establishing clear narratives within and across the periods they study.
● To regularly address and sometimes devise historically valid questions about change, cause, similarity and difference, and significance.
● To construct informed responses that involve thoughtful selection and organisation of relevant historical information.
● To understand how our knowledge of the past is constructed from a range of sources.

Expected outcomes

● All children can write questions to ask local people about the local history topic.
● Most children can use interviews or surveys to gather historical evidence.
● Some children can draw valid conclusions about the past from the evidence collected.

Resources

Tools for creating interviews and surveys

2: What can local people tell us about local history?

Session 1

● Introduce this lesson's focus question: *What can local people tell us about local history?*
● Present the following questions one at a time, asking the children to discuss each question in their group, before coming back together as a class to share ideas.
  ● *Which of our focus questions might local people be able to help us answer?*
  ● *Who could we ask about this subject?* Decide on the most appropriate population to target.
  ● *How could we ask them?* This might be through a face-to-face interview or through a written survey (on paper or online).
  ● *What questions could we ask?*
  ● *How could we record answers?*
● Discuss the features of good survey questions. They ask only one question at a time, and its meaning is unambiguous. Using multiple-choice rather than open-ended questions makes it easier to collate, graph and interpret the data. If using multiple-choice, the choices must be mutually exclusive and cover all possible answers. Surveys must be quick and easy to fill in, so they should be presented clearly, and be fairly short.
● Ask groups to work together to write a set of interview questions or survey questions.

Session 2

● Arrange time for the children to conduct the interviews or surveys.
● Emphasise the importance of conducting interviews and surveys respectfully – the need to gain consent and to ensure privacy and anonymity.
● Ask groups to collect responses to their questions. If this involves direct contact with members of the public ensure adequate adult supervision, and if it involves going off the school premises, ensure the relevant guidelines are followed.

Session 3

● Ask groups to collate the data they have collected and present it in the form of a table or a graph.
● Ask children to interpret their data in relation to the focus question(s) they were trying to answer. Children may need help with this.

Differentiation
● Support: mixed-ability groups may be helpful.

Review

● Session 1: Review each group's survey questions. Ask: *Will this question help us to find out what we want to know? Do the answer options cover the whole range of possible answers? Will the survey be easy to fill in? Will the survey be quick to complete?*
● Session 2: Ask children to feed back on the experience of conducting the interview or survey. Discuss any problems encountered, and ways of dealing with them.
● Session 3: Ask each group to share with the rest of the class what they have found out from their interview or survey. Ask: *Did you find out what you wanted to know? If you were to repeat the survey or interview, what would you do differently? Why?*

Week 4 lesson plans

This week's lessons are visit-based. It is likely that one of the lessons will be more appropriate for your chosen topic than the other, so they are offered as alternatives. In Lesson 1 the children visit a building and in Lesson 2 they visit an archaeological site. Some sites of historical interest contain both a building and an archaeological site, of course! In both lessons the children use the visit to gather evidence for one of their local history questions.

1: What can buildings tell us about local history?

Lesson objectives
● To develop a chronologically secure knowledge and understanding of British, local and world history, establishing clear narratives within and across the periods they study.
● To understand how our knowledge of the past is constructed from a range of sources.

Expected outcomes
● All children can record their observations on a visit to [building].
● Most children can use the visit to [building] to gather evidence about [specific aspect of local history].
● Some children can say whether the evidence they collected suggests possible answers to any other questions about the past.

Resources
Information about your chosen building to share with the class (such as a presentation, a video clip, an information leaflet or a web page)

Preparation
● Choose a local building that relates to the study topic the children have chosen.
● Collect as much information as you can about the building.
● Arrange for the class to visit to the building.
● If possible, go on a fact-finding visit before you visit with the class.
● Review the historical questions the children have chosen to investigate and decide which is the most suitable focus for a visit to the building.
● Rewrite the lesson's focus question and expected outcomes to make them specific to the building you are visiting and the aspect of local history you are investigating.
● Decide on appropriate activities during the visit that will enable children to collect the evidence they need. Activities could include: answering questions (for example, their own from Week 1), making notes, drawing plans, taking photographs, shooting video, or following activities devised by the venue's education officer.

Introduction
● Introduce this lesson's focus question: *What can [building] tell us about [specific aspect of local history]?*
● Ask the children what they know about the building already and its relationship to the aspect of local history in the focus question.
● Share some of the information about the building that you have collected.

Paired work or Group work
● Ask children, working in pairs or small groups, to make a list of what else they would like to find out about the building during their visit.

Whole-class work
● Go on the visit.

Differentiation
● Support: mixed-ability groups are recommended throughout this lesson.

Review
● Review the focus question for this lesson.
● Ask the children to share the evidence they collected during the visit. Discuss whether this evidence helps to answer the focus question. Ask the children whether the evidence they collected suggests possible answers to any other questions about the past.
● Taking into account the final outcome of the local history study, help the children to decide what they will do with the evidence they have collected.

Lesson objectives
- To develop a chronologically secure knowledge and understanding of British, local and world history, establishing clear narratives within and across the periods they study.
- To understand how our knowledge of the past is constructed from a range of sources.

Expected outcomes
- All children can record their observations on a visit to [archaeological site].
- Most children can use the visit to [archaeological site] to gather evidence about [specific aspect of local history].
- Some children can say whether the evidence they collected suggests possible answers to any other questions about the past.

Resources
Materials for creating a mock archaeological dig (such as area of bare earth, objects to bury such as bones and broken pottery, trowels, sieves, plastic trays, old brushes, glue; grid marking equipment such as canes and twine)

2: What can a visit to an archaeological site tell us?

Preparation
- Follow the directions in the Preparation section of the previous lesson (Week 4, Lesson 1), replacing *building* with *archaeological site*.
- In addition, prepare a mock archaeological dig for the children to investigate. Find an area of bare earth in the school grounds or create one by shovelling earth into a large, shallow container such as a paddling pool or sandpit. Bury objects in the area of bare earth, such as animal bones or items of pottery broken into several pieces. Mark out a co-ordinate grid over the area of the dig (for example, using canes and twine).

Introduction
- Introduce this lesson's focus question: *What can [archaeological site] tell us about [specific aspect of local history]?*
- Discuss the terms *archaeological site*, *archaeology* and *archaeologist*.
- Draw out key information about the work of archaeologists, for example by hot seating in character as an archaeologist or watching a video clip (see *Resources*).
- Make sure you mention the following: Archaeologists study the past by looking for the remains that people have left behind by living in a particular place. They do this by digging, and the further down they dig, the further back in time they go. Archaeologists use a sieve to help them find small objects they might not otherwise find. Archaeologists don't just find small objects; they can find large features, too, such as the remains of walls and buildings. They try to find as many pieces of evidence as they can, because the more clues they find, the more they can find out about people who lived in the past.

Paired work or Group work
- Give pairs or small groups of children the opportunity to explore the mock archaeological dig, record the location of their finds, and attempt to piece together any broken objects.

Whole-class work
- Go on the visit.

Differentiation
- Support: mixed-ability groups are recommended throughout this lesson.

Review
- After the visit, review the focus question for this lesson.
- Ask the children to share the evidence they collected during the visit. Discuss whether this evidence helps to answer the focus question. Ask the children whether the evidence they collected suggests possible answers to any other questions about the past.
- Taking into account the final outcome of the local history study, help the children to decide what they will do with the evidence they have collected.

Week 5 lesson plans

This week the children investigate two more sources of historical evidence: artefacts and gravestones. In Lesson 1 the children play a game in which they examine artefacts relating to the local history topic they are studying, practise asking historically relevant questions about them and then develop historical theories to answer these questions. This lesson should be appropriate for all classes. Lesson 2 may only be appropriate for some classes. It is a three-part lesson involving a visit to a local graveyard or cemetery during which the children collect evidence from gravestones about the aspect of local history they are investigating.

1: What can artefacts tell us about local history?

Lesson objectives
● To develop a chronologically secure knowledge and understanding of British, local and world history, establishing clear narratives within and across the periods they study.
● To understand how our knowledge of the past is constructed from a range of sources.

Expected outcomes
● All children can ask questions about artefacts.
● Most children can use artefacts to gather historical evidence.
● Some children can evaluate the artefacts for richness and relevance.

Resources
Nine artefacts relating to the subject of the local history study; a container to put the objects in that is appropriate for the topic; masking tape; sticky labels; large counters made from coloured card; ten-sided dice; question word prompt sheets; timer

Preparation
● Just before the lesson, lay out a 3 by 3 grid of squares on the classroom floor using masking tape (the game board). The idea for this game is taken from Teachers TV as shown on YouTube (Crown Copyright).

Introduction
● Introduce this lesson's focus question: *What can artefacts tell us about local history?* Revise the term *artefact* (a made object).
● Open the container with the nine artefacts inside, take out one artefact at a time and ask the children a question about it. Vary the types of question you ask by using a different word to start each question (Who? Where? Why? How? When? Which? Whose? What?). Place each artefact in a different square on the game board.

Group work
● Explain the game to the children:
  ● Each group has a coloured counter and a ten-sided dice;
  ● They roll the dice to find out which square to take an artefact from;
  ● They put their counter in the square they take the artefact from;
  ● Take the artefact back to their table, and write and answer as many questions about the artefact as they can in the time available.
● Organise the class into groups and give children a total length of time (such as 30 minutes) in which to examine a minimum number of artefacts, or alternatively set the timer for short intervals (such as five minutes), after which time the children roll the dice again and examine a different artefact.

Whole-class work
● Hold up each artefact in turn, asking the children to share the questions they asked about it. Discuss their suggested answers. Explain that their suggested answers are historical theories. Ask: *How could we find out whether our historical theories are correct?* (Check other sources to see if they support our theory.) *Which sources could we use?*

Differentiation
● Support: ensure mixed-ability groupings during the group activity. You may wish to group less confident learners together so that they can work with an adult.

Review
● Ask: *How could we use what we have found out in our [the final outcome you are working towards]? Out of the artefacts you have examined so far, which one is the richest source of evidence? Why? Which one is the most relevant? Why?*

■ SCHOLASTIC
www.scholastic.co.uk

Lesson objectives
● To develop a chronologically secure knowledge and understanding of British, local and world history, establishing clear narratives within and across the periods they study.
● To understand how our knowledge of the past is constructed from a range of sources.

Expected outcomes
● All children can record observations of gravestones.
● Most children can use gravestones to gather evidence about [the aspect of local history you are studying].
● Some children can use research skills to find out more about one or more of the people commemorated on the gravestones.

Resources
Photos of local gravestones; optional resources for the class visit: digital cameras, sketchbooks and art pencils, large plain paper, jumbo crayons, scissors, masking tape

2: What can gravestones tell us about local history?

Preparation
● Visit a local graveyard or cemetery and take photos of inscriptions and other possible sources of evidence relating to the local history topic you are studying.
● Arrange for the class to visit the local graveyard or cemetery.
● Decide on appropriate activities during the visit that will enable children to collect the evidence they need. Activities could include: drawing sketches, copying inscriptions, taking photographs and taking rubbings.
● Rewrite the lesson's focus question and expected outcomes to make them specific to the aspect of local history you are studying.

Introduction
● Introduce this lesson's focus question: *What can gravestones tell us about [the aspect of local history you are studying]?*

Paired work or Group work
● Display a photograph you took at the local graveyard or cemetery. Ask the children, working in pairs or groups, to discuss what the photograph tells them about the aspect of local history you are studying. Discuss ideas as a class, drawing out those pieces of evidence that relate to the specific questions children have chosen to investigate.
● Discuss the upcoming visit with the children, emphasising the importance of showing respect to the people who are buried and commemorated in the graveyard or cemetery, and suggesting ways to do this.

Whole-class work
● Go on the visit.
● If children will be taking rubbings of the gravestones, you will need jumbo crayons (preferably in dark colours), large plain paper (for example, flip chart sheets or a roll of white display-board paper), scissors to cut the paper to size, and masking tape to secure it to the gravestone. For the most effective rubbings, instruct children to attach the paper securely so that it doesn't slip, and rub evenly and systematically, with all their strokes going in the same direction.

Differentiation
● Support: mixed-ability groups are recommended throughout this lesson.
● Challenge: ask children to use research skills to find out more about one or more of the people commemorated on the gravestones.

Review
● Ask the children to share their observations from the visit to the graveyard or cemetery.
● Review the focus question: *What can gravestones tell us about [the aspect of local history you are studying]?* Discuss which observations are pieces of evidence that help us to answer the focus question.
● Taking into account the final outcome of the local history study, help the children to decide what they will do with the evidence they have collected.

Week 6 lesson plans

Lesson 1, which involves a visit to a local museum, may or may not be relevant for your class. Contact your local museums to find out which, if any, have relevant exhibits. Even if they do not carry enough relevant material to make a visit worthwhile, they may be able to loan you artefacts, images or documents that the children can investigate in class. Lesson 2, which is appropriate whichever aspect of local history you're studying, offers a valuable opportunity for the children to learn about history and the skills of historical enquiry from a subject specialist. It is advisable to cover this lesson if possible.

1: What can a museum visit tell us about local history?

Lesson objectives
● To develop a chronologically secure knowledge and understanding of British, local and world history, establishing clear narratives within and across the periods they study.
● To understand how our knowledge of the past is constructed from a range of sources.

Expected outcomes
● All children can record their observations on a visit to [museum].
● Most children can use a visit to [museum] to gather evidence about [aspect of local history].
● Some children can evaluate the evidence they collect.

Resources
Information leaflets about the museum you will be visiting or the link to the museum website

Preparation
● Make a preliminary visit to a local museum, assessing which exhibits relate to the aspect of local history you are studying.
● Arrange for the class to visit to the museum.
● Rewrite the lesson's focus question and expected outcomes to make them specific to the museum you are visiting and the aspect of local history you are studying.

Introduction
● Introduce this lesson's focus question: *What can a visit to [name of museum] tell us about [the aspect of local history you are studying]?*
● Ask the children whether any of them have already visited the museum, and if so, what they remember, and what they found out about local history.

Paired work
● Give out information leaflets about the museum or give children the link to the museum website. Ask children, working in pairs, to discuss which exhibits and/or activities might be relevant to the aspect of local history they are studying. Share ideas.
● Sketch a timeline on the board showing the block of time you will be at the museum. Mark in any essential events (such as lunch) and then ask pairs of children to sketch out a timetable to help you plan the rest of the time. Ask them to consider what order to do things in, and how much time to spend on each area or activity.

Whole-class work
● Go on the visit.

Review
● Review the focus question for this lesson: *What can a visit to [name of museum] tell us about [the aspect of local history you're studying]?*
● Ask children to share the evidence they collected during the museum visit. Discuss whether this evidence helps to answer the focus question.
● Taking into account the final outcome of the local history study, help the children to decide what they will do with the evidence they have collected, and then facilitate them doing it.

2: What can a local historian tell us about local history?

Lesson objectives
● To develop a chronologically secure knowledge and understanding of British, local and world history, establishing clear narratives within and across the periods they study.
● To understand how our knowledge of the past is constructed from a range of sources.

Expected outcomes
● All children can write relevant questions to ask an historian.
● Most children can use a visit by a local historian to gather historical evidence.
● Some children can ask the historian relevant follow-up questions.

Resources
Film recording equipment (optional)

Preparation

● Arrange for a local historian to visit the school to give a talk on a subject relating to the aspect of local history you are studying. See www.local-history.co.uk/Groups for a list of local history societies in the UK.
● You might want to arrange for the historian to talk to your class or year group only. Alternatively, if the subject they will be talking about is of wider interest, you could invite them to give their presentation to the whole school, or the whole of Key Stage 2.
● Rewrite the lesson's focus question to make it specific to the aspect of local history you are studying.

Introduction

● Introduce this lesson's focus question: *What can a local historian tell us about [aspect of local history you are studying]?*
● Give the children some information about the historian who will be coming to talk to them and what their talk will be about.
● Tell the children they are going to write a list of questions they would like to ask the historian. Ask: *What makes a good question?* Work with the children to create a list of criteria.

Paired work

● Organise children into pairs to write their questions, and then ask pairs to share their best questions with the class, asking the rest of the class to provide feedback.
● Give pairs time to revise their questions, taking into account the feedback they received.

Whole-class work

● The rest of the lesson will take place on the day of the historian's visit.
● Just before the historian arrives explain to the children your expectations of their behaviour during the visit.
● Welcome the visitor and listen to their presentation.
● Give the children time after the historian's presentation to ask any prepared questions that have not already been answered, as well as any follow-up questions they may have.
● You could ask a competent child to film the presentation and the question session for use as a future school resource, or to incorporate into your final outcome.

Review

● Review the focus question for this lesson: *What can a visit from a local historian tell us about [the aspect of local history you're studying]?*
● Ask children to share the evidence they collected during the historian's visit. Discuss whether this evidence helps to answer the focus question.
● Taking into account the final outcome of the local history study, help the children to decide what they will do with the evidence they have collected, and then facilitate them doing it.

Curriculum objective
● To understand how our knowledge of the past is constructed from a range of sources.

Resources
Interactive activity 'Timeline maker' on the CD-ROM (optional)

Timelines

Revise

● Ask the children: *What sources of evidence have we investigated so far?*
● Give the children a few minutes working in pairs or groups to list all the sources of evidence they have investigated during the local history study.
● Collate answers to produce a full list on the board.

Assess

● Introduce the assessment task. On the board write: *What does this source tell us about [the aspect of local history you're studying]?* Ask children to choose TWO of the sources written on the board, and write an answer for each of them.
● Give the children a set length of time (for example, 20 minutes) to complete the task. Emphasise the importance of working independently.
● If you have any children who struggle with writing you might want to give them an alternative way of recording what they know (perhaps explaining their answer to a teaching assistant who makes an audio recording of it).
● If any children finish ahead of time you could ask them to choose and write about one more source.

Further practice

● If appropriate for the aspect of local history you are studying, ask the children to use the interactive activity 'Timeline maker' on the CD-ROM to create a timeline outlining key events in local history.
● During the next chapter, children could add more events to the timeline and incorporate the completed timeline into their final outcome for the study.

Curriculum objective
● To develop the appropriate use of historical terms.

Resources
Multiple sets of cards in which each card features an historical term from the local history study

Historical terms

Revise

● Organise the class into groups, giving each group a set of historical term cards.
● Ask each group to work together collaboratively to sort the cards into groups.
● Discuss with children the criteria they have used for sorting the cards.

Assess

● Introduce the assessment task: children are going to choose four of the words from the cards. Each word must belong to a different group from the sorting activity. For each word, the children write a definition and then use the word in context, in a sentence or short paragraph.
● Demonstrate the task, choosing one of the words from the cards. Encourage children to help you write the definition and suggest a sentence or short paragraph in which to put the word in context. Tell children this word is now 'off limits'.
● Give the children a set length of time (for example, 20 minutes) to complete the task. Emphasise the importance of working independently.

Further practice

● Play historical term bingo in groups or as a whole class.
● Each player draws a 3 by 3 grid, writing a different historical term from the cards in each cell. One person acts as caller. The caller draws one historical term card at a time, at random. Instead of reading out the historical term on the card, they define it.

What is a good question for a historical investigation?

- A good question for an historical investigation is one that is specific.

For example:

How has our local area changed? is not specific enough. It does not put definite boundaries on the subject or the time you are investigating, and it would be difficult to know where to start looking for answers.

How has our classroom changed since last year? is too narrow in its scope. It does not give you much to find out.

How has our school changed since the 1950s? is a good question. It is clear which subject and time you are investigating, so you can work out where to start looking for answers. There is also plenty to find out.

- A good question for an historical investigation is historically relevant.
- A good question is based on one of the following historical concepts: change, cause, similarity or difference and significance.

For example:
Change
How did... change/develop between/during...?
How has... changed/developed since...?

Cause
Why did...?
What were the causes of...?
How did... affect...?

Similarity or difference
How is/was... different from...?
In what ways is/was... the same as...?

Significance
What does/did... mean for...?
Why was... important during...?
Why is... still significant today?

Where could we find answers to our questions?

Focus question:	**Focus question:**
Possible sources (circle those that apply)**:** online, documents in school, artefacts, historical buildings, archaeological sites, libraries, museums, local people, other	**Possible sources** (circle those that apply)**:** online, documents in school, artefacts, historical buildings, archaeological sites, libraries, museums, local people, other
Specific sources:	**Specific sources:**
Focus question:	**Focus question:**
Possible sources (circle those that apply)**:** online, documents in school, artefacts, historical buildings, archaeological sites, libraries, museums, local people, other	**Possible sources** (circle those that apply)**:** online, documents in school, artefacts, historical buildings, archaeological sites, libraries, museums, local people, other
Specific sources:	**Specific sources:**
Focus question:	**Focus question:**
Possible sources (circle those that apply)**:** online, documents in school, artefacts, historical buildings, archaeological sites, libraries, museums, local people, other	**Possible sources** (circle those that apply)**:** online, documents in school, artefacts, historical buildings, archaeological sites, libraries, museums, local people, other
Specific sources:	**Specific sources:**

Name: _____ Date: _____

Evaluating evidence flowchart

START

Might this source help us answer one of our questions?

Yes

No → Try another source.

Does this source contain writing or speech?

Yes

No

Who wrote/said this?

What might the source tell us?

What are they trying to tell us?

Could the source be interpreted in a different way?

How reliable might their facts be?

How biased might their opinions be?

A local history study (2)

This chapter continues the local history study started in the previous chapter. The lessons in the first four weeks of this chapter are optional. Choose the lessons that are appropriate for the local history topic the children are investigating and for the range of evidence you have access to, and cover them in whichever order suits you. The lessons in weeks 5 and 6 wrap up the whole term's work, and are essential for every class. You should teach them in the order in which they are presented.

Chapter at a glance

Curriculum objective
• A local history study.

Week	Lesson	Summary of activities	Expected outcomes
1	1	• Children examine old newspapers related to their chosen topic and use what they find out as evidence to answer their focus questions.	• Can use old newspapers to gather historical evidence.
	2	• Children examine old maps related to their chosen topic and use what they find out as evidence to answer their focus questions.	• Can use old maps to gather historical evidence.
2	1	• Children examine old photographs related to their chosen topic and use what they find out as evidence to answer their focus questions.	• Can use old photographs to gather historical evidence.
	2	• Children examine public records (such as census returns, wills, and certificates of births and marriages and deaths) and use what they find out as evidence to answer one or more of their focus questions.	• Can use public records to gather historical evidence.
3	1	• Children examine old school logbooks and use what they find out as evidence to answer one or more of their focus questions.	• Can use old school logbooks to gather historical evidence.
	2	• Children examine personal documents (such as diaries and letters) and use what they find out as evidence to answer one or more of their focus questions.	• Can use personal documents to gather historical evidence.
4	1	• Children examine books on local history and use what they find out as evidence to answer one or more of their focus questions.	• Can use books on local history to gather historical evidence.
	2	• Children compare the aspect of local history they have been studying with the same aspect of the locality today.	• Can make connections between their locality's past and present.
5	1	• Children use what they have found out during the local history study to make wider inferences about British history.	• Can make connections between local history and British history.
	2	• Children work together to prepare to present their findings about local history.	• Can prepare a local history presentation.
6	1	• Children take part in/complete the presentation and collect feedback from their audience.	• Can present the results of their local history study.
	2	• Children reflect on the knowledge and skills they have gained over the course of the study. • They evaluate the success of their presentation. • They identify next steps for learning in history.	• Can evaluate their learning.
Assess and review		• To review the half-term's work.	

■SCHOLASTIC
www.scholastic.co.uk

Expected prior learning

● Children need to have completed at least the first five lessons from the previous chapter Year 5, Summer 1: A local history study (1).

Overview of progression

● This chapter, in conjunction with the previous chapter, provides children with knowledge and understanding of an aspect of local history.
● The children continue to address historically valid questions about change, cause, similarity and difference, and significance.
● They have the opportunity to note connections, contrasts and trends over time and develop the appropriate use of historical terms.
● They use a range of sources to construct informed responses that involve thoughtful selection and organisation of relevant historical information.

Creative context

● The children continue working towards a final outcome that allows them to share what they have found out with a wider audience. It is in guiding the children towards this final outcome that you will be able to make the most of creative opportunities and cross-curricular links. Some possible final outcomes might be: turning the classroom into a museum, creating a documentary film, publishing an e-book, creating a website or putting on an assembly.

Background knowledge

● As in the previous chapter, the focus here is on developing skills of historical enquiry. It is not essential that you as the teacher know a lot about the aspect of local history the children are investigating; but you do need to be able to provide children with a wide variety of sources from which they can gather and interpret evidence.
● During this chapter the children will continue to work towards an end of term presentation that allows them to share what they have found out with a wider audience. The possible final outcomes that were suggested in the previous chapter will be supported by lesson plans in this chapter. Of course, there are many ways in which the children could present what they have found out, but many of the suggestions given here are easily adaptable to other situations.

Week 1 lesson plans

In this week's lessons the children continue their examination of primary sources in order to gather evidence to answer the questions they have chosen to investigate about an aspect of local history. One, both or neither of this week's lessons may be appropriate for your class. In Lesson 1 the children examine an article from an old newspaper and then search through one or more old newspapers in an attempt to find relevant sources of information. In Lesson 2 they study an old map and consider how it might help them with their investigation.

1: What can old newspapers tell us about local history?

Lesson objectives
● To develop a chronologically secure knowledge and understanding of British, local and world history, establishing clear narratives within and across the periods they study.
● To understand how our knowledge of the past is constructed from a range of sources.

Expected outcomes
● All children can read old newspapers.
● Most children can use old newspapers to gather historical evidence.
● Some children can describe several strengths and limitations of newspapers as sources of historical evidence.

Resources
Copies of one or more old local newspapers; a newspaper article; an audio recording of the article, audio playing equipment, headphones; photocopiable page 113 'Gathering evidence from old newspapers'; useful information, including a list of online newspaper collections, can be found at the National Archives website

Introduction
● Introduce this lesson's focus question: *What can old newspapers tell us about local history?*, rewording the question so that it refers to the aspect of local history the children are studying.
● Display the article you have selected and give children time to read it independently.
● Write on the board: *What does the article tell us about* [the aspect of local history you are studying]? When the children have read the article, ask them to discuss the question with a partner. Discuss ideas as a class.

Paired work
● Ask pairs to look through the newspaper and identify any articles, adverts or other features that might be relevant to their local history topic. Share ideas as a class.
● Ask each pair to choose one relevant article, advert or other feature from the newspaper, and answer the questions about it on photocopiable page 113 'Gathering evidence from old newspapers' from the CD-ROM.

Whole-class work
● Ask pairs to report back to the class on what they have found out.
● Ask: *What are the limitations of newspapers as a way of gathering historical evidence?* Limitations include: with lots of features and no indexing system it can be difficult to find the information you need; newspapers are written to deadlines, so facts are not always checked thoroughly; article choice and content shows the bias of the reporter, editor and/or newspaper owner; and newspapers are subject to political pressure (local newspapers less so than national newspapers).

Differentiation
● Support: for the introduction, children requiring support will benefit from access to an audio recording of the article, so they can follow the text as they listen.
● Challenge: encourage some children to identify several strengths of newspapers as a source of evidence.

Review
● Discuss with children what they will do with the evidence they have gathered from this activity, and how they will incorporate it into the presentation they are preparing for the end of term.

Lesson objectives

● To develop a chronologically secure knowledge and understanding of British, local and world history, establishing clear narratives within and across the periods they study.
● To understand how our knowledge of the past is constructed from a range of sources.

Expected outcomes

● All children can read old maps.
● Most children can use old maps to gather historical evidence.
● Some children can gather further historical evidence by comparing old maps with a map of the same area today.

Resources

One or more old maps of the local area; a current map of the local area; useful information and maps to purchase can be found online at the British Library, National Archives and Ordnance Survey websites

2: What can old maps tell us about local history?

Introduction

● Introduce this lesson's focus question: *What can old maps tell us about local history?*, rewording the question so that it refers to the aspect of local history the children are studying.
● Ensure everyone can see a copy of the map at close quarters.
● Ask questions about the map, as appropriate, such as: *What physical features are shown on the map? What human features are shown? When was the map created? Who created it? Did they draw it by hand? Why was the map created? Who was the intended audience? What symbols does the map-maker use? What do they mean? How do you know? Could symbols be misinterpreted because of modern assumptions about symbols?*

Group work

● Ask groups to examine the map and make notes about the information it gives them about the aspect of local history they are studying in general, and the class's focus questions in particular. If you have more than one map, some groups could examine a different map from the one used in the introduction.
● You might want to provide each group with a list of questions to answer about the information the map provides on the local history topic. Suitable questions will depend on the aspect of local history you are studying, the class's focus questions, and the information contained in the map.
● When each group has finished writing notes and/or answering questions, give them a map showing the same part of the local area today. Ask them to compare and contrast the old and new maps, drawing further conclusions about the aspect of local history they are studying. This is a particularly valuable activity if one or more of this term's focus questions are on the theme of change.

Whole-class work

● Ask groups to report back to the class on what they have found out.
● Ask: *How does this map compare with other sources? Is the information it provides consistent with other sources? What do you still not know – and where can you find that information?*

Differentiation
● Support: organise children into mixed-ability groupings for the group activity.
● Challenge: encourage children to compare the old map(s) with a map of the same area today, and draw conclusions about the aspect of local history they are studying.

Review

● Finally, discuss with children what they will do with the evidence they have gathered from this activity, and how they will incorporate it into the presentation they are preparing for the end of term.

Week 2 lesson plans

In this week's lessons the children collect evidence about the past of their locality from old photographs and from public records. While public records are not as immediately accessible for children as old photographs, they are a valuable source of evidence used extensively by historians, and it is recommended that you cover both of this week's lessons if they are appropriate for the aspect of local history the children are investigating.

1: What can old photographs tell us about local history?

Lesson objectives
- To develop a chronologically secure knowledge and understanding of British, local and world history, establishing clear narratives within and across the periods they study.
- To understand how our knowledge of the past is constructed from a range of sources.

Expected outcomes
- All children can ask and answer questions about old photographs.
- Most children can use old photographs to gather historical evidence.
- Some children can collect further evidence to support historical theories suggested by old photographs.

Resources
Collection of old photographs relating to the aspect of local history you are investigating; theory cards about the photographs (see *Preparation*)

Preparation
- Collect a large selection of old photographs relating to the aspect of local history you are investigating.
- Choose a subset of about a dozen photographs to use in the introductory activity. Arrange them on a single page/screen and number each photo. Write a separate 'theory card' for each of these photos. This should contain a theory about local history, in the form of a short statement, which could be inferred from looking at the photograph, for example: *The school playing field used to be larger, The local economy was depressed in the 1970s because lots of shops were empty*, or *The village used to have a railway station.*

Introduction
- Introduce this lesson's focus question: *What can old photographs tell us about local history?*, rewording the question so that it refers to the aspect of local history the children are studying.
- Organise the class into groups. Give each group a copy of the numbered set of photographs and a set of theory cards. Ask them to match each theory card with the correct photograph and then write a second historical theory for each photograph.

Whole-class work
- Go through the answers to the introductory activity, and then discuss the children's own ideas for theories. If any of these are interesting and might merit further investigation, make a note of them.

Paired work
- Organise children into pairs and give them access to your complete collection of old photographs.
- Ask each pair to look through the photographs and choose three to examine in greater detail. For each photograph they examine in detail ask them to write as many historical theories as they can.

Whole-class work
- Ask pairs to share their theories with the class.

> **Differentiation**
> - Challenge: ask children to look for further evidence to support any interesting theories suggested during the introductory activity.

Review
- Discuss with children what they will do with the evidence they have gathered from this activity, and how they will incorporate it into the presentation they are preparing for the end of term.

2: What can public records tell us about local history?

Introduction
● Display a public record document. Ask: *What can you tell me about this document?* Ask children to discuss the document with a partner, and then share their ideas with the class.
● Tell the children what type of document it is, explaining that it is an example of a public record. Ask: *What are public records?*
● Introduce this lesson's focus question: *What can public records tell us about local history?*, rewording the question so that it refers to the aspect of local history the children are studying.

Paired work
● Give each pair a public record document. Ideally, give out several documents throughout the class.
● Display photocopiable page 'Assessing public record documents' from the CD-ROM.
● Ask pairs to examine the document you have given them, discuss the questions on the photocopiable sheet, and record their answers.
● As children are working, discuss the questions with them, focusing in particular on the first five. (The final three questions will be the focus of the whole-class work towards the end of the lesson.)

Whole-class work
● Ask pairs to describe to the rest of the class the public record document they have been studying, and explain what they have found out from it.
● Question the children about their conclusions, and in particular about their answers to the final three questions from the paired activity, asking: *Does the document help you answer one of the focus questions? Does it give any other information about the aspect of local history we are studying?* and *Does it raise any further questions? If so, what are they?*
● Collate a set of class notes relating to these three questions for each of the documents studied.
● Tell children that public records are important sources of evidence for historians and ask them to suggest why. (They are factual, usually reliable, dated, designed for the fast retrieval of information, and they are kept centrally, so they are easy to find.)

Review
● Discuss with children what they will do with the evidence they have gathered from this activity, and how they will incorporate it into their presentation.

Week 3 lesson plans

In this week's lessons the children continue their examination of primary sources. In Lesson 1 they investigate old school logbooks, and in Lesson 2 they look at a range of personal documents, including official documents (such as passports, driving licences and ration books), and non-official documents (such as letters and diary entries). All these types of documents are rich and often fascinating sources of evidence, and it is recommended you cover both lessons, providing they are appropriate for the aspect of local history the children are studying.

Lesson objectives
● To develop a chronologically secure knowledge and understanding of British, local and world history, establishing clear narratives within and across the periods they study.
● To understand how our knowledge of the past is constructed from a range of sources.

Expected outcomes
● All children can ask and answer questions about old school logbooks.
● Most children can use old school logbooks to gather historical evidence.
● Some children can describe some of the limitations of school logbooks as a source of evidence.

Resources
Pages from a school logbook; paper-based or digital writing materials

1: What can old school logbooks tell us about local history?

Introduction
● Introduce this lesson's focus question: *What can old school logbooks tell us about local history?*, rewording the question so that it refers to the aspect of local history the children are studying.
● Discuss school logbooks in general, and introduce the logbook you will be examining.
● Display an extract from the logbook. Ask volunteers to read the text aloud, helping them to decipher handwriting as necessary. Encourage children to ask questions about anything they do not understand.

Whole-class work
● Ask: *What is surprising about this text?* Draw out differences between school life at the time of the logbook entry and school life now.
● Ask: *What does this text tell you about* [the aspect of local history you are studying]*?* Give children a few minutes to discuss this with a partner, and then ask them to share their ideas.

Group work
● Give each group a different extract from the logbook. Write the questions from the whole-class activity on the board. Ask groups to discuss these questions about this logbook extract.

Independent work
● Ask individuals to choose a short passage from the group's extract and transcribe it. The passage should be relevant to the local history topic, and if possible, to one of the focus questions.

Differentiation
● Support: group the class according to ability. Give less confident groups shorter and less challenging extracts to study, and arrange for them to work with an adult.
● Challenge: encourage some children to identify some of the limitations of school logbooks as a source of evidence.

Review
● Ask several children to read out the passage they have transcribed, explaining its relevance, and then answering questions about it from the rest of the class.
● Discuss with children what they will do with the evidence they have gathered from this activity, and how they will incorporate it into their end-of-term presentation.

Lesson objectives

● To develop a chronologically secure knowledge and understanding of British, local and world history, establishing clear narratives within and across the periods they study.
● To understand how our knowledge of the past is constructed from a range of sources.

Expected outcomes

● All children can ask and answer questions about personal documents.
● Most children can use personal documents to gather historical evidence.
● Some children can describe limitations of non-official personal documents, such as letters and diaries, as a source of evidence.

Resources

An official personal document (for example passport, driving licence or ration book); several non-official personal documents (such as letters or diary extracts); paper-based or digital writing materials

2: What can personal documents tell us about local history?

Introduction

● Introduce this lesson's focus question: *What can personal documents tell us about local history?*, rewording the question so that it refers to the aspect of local history the children are studying.
● Display an official personal document, such as a passport, driving licence or ration book. Ask: *What can you tell about the person who owned this document?* Ask children to discuss this question with a partner, and then to share their ideas with the rest of the class.
● Ask: *What does this document tell you about* [the aspect of local history you are studying]? and repeat the discussion process.

Group work

● Give each group a different non-official personal document, such as a letter or diary extract. Ask groups to read the document and then write questions about it. Challenge them to write a minimum number of questions and to make the questions as varied as possible.
● Ask groups to pair up to swap documents and answer each other's questions.

Paired work

● Tell children they will be producing a piece of creative writing in response to one of the non-official personal documents they have read. For example, in response to a letter they could write a letter in reply; in response to a diary extract they could write the next day's entry in the diary.
● Ask children, working in pairs, to use the documents they have just read, together with their knowledge of text types from English lessons, to brainstorm the features of the type(s) of text they will be writing. Discuss ideas as a whole class, ensuring children are clear about the features of the relevant text type(s).

Independent work

● Give children time, working independently, to draft, review and revise their piece of creative writing.

Differentiation

● Support: in the independent creative writing activity support children with appropriate scaffolding to help them write their letter or diary entry.
● Challenge: ask children to consider and describe the limitations of non-official personal documents, such as letters or diaries, as sources of evidence. (They only present one, limited viewpoint; they are inevitably biased as they reflect the opinions and prejudices of the author; if the author is writing about events a while after they happened, their memories may not be reliable.)

Review

● Ask selected children to share their creative writing.
● Discuss with children what they will do with the evidence they have gathered from this lesson, and the letters or diary entries they have written, and how they will incorporate them into their presentation.

Week 4 lesson plans

In Lesson 1 the children use local history books to gather evidence on the topic they are studying. You could teach this lesson as an alternative to, or in conjunction with, the lesson featuring a visit by a local historian (see page 93). In Lesson 2 the children begin wrapping up the project, by comparing the aspect of local history they have studied with the same aspect of the locality today. This lesson is recommended for all classes, unless the children have already covered it through one of their focus questions.

Lesson objectives
● To develop a chronologically secure knowledge and understanding of British, local and world history, establishing clear narratives within and across the periods they study.
● To understand how our knowledge of the past is constructed from a range of sources.

Expected outcomes
● All children can find information in books on local history.
● Most children can use books on local history to gather historical evidence.
● Some children can evaluate local history books in terms of richness, reliability and relevance.

Resources
Various books on local history (one with multiple copies); questions whose answers can be found in the book you have multiple copies of

1: What can books tell us about local history?

Introduction
● Introduce this lesson's focus question: *What can books tell us about local history?*, rewording the question so that it refers to the aspect of local history the children are studying.
● Organise the class into groups, giving each group a copy of the book you have multiple copies of.
● Read out the prepared questions one at a time, asking children to find the answer in the book, write it on a piece of paper and hand it to you. Devise a scoring system that rewards quick correct answers.
● At the end of the game ask: *How did you find the information you needed? Were any ways quicker than others?*

Whole-class work
● Ask: *How is this book different from most of the other sources we have investigated?* Establish that it is a *secondary source* rather than a *primary source*, revising these terms if necessary.
● Ask: *How might the fact that it is a secondary source affect the quality of the information it provides?* (It is not based on direct experience, so it may not be as reliable, but it may provide a more balanced and complete view.)

Paired work
● Ask pairs to choose one focus question (from the class list or one of their own), and look for information about it in the local history books.
● Ask children to note any differences of opinion or factual information in the books.

> **Differentiation**
> ● Challenge: children to evaluate the various local history books in terms of richness, reliability and relevance.

Review
● Ask pairs to discuss the progress they have made towards answering their chosen question.
● Ask the children to describe any differences they noted between books, and discuss possible reasons for these differences. If books disagree over factual information, ask the children to suggest how they might be able to find out what the correct facts are.

Lesson objectives
- To develop a chronologically secure knowledge and understanding of British, local and world history, establishing clear narratives within and across the periods they study.
- To note connections, contrasts and trends over time.
- To understand how our knowledge of the past is constructed from a range of sources.

Expected outcomes
- All children can research present-day information about the locality.
- Most children can make connections between the locality's past and present.
- Some children can carry out independent research into the present-day locality in order to make further connections with the past.

Resources
Internet access; sources of present-day information about the aspect of the locality children have been investigating; teaching assistant (optional)

2: How does the aspect of local history we have studied compare with the same aspect of the locality today?

Introduction
- Introduce this lesson's focus question: *How does the aspect of local history we have studied compare with the same aspect of the locality today?*, rewording the question so that it refers to the aspect of local history the children are studying.
- On the board write the title *[The aspect of the locality you have been studying] today*. Under the title write two headings: *What we already know* and *What we need to find out*.
- Ask the children, working with a partner, to jot down ideas for what to write under each heading. Collate ideas to produce a class list. Keep the *What we already know* list to refer to in the final lesson of the chapter.
- Look at each of the questions listed in *What we need to find out*. Ask: *How could you find out the answer?* Establish whether there are any questions that cannot be answered using the internet or the printed sources you have available. If there are, assign these questions as extension activities for children to pursue in their own time.

Whole-class work
- Revise what is meant by *research* (searching carefully, with a method, in order to answer a question).
- Ask the children where they could research the information they need in order to answer the remaining questions. (For example, they could look in printed materials in the classroom or school library, or they could search online.)
- Ask children to suggest what skills they need in order to do effective research in books. (For example, understanding the library's classification system, knowing where to find and how to use a book's index, and being able to skim read to pinpoint relevant information.) Repeat the question for effective online research skills. (For example, understanding how search engines work, knowing how to use advanced search options, and being able to assess websites and information for credibility.)

Group work
- Divide the class into groups and share the remaining questions between them. Ask each group to research the answers to the questions they have been given.

Whole-class work
- Bring the class back together and ask groups to report back on what they have found out. Record the answers on the board.
- Discuss the following questions: *What is different about then and now? Why has it changed? Do you know? Can you guess? Could you find out?*

> **Differentiation**
> - Support: use mixed-ability groupings. Some children may need adult support with the research.

Review
- Discuss with children what they will do with the evidence they have gathered from this lesson, and the letters and how they will incorporate it into their presentation.

Week 5 lesson plans

The lessons this week continue to wrap up the project, and it is recommended that you teach both of them. In Lesson 1 the children review what they have learned over the whole local history study, and then use their knowledge to draw conclusions about British history. If you have already made connections to British history over the course of the study, you may want to adapt this lesson, basing it solely around a review of the children's learning. In Lesson 2 the children make the final preparations for their end of term presentation. This lesson may take several sessions to complete.

1: What does our local history study tell us about British history?

Introduction
● Introduce this lesson's focus question: *What does our local history study tell us about British history?*
● Ask: *What have you found out about [the aspect of local history you have been studying]?* Ask children to work with a partner to write a list of statements summarising what they have found out. (For example, *The school was built in 1865. Caning was a form of punishment. Children took time off school in the autumn to help with the apple harvest.*)

Whole-class work
● Collect between six and eight of the children's statements, and write them on the board.
● Ask: *Which of these statements tell you something about the country as a whole?* (For example, taking the statements above, the first doesn't apply to the country as a whole, the second does, and the third does in a modified form, such as *Children in rural areas sometimes took time off school to help on the land.*) Establish which statements tell us something about the country as a whole, and what they tell us.

Group work
● Ask pairs to form groups of four or six. Ask each pair to share with the group the statements they have written. The group should then discuss the statements, deciding which of them tells us something about the country as a whole, and for those that do, what they tell us.
● Ask each group to produce a separate list of statements about the country as a whole.

Whole-class work
● Bring the class back together and ask groups to report back on what they have found out.

Differentiation
● Support: use mixed-ability groupings.
● Challenge: encourage children to devise relevant questions to ask about British history.

Review
● Discuss with children what they will do with the conclusions they have drawn this lesson, and how they will incorporate them into their presentation.

Lesson objectives
● To develop a chronologically secure knowledge and understanding of British, local and world history, establishing clear narratives within and across the periods they study.
● To note connections, contrasts and trends over time.

Expected outcomes
● All children can explain what they have found out about the aspect of local history they have been studying.
● Most children can make connections between local history and British history.
● Some children can devise relevant questions to ask about British history.

Resources
Writing materials

Lesson objective
● To develop a chronologically secure knowledge and understanding of British, local and world history, establishing clear narratives within and across the periods they study.

Expected outcomes
● All children can make a contribution to the end of term presentation.
● Most children can work together effectively to prepare the presentation.
● Some children can lead the work of a group.

Resources
The resources will vary

2: Can we prepare to share what we have found out?

Introduction
● Introduce this lesson's focus question: *Can we prepare to share what we have found out?*
● Facilitate the children in whatever they need to do to prepare for the presentation. Make clear how much class time you will be able to give them in order to complete their preparations.

Whole-class work
● Appropriate activities for this will vary widely, depending on the chosen form of the presentation, and on how much planning and preparation the children have already done. Below are some suggestions for activities based on some possible final outcomes for the project.
● **Museum**
  ● Decide what work will go into the museum and how pieces of work will be grouped together to form exhibits.
  ● Draw up a plan of where each exhibit will go. Think about possible routes visitors will take around the exhibits, and try to ensure a logical flow.
  ● Work in groups to create the exhibits.
  ● Decide on opening times, and advertise these to teachers and parents.
  ● Train a couple of children to act as guides. Ask them to train more guides.
  ● Record an audio tour of the museum for visitors to use.
● **Filming documentary**
  ● Decide what work will be featured in the video.
  ● Draw up a storyboard.
  ● Write script notes or a full script.
  ● Allocate roles (both on- and off-camera).
  ● Practise using film equipment and video editing software.
  ● Rehearse the documentary.
  ● Film the documentary.
  ● Allow plenty of time for children to edit the video and to shoot and incorporate extra footage if needed.
  ● Show the documentary to a trial audience (such as, a parallel class), get feedback from them, and make final changes in the light of this.
  ● Arrange a premier screening of the documentary.
● **E-book/website**
  ● Decide what work will be featured in the book or on the website.
  ● Divide the book/website into sections, allocating each section to a group.
  ● Organise (and if necessary, create) written, visual and multimedia content.
  ● Proofread and evaluate each other's work, and then edit work in response.
  ● Arrange an event to celebrate the publication of the e-book or launch of the website.
● **Assembly**
  ● Invite parents.
  ● Decide what work will be included in the assembly.
  ● Plan the running order for the assembly and allocate roles to groups.
  ● Rehearse in groups and as a whole class.
  ● Arrange for one or more children to film the assembly (best done at a final rehearsal).

Review
● Hold plenary sessions to review how the preparations are progressing, to change plans if necessary, and to help children to address any problems that may have arisen.

Week 6 lesson plans

In Lesson 1 the children present the final outcome of the local history study, sharing what they have discovered over the past term with their chosen audience. In Lesson 2 the children evaluate the presentation they gave in Lesson 1, and assess their learning over the course of the study.

1: Can we share what we have found out?

Lesson objective
● To develop a chronologically secure knowledge and understanding of British, local and world history, establishing clear narratives within and across the periods they study.

Expected outcomes
● All children can contribute to the presentation.
● Most children can make an effective contribution to the presentation.
● Some children can play a leading role in the presentation.

Resources
The resources will vary

Introduction
● Introduce this lesson's focus question: *Can we share what we have found out?*
● Praise the children for all their hard work over the course of the study, and during their preparations for presenting what they have found out. Encourage them to do their best during the presentation, and to have fun!

Whole-class work
● Appropriate activities for this lesson will vary widely, depending on the chosen form of the presentation. Below are some suggestions based on some possible final outcomes for the project.
● **Museum**
  ● Open the museum to the rest of the school and to parents. You could have a grand opening, asking a VIP to cut a ribbon.
  ● If children have trained as museum guides, ask them to post a rota to show the times each child will be on guiding duty.
  ● If children have recorded an audio tour, ask them to ensure appropriate equipment is available so that visitors can listen to it.
  ● You could put a visitor's book and pen at the exit to the museum and ask visitors to record their impressions.
  ● Ask children to create a photographic record of the museum.
● **Filming documentary**
  ● Show the premier of the documentary to your chosen audience.
  ● After the premier hold a reception where the audience can mingle with the film makers over squash and biscuits.
  ● Release the documentary to a wider audience. You could hold further screenings in school, and/or upload the film to the school learning platform or a video-sharing site. If the film is to be shared publicly, make sure appropriate guidelines are followed.
  ● **E-book or website**
  ● Hold a launch party for your e-book or website.
  ● Use laptops and tablets to display multiple copies of the e-book or website, making them available to visitors.
  ● If the children have written an e-book you may want to publish it in the public domain. Charging a small fee to download the book might be a way of raising money for school or class funds. You could discuss this possibility with your headteacher.
● **Assembly**
  ● Present your assembly to your chosen audience.
  ● If children did not film the assembly during a final rehearsal you might want to ask a colleague to record the actual assembly.

Review
● After the presentation, review how it went. Ask, for example: *Did you enjoy giving the presentation? Did the audience enjoy the presentation? How can you tell? What did they learn? How do you know? If you were doing the presentation again, what would you keep the same? What would you change, and why?*

Lesson objective
● To develop a chronologically secure knowledge and understanding of British, local and world history, establishing clear narratives within and across the periods they study.

Expected outcomes
● All children can evaluate the presentation.
● Most children can assess their learning over the course of the project.
● Some children can suggest next steps in their learning.

Resources
Photocopiable page 114 'Evaluating the presentation'; photocopiable page 115 'Self-assessment'

2: What have we learned?

Introduction
● Introduce this lesson's focus question: *What have we learned?*
● Display photocopiable page 114 'Evaluating the presentation' and read through it together, ensuring the children understand what they need to do.

Paired work
● Ask the children to work in pairs to evaluate the presentation and record their opinions on the photocopiable page.

Whole-class work
● Ask pairs to feed back on their evaluation of the presentation. Ask: *If you were to do the project again, would you choose the same type of presentation? If not, what type of presentation would you choose, and why?*
● Display the *What we know* list drawn up at the beginning of the local history study (in Summer 1, Lesson 1). Next to it display the *What we already know* list created during Week 4 Lesson 2 of this chapter.
● Help the children to compare these lists and gain an overview of what they have learned over the course of the study. Ask: *How does what you have learned compare with what you thought you would learn? Have you learned more/less/about the same as you thought you would?*
● Emphasise the fact that these lists only show facts that the children have learned – not skills. Ask: *Have you learned any new skills? If so, what are they?*

Independent work
● Display photocopiable page 115 'Self-assessment' and read through it together, ensuring the children understand how to fill it in.
● Give individuals time to complete the self-assessment independently.

Differentiation
● Support: give children the opportunity to discuss their self-assessment with an adult before filling in the form.
● Challenge: ask some children to suggest next steps in their learning, and to draw up specific targets to work on during Year 6.

Review
● Ask the children to suggest ways in which the local history study could be improved in future. As part of this, you could ask them to suggest ways in which the work they have done this term could be used to enhance the experience of the project for subsequent classes. Make notes about the children's suggestions, keeping them to refer to next time you teach the project, or passing them on to the next teacher to do so.

Curriculum objectives
● To develop a chronologically secure knowledge and understanding of British, local and world history, establishing clear narratives within and across the periods they study.

Resources
A quiz you have written on the aspect of local history the children have been studying; equipment and materials for creating paper-based and/ or digital quizzes and games; interactive activity 'Timeline maker' on the CD-ROM (optional)

Local history quiz

Revise

● Divide the class into mixed-ability teams for a quiz about the aspect of local history the children have been studying.
● The quiz is more fun if you read out the quiz questions, but if you prefer, you can give each team a copy of the questions and let them work through the questions in their own time.
● At the end of the quiz, go through the answers, asking teams to swap papers and mark each other's answers.

Assess

● Note: This activity is likely to take the children several sessions to complete.
● Organise the class into pairs or small groups and set children the task of designing and creating a resource that can be used to test future classes' knowledge of the local history topic. For example, they might design and create a paper-based or digital quiz or game.

Further practice

● If you have not already created a timeline, and it is appropriate for the aspect of local history you have been studying, ask the children to use the interactive activity 'Timeline maker' on the CD-ROM to create a timeline outlining key events to do with the topic.

Curriculum objectives
● To regularly address and sometimes devise historically valid questions about change, cause, similarity and difference, and significance.

Resources
Audio recording equipment (optional)

Writing historical questions

Revise

● Revisit some of the questions children devised for the local history topic. Encourage children to discuss the answers to the questions, explain how they found out the answers, what else they found out while doing the research, and what other questions their research led them to ask.

Assess

● On the board, write a question relating to the topic of the local history study that focuses on change, cause or significance.
  ● A question about *change* could ask about change in the locality over the period of local history studied, or about changes in the locality between the period studied and today.
  ● A question about *cause* could ask about the causes of events that took place during the period studied, or their effects.
  ● A question about *significance* could ask why certain local people or events are still important today locally, nationally or even internationally.
● Give the children a set length of time (such as 15 minutes) to write an answer to the question, answering as fully as they can, and supporting their answer with evidence from the historical sources they have investigated. Emphasise the importance of working independently.
● If you have any children who struggle with writing you might want to give them an alternative way of recording what they know (such as explaining their answer to a teaching assistant who makes an audio recording of it).

Further practice

● Ask the children to put together a list of recommended focus questions for subsequent classes studying the same local history topic.

Gathering evidence from old newspapers

Name of newspaper _____

Date of newspaper _____

Title of text _____

Page number _____

■ Work with your partner to answer these questions about the article you have chosen.

1. What sort of text is it? _____

_____

2. Who wrote it? _____

_____

3. Why did they write it? _____

_____

4. How does the writer convey information and make his or her point?

_____

_____

5. What do you believe and disbelieve from this text? _____

_____

6. How might others at the time have reacted to this text? _____

_____

7. What does the text tell you about the aspect of local history you are

studying? _____

_____

I can collect evidence from newspapers.

How did you do?

Name: _____   Date: _____

Evaluating the presentation

■ Work with your partner. Answer these questions to evaluate your presentation.

I. Describe how you both contributed to the presentation.

_____

_____

_____

2. What problems did you or your group(s) have?

_____

_____

_____

3. How did you solve them?

_____

_____

_____

4. Think about the final result. What do you think are its strongest points?

_____

_____

_____

5. What advice would you give to another class making a similar presentation?

_____

_____

_____

I can evaluate my presentation.

How did you do?

PHOTOCOPIABLE

Name: _____   Date: _____

Self-assessment

■ For each numbered row, tick the statement that best describes what you can do.

1.	I can describe some of the main features of different periods of time.	I can pick out things that are the same or different between different periods of time.	I can suggest reasons for some of these differences and similarities.	
2.	I can give some reasons for some of the main events in the past.	I can give some reasons for and some results of events and changes.	I can give well thought-out reasons for and results of events and changes.	
3.	I can pick out information from historical sources.	I can pick out information from different sources and put it together.	I can judge sources of information and decide which will be most useful.	
4.	I know that the past has been interpreted in different ways.	I know that the past has been interpreted in different ways and I can describe some of the different interpretations.	I know that the past has been interpreted in different ways and I can suggest why this has happened.	

I can write a self-assessment.

How did you do?

The Vikings (1)

This chapter continues the chronological narrative of the history of Britain. Children begin by explaining what they already know about the Vikings, and evaluating the reliability of their sources of knowledge. They discover who the Vikings were, where they came from, and why they came to Britain. They investigate Viking raids and warfare, as well as home life and the role of women and children. They consider how historians know about the Vikings, and examine both archaeological and written sources in order to draw their own conclusions.

Chapter at a glance

Curriculum objective

• The Viking and Anglo-Saxon struggle for the Kingdom of England to the time of Edward the Confessor.

Week	Lesson	Summary of activities	Expected outcomes
1	1	• Children discuss what they already know about the Vikings, and where this knowledge comes from. They identify 'facts' which may need checking for accuracy.	• Can evaluate the accuracy and reliability of their own sources of historical knowledge.
	2	• Children evaluate the proposition 'All Vikings were bloodthirsty'. They conduct research and hold a class debate.	• Can debate a statement about the Vikings.
2	1	• Children look at historical sources telling us what Viking warriors wore. • They draw the typical dress of a Viking warrior.	• Can describe the dress of a Viking warrior.
	2	• Children watch video clips showing Viking armour, weapons and fighting style, and read about Viking battle tactics.	• Can describe the weapons, armour and battle tactics of Viking warriors, and suggest why they were so feared.
3	1	• Children read and discuss a text describing the Viking raids and invasions. • They explore an interactive text about the Viking raid on Lindisfarne in AD793.	• Can describe Viking attacks in general terms and identify when and where some of them took place.
	2	• Children read about Viking longships. • They design a figurehead for a Viking longship.	• Can describe Viking longships and identify aspects of their design that contributed to the Vikings' success in raids.
4	1	• Children use role play to investigate the reasons why the Vikings raided, invaded and settled in Britain.	• Can explain some of the reasons why the Vikings came to Britain.
	2	• Children examine pictures of archaeological evidence left behind by the Vikings, making inferences about Viking life.	• Can describe relevant archaeological evidence and explain what it tells us about Viking life.
5	1	• Children read excerpts from writing left behind by the Vikings and from accounts written about them by others. • They experiment with kennings and use them to write a poem.	• Can describe some of the written sources we have for our knowledge about the Vikings and can explain what they tell us.
	2	• Children consider some facts about the role of women in Viking society.	• Can say whether they think women were treated fairly in Viking society, using evidence to support their argument.
6	1	• Children explore an interactive Viking longhouse. • They design and make a model of a longhouse.	• Can describe the features of a Viking longhouse.
	2	• Children conduct research on the features of a Viking village and the role of children in Viking society.	• Can describe some of the features of daily life for children in a Viking village.
Assess and review		• To review the half-term's work.	

Expected prior learning

● Children do not need any prior knowledge about the Vikings, although it is highly likely they will have picked up some information about them informally outside school (only some of which may be accurate).

● It is assumed that children have a thorough knowledge of Anglo-Saxon Britain (for example, from covering the first two chapters in this book).

Overview of progression

● Children will build on their enquiry skills, using a variety of different methods to research what life was like in Viking Britain. They will respond to written, pictorial and video accounts of Viking life, and learn about the way both archaeological and written evidence has contributed to our historical knowledge of the Viking age.

● Children will also develop their ability to draw comparisons, as they consider similarities and differences between the daily life of a Viking child and their own daily lives.

● Children will demonstrate their knowledge of the past in different ways, including discussions, notes, lists, tables, reports, drawings, collaborative articles, maps, timelines, poems, diagrams, ideas boards, designs and models.

Creative context

● In this chapter children apply English skills across the domains of spoken language, reading and writing. These include taking part in discussions and role play, reading for information, exploring kennings, and writing a poem.

● Children develop their geographical skills as they locate Viking raids and invasions on a map of Britain.

● There are links to design and technology, with children designing and making a Viking longhouse.

● Applying their skills in art and design, children draw a picture of a Viking warrior and design a figurehead for a Viking longship.

● Children undertake historical research online, which addresses several requirements of the computing curriculum, including using the internet safely and responsibly, using search engines effectively and evaluating online content.

● There are links to personal, social, health and economic education with children exploring and discussing the treatment of women and the role of children in Viking society.

Background knowledge

● Children examine historical sources. These can include: documents (for example, books, letters, diaries, stories and poems), buildings, human and animal remains, made objects (historians call these artefacts), images (paintings, drawings and photographs) and oral testimony (eyewitness accounts). Primary sources come from the time being studied. Secondary sources come from a later time. An historical source becomes historical evidence when a historian uses it to support a theory about the past.

● In Week 5 children investigate the written evidence we have about the Vikings. There is not a lot from this period, which is why historians call it the 'Dark Ages'. From the Vikings themselves we have runic inscriptions, sagas and poems. Inscriptions are very short and so do not tell us much. Sagas and poems tell us more, but these were part of an oral tradition, and were not written down until several hundred years later. A few contemporary accounts remain, describing Viking raids on churches and monasteries. They were written by churchmen, and they understandably present a rather biased and one-dimensional view of the Vikings.

● Most of the written evidence we have about the Vikings comes from historical accounts written several hundred years after the events they describe. One of the most important of these is the *Anglo-Saxon Chronicle*.

Week 1 lesson plans

This week's lessons have an emphasis on evaluating the reliability of historical sources. In Lesson 1 children consider what they already know about the Vikings, identify where they got their knowledge from, and consider how reliable each source of historical information is likely to be. Using this evaluation they draw up a list of Viking 'facts' that need checking. In Lesson 2 children evaluate a commonly held assumption about the Vikings before debating the statement 'All Vikings were bloodthirsty'.

1: What do we already know about the Vikings?

Lesson objectives
● To develop a chronologically secure knowledge and understanding of British, local and world history, establishing clear narratives within and across the periods they study.
● To understand how our knowledge of the past is constructed from a range of sources.

Expected outcomes
● All children can describe what they already know about the Vikings.
● Most children can identify some of the sources of their knowledge about the Vikings.
● Some children can judge how reliable each source is likely to be.

Resources
Writing materials

Introduction
● Introduce this lesson's focus question: *What do we already know about the Vikings?*
● Ask the children, working in pairs, to discuss and write down what they already know (or think they know!) about the Vikings.

Paired work
● Ask children to look at each fact they wrote down about the Vikings, and add a note, maybe in a different colour, about how they know it (where they got the information from).
● Common sources include: told by a teacher/parent/friend; read it in a book; saw it on television; saw it in a film; saw it in a museum/at an archaeological site; saw/read it on the internet.
● Ask the children questions to get them to evaluate the relative reliability of the information they 'know'. For example:
  ● *Are some people more reliable sources of historical information than others? If so, who?*
  ● *Are some types of books more reliable than others? If so, which?*
  ● *If you got the information from TV, does it make a difference what type of TV programme it was?*
  ● *Is information on the internet more or less reliable than information on TV?*
  ● *Does it make a difference which website it came from?*
● Ask the children to consider these questions and use their answers to sort their list of 'facts' into two groups: 'Probably true' and 'May not be true – need checking'.

Whole-class work
● Ask pairs to share their ideas with the rest of the class. Create a class list in two columns: facts that pupils judge are 'probably true' and facts that 'need checking'.
● It is possible that some 'probably true' facts given by one pair may contradict facts given by another pair. If so, move these facts to the 'need checking' list.

Differentiation
● Support: use mixed-ability pairings throughout this lesson.

Review
● Ask: *If one fact is 'known' by more people than another fact, does this mean it is more likely to be true? Why? Why not?*
● Ask the children to copy down the class list, for use in the following lesson.

Lesson objectives
● To develop a chronologically secure knowledge and understanding of British, local and world history, establishing clear narratives within and across the periods they study.

Expected outcomes
● All children can explain why the Vikings have a reputation for being bloodthirsty.
● Most children can discuss whether or not all Vikings were bloodthirsty.
● Some children can put forward a compelling argument in support of their point of view.

Resources
Books on the Vikings and/or internet access; writing materials (paper-based or electronic)

2: Were all Vikings bloodthirsty?

Introduction
● Explain to the children that the Vikings have a reputation for being bloodthirsty, and that in this lesson they will be considering whether or not this reputation is deserved.
● Introduce this lesson's focus question: *Were all Vikings bloodthirsty?*

Paired work
● Group children into pairs, asking each pair to use books or the internet to find evidence supporting or refuting the Vikings' bloodthirsty reputation. Ask pairs to discuss what they find out.

Group work
● Propose the statement: *All Vikings were bloodthirsty.*
● Divide the class into two groups, according to whether they want to support or challenge the motion.
● Ask each group to think of arguments to support their position, and then divide up into smaller groups, with each small group preparing a short presentation based on one of the arguments.

Whole-class work
● Conduct a class debate, with groups on either side presenting their arguments.
● Explain to the children how you expect them to behave during the debate, perhaps displaying a list of rules, or working together to draw one up.
● Choose a moderator to lead the debate. You could do this yourself, or select a child for the role. The moderator needs to be able to speak clearly, communicate assertively but respectfully, keep everyone on task, and ensure all participants get a fair say.
● The moderator introduces the topic of debate, and invites representatives from each side of the issue to present their arguments, alternating between the two sides.
● Once all the prepared arguments have been presented give teams the opportunity to prepare and present rebuttals in response to the opposing side's arguments.

Differentiation
● Support: mixed-ability pairings may be useful for the paired work. In the group work, children may benefit from being grouped together and working with the support of an adult.

Review
● Complete the debate by asking children to vote for the point of view that was supported by the most compelling arguments. Ask: *Which way did you vote? Did you find the decision about which way to vote difficult to make? Why? Why not?*

Week 2 lesson plans

This week's lessons focus on Viking warfare. In Lesson 1 children look at various visual sources of evidence for what Viking warriors wore. They sort the images into primary and secondary sources. They piece together evidence from several primary sources to draw a picture of a Viking warrior. They then evaluate the secondary sources for accuracy. In Lesson 2 children watch a video clip showing Viking fighting style, and read and discuss a text about Viking battle tactics. They begin work on a class resource on the Vikings, collaborating to incorporate what they have found out this week about Viking warfare into an article.

1: Did Viking helmets have horns on?

Introduction
- Introduce this lesson's focus question: *Did Viking helmets have horns on?*
- Ask: *What do you think the answer to the focus question is?* and take a quick straw poll.
- Ask: *What do you think a Viking warrior looked like?* Give children a short time to draw a quick pencil sketch of a Viking warrior (independently, and without referring to any images). Emphasise the fact that this is not a test of their artistic skills. Remind them to include the warrior's footwear, headgear, clothing, armour and weapons. Ask children to keep their sketches for use later in the lesson.

Whole-class work
- Revise the terms primary source and secondary source. Discuss which of these types of source is likely to be more reliable when working out what Viking warriors wore.
- Display the media resource 'Viking warriors' on the CD-ROM.
- Work together to examine and discuss the images, sorting them into two groups: secondary sources and primary sources.

Independent work
- Ask children to use the primary sources to help them to draw an accurate and detailed pencil drawing of a Viking warrior, showing what he would have worn on each part of his body (feet, legs, body, head, hands) and what armour he would have carried.

> **Differentiation**
> - Challenge: ask children to research dyes used by the Vikings and add appropriate colours to their drawing.

Review
- Using the media resource, display the images that show secondary sources. Ask children to evaluate them for accuracy based on the evidence provided by the primary sources. Ask: *Which picture(s) is most accurate? Which picture(s) is least accurate? Why?*
- Ask: *What have you learned?* Encourage children to be specific in their answers by comparing the sketch they drew at the beginning of the lesson and their drawing from later in the lesson.
- Revisit the focus question, *Did Viking helmets have horns on?*

Lesson objectives
- To develop a chronologically secure knowledge and understanding of British, local and world history, establishing clear narratives within and across the periods they study.
- To construct informed responses that involve thoughtful selection and organisation of relevant historical information.
- To understand how our knowledge of the past is constructed from a range of sources.

Expected outcomes
- All children can say whether Vikings had horns on their helmets.
- Most children can describe what a Viking warrior wore.
- Some children can draw an accurate picture of a Viking warrior.

Resources
Media resource 'Viking warriors' on the CD-ROM; plain paper; colouring pencils; erasers

Lesson objectives

● To develop a chronologically secure knowledge and understanding of British, local and world history, establishing clear narratives within and across the periods they study.
● To regularly address and sometimes devise historically valid questions about change, cause, similarity and difference, and significance.

Expected outcomes

● All children can describe the weapons and armour of Viking warriors.
● Most children can describe the battle tactics of Viking warriors.
● Some children can suggest why Viking warriors were so feared.

Resources

Viking sword fighting video (such as from http://www.museumsecrets. tv -optional); photocopiable page 131 'Viking battle tactics'; materials for creating a class article, such as wiki tools

2: Fighting like a Viking: what was so scary about a Viking warrior?

Introduction

● Introduce this lesson's focus question: *Fighting like a Viking: What was so scary about a Viking warrior?*
● Show children a sword fighting video (see *Resources*).
● Ask questions about the clip; for example: *What 'Hollywood' style fighting moves would Vikings not have made?* (lifting swords over their head, spinning around) *Why not?* (These moves give a real opponent an easy chance to strike.)

Paired work

● Organise the children into pairs, providing each pair with a copy of photocopiable page 131 'Viking battle tactics'.
● Ask children to read the text and then talk through the discussion questions with their partner.

Whole-class work

● Ask pairs to share their thoughts about the discussion questions from the photocopiable page with the whole class.
● Tell the children they will be collaborating to write an article about what they have learned over the course of the last two lessons about Viking warriors and how they fought. Explain that this will be the first article in a class resource about the Vikings that the children will be adding to over the rest of the study (this chapter and the following chapter).
● There are several forms the collaborative class resource could take. You could use wiki tools (hosted online or on your school network), or you could use a word-processed document hosted on a platform that is built for collaboration (such as a Google Docs document shared via Google Drive). Creating a document in a standard word-processing program would also be an option, but is not so collaboration-friendly.

Group work

● Organise the class into groups. Help the class as a whole to make decisions about what each group will write about.
● Allow groups to decide for themselves how they will divide up the work between the individual members of the group, but emphasise the importance of distributing tasks fairly and also of taking into account group members' knowledge, skills and interests when deciding which tasks to allocate to whom.

Differentiation

● Support: use mixed-ability groups throughout the lesson.

Review

● Display the current version of the collaborative article. Ask the children to read and review the article, discussing their ideas with a partner before sharing them with the whole class. Draw up a list of revisions to make during the next stage of the writing process.

Week 3 lesson plans

In Lesson 1 children read and discuss a text describing the Viking attacks on Britain. They locate and mark some of the most significant attacks on a map of the British Isles and on a timeline. They explore an interactive telling the story of the Viking raid on Lindisfarne in AD793. In Lesson 2 the children read about Viking longships and discuss how their design contributed to the Vikings' effectiveness in raids. They design a figurehead for a Viking longship and play a game to consolidate their knowledge.

1: Raid! What do we know about the Viking attacks?

Lesson objective
● To develop a chronologically secure knowledge and understanding of British, local and world history, establishing clear narratives within and across the periods they study.

Expected outcomes
● All children can describe what we know about the Viking attacks on Britain and how we know it.
● Most children can identify when and where some of the Viking attacks took place.
● Some children can use their understanding to write a gripping account of the Viking raid on Lindisfarne.

Resources
Photocopiable page 'The Vikings attack Britain' from the CD-ROM; interactive activity 'Timeline maker' on the CD-ROM; map of Britain; computers or laptops

Introduction
● Introduce this lesson's focus question: *Raid! What do we know about the Viking attacks?*
● Ask the children to suggest how we might know about the Viking attacks. Ask: *What sources of evidence might there be?*

Whole-class work
● Display the photocopiable page 'The Vikings attack Britain' from the CD-ROM. Read through the text together, and ask comprehension questions. At the end ask: *Where did the invading army come from that is mentioned at the very end of the text (the army that wasn't made up of Norsemen)?* (Normandy.) *Who was their leader?* (Duke William II of Normandy.) *Where did the battle take place?* (Hastings, in East Sussex.) *What happened?* (The English army was defeated, and William became King William I of England. He is commonly known as William the Conqueror.)
● Display a map of Britain. Ask a volunteer to mark the location of the raid on Lindisfarne on it.
● Demonstrate the interactive activity 'Timeline maker' on the CD-ROM. Ask a volunteer to use it to mark the date of the raid on Lindisfarne on a timeline.

Paired work
● Organise the class into pairs, giving each pair a map of Britain and a computer with access to the interactive activity.
● Ask children to mark the rest of the attacks mentioned in the photocopiable text, first on a map of Britain and then on a timeline.

Differentiation
● Support: use mixed-ability pairings.
● Challenge: ask children to write an account of the Viking raid on Lindisfarne, for example an eyewitness account in the form of a letter.

Review
● Say to the children: *Imagine that you witnessed a Viking raid. How would you have felt at the time? What would you have done? How would you have felt afterwards? How might the raid have affected your life? What would you have thought of the Vikings?*
● If any children have written an eyewitness account of the Viking raid on Lindisfarne, ask them to share what they have written.

2: How did the design of longships help the Vikings?

Introduction

- Introduce this lesson's focus question: *How did the design of longships help the Vikings?*
- Explain that the way the Vikings designed their longships made them particularly good for carrying out raids. Ask the children what they already know about Viking longships, whether any of these features might have helped the Vikings when they were raiding, and if so, how.

Whole-class work

- Display or give out copies of the photocopiable page 'Tour of a Viking longship' from the CD-ROM.
- Further information about Viking longships is available online. Search for 'Viking ships' and 'longships'.
- Ask the children, referring to the photocopiable page (and information in video clips if watched), to discuss how the design of longships contributed to the Vikings' effectiveness in raids. (For example, longships had oars as well as a sail, so did not rely on the wind being strong or in the right direction; the shallow and narrow hull meant they could navigate up rivers, closer to their targets; longships could be sailed either way round, which helped with a quick getaway; and they were light enough for the crew to haul on dry land).

Independent work

- Ask children to design a figurehead for a Viking longship. Discuss the features the figurehead will need to have (for example, it needs to be able to be carved from a single piece of wood; it needs to depict a scary beast; it needs to fit on the prow or stern of a longship).
- Children could create their designs on paper, or could use a computer-based drawing program. Encourage children to draw two views of their figurehead: one front-on, and the other side-on.
- Children who complete their design could attempt to create it in modelling materials, such as plasticine, clay or papier-mâché.

> **Differentiation**
> - Challenge: encourage children to find out about some of the beasts from Norse mythology such as dragons, sea serpents, wurms, or the Kraken, and base the design of their figurehead on one of these, or a combination of them.

Review

- Play a game using photocopiable page 'Viking longship hangman'. The sheet provides quiz questions based on the children's knowledge of longships, plus a simple eight-step longship cartoon which can be added to the board during the game. Add the eye in the figurehead as the final stage to indicate a player's failure. Play with the children in teams, or simply you teacher as questioner.

Lesson objectives

- To develop a chronologically secure knowledge and understanding of British, local and world history, establishing clear narratives within and across the periods they study.
- To regularly address and sometimes devise historically valid questions about change, cause, similarity and difference, and significance.

Expected outcomes

- All children can describe Viking longships in general terms.
- Most children can describe in detail specific features of Viking longships.
- Some children can identify aspects of the design of longships that contributed to the Vikings' success in raids.

Resources

Photocopiable page 'Tour of a Viking longship' from the CD-ROM; internet access (optional); art materials (paper-based or electronic); modelling materials (optional); photocopiable page 'Viking longship hangman' from the CD-ROM

Week 4 lesson plans

In Lesson 1 children investigate the reasons why the Vikings raided, invaded and settled in Britain. In Lesson 2 children examine various examples of archaeological evidence the Vikings left behind and infer what each piece of evidence tells us about Viking life. The class then chooses a set of objects to put in a 'time capsule'.

1: Why did the Vikings come to Britain?

Lesson objectives
● To develop a chronologically secure knowledge and understanding of British, local and world history, establishing clear narratives within and across the periods they study.
● To regularly address and sometimes devise historically valid questions about change, cause, similarity and difference, and significance.

Expected outcomes
● All children can suggest reasons why people come to Britain today.
● Most children can explain some of the reasons why the Vikings came to Britain.
● Some children can arrange the reasons why the Vikings came to Britain in order of importance, justifying their decision-making.

Resources
Photocopiable page 132 'Messages'

Introduction
● Introduce this lesson's focus question: *Why did the Vikings come to Britain?*
● Discuss why people come to Britain today. Discuss both the purposes for which they come (perhaps for a holiday, to do business, or to come and live) and their reasons for coming (such as interesting history and culture, good business opportunities). In particular, draw out the various reasons why people might decide to migrate to Britain (for example, more job opportunities, or war or persecution in their homeland).

Paired work
● Organise the class into pairs. Ask each pair to discuss and make notes about possible reasons why the Vikings might have come to Britain.

Whole-class work
● Ask pairs to share their ideas with the rest of the class. Make a list of suggestions on the board.
● Clarify the various purposes of the Vikings' visits to Britain: distinguish between raiding, invading, trading, and settling.
● In particular, draw out possible reasons why Viking people might have decided to settle in Britain. (Escaping problems at home; or simply searching for a better life, in a place with better weather, a longer growing season, and more farming land.)

Group work
● Tell the class that they are the inhabitants of a Viking village on the south-western coast of Norway. Organise the class into groups of three or four, explaining that each group represents a separate family in the village.
● Present each group with a copy of the first message from photocopiable page 132 'Messages'. Give each family a short time to discuss what to do. The whole village meets and a spokesperson from each family presents their case. The village then votes on what to do.
● Give children the second message from the photocopiable page, and repeat the whole process.

> **Differentiation**
> ● Challenge: ask children to arrange the reasons why the Vikings came to Britain in order of importance, explaining their reasoning.

Review
● Conclude the work on the photocopiable page by taking a class vote on whether to Fight, Surrender or Flee for each scenario. Ask: *What were your reasons for that decision? What further problems might that decision create?*
● Revisit the focus question, *Why did the Vikings come to Britain?* Establish that some left their homelands because they were fleeing persecution, but that others may have left because they were simply looking for a better life.

Lesson objectives
• To develop a chronologically secure knowledge and understanding of British, local and world history, establishing clear narratives within and across the periods they study.
• To develop the appropriate use of historical terms.
• To understand how our knowledge of the past is constructed from a range of sources.

Expected outcomes
• All children can describe some of the archaeological evidence the Vikings left behind.
• Most children can explain what archaeological evidence tells us about Viking life.
• Some children can explain how the range of evidence archaeologists find affects the conclusions they are able to draw about the past.

Resources
Several rubbish bins (such as waste-paper baskets) each containing a different variety of (clean) rubbish; media resource 'Photos of archaeological evidence from the Vikings' on the CD-ROM

2: What archaeological evidence did the Vikings leave behind?

Introduction
• On the board write the phrase 'archaeological evidence'. Give children a couple of minutes to discuss with a partner what this phrase means, and then share their ideas as a class. Establish that 'archaeological evidence' refers to evidence about the past in the form of objects (rather than writing). It can include artefacts, built structures, and the remains of humans, animals and plants.
• Introduce this lesson's focus question: *What archaeological evidence did the Vikings leave behind?*
• Organise the class into groups, giving each group a rubbish bin containing a different variety of rubbish. Ask: *What can you tell me about the person this rubbish bin belongs to?*

Group work
• Display the media resource 'Photos of archaeological evidence from the Vikings' on the CD-ROM.
• Ask each group to examine the archaeological evidence and discuss and make notes on what each piece of evidence tells them about Viking life.

Whole-class work
• Ask groups to share the conclusions they have drawn. Focus discussion around any pieces of evidence that have been interpreted differently by different groups.
• Discuss what archaeological evidence we are likely to leave behind, and what people in the future might infer about us from it.

Paired work
• Ask each pair to write a list of objects to put in a 'time capsule' for archaeologists to open in a thousand years' time.

Differentiation
• Support: organise pairs and groups so that they are mixed ability.

Review
• Bring the class together to discuss the choice of objects to put in a 'time capsule'. Ask: *How will the objects chosen affect the conclusions that future historians draw?*

Week 5 lesson plans

In Lesson 1 children read excerpts from sources written by Vikings and from accounts about them written by others. They consider what view each source gives us of the Vikings, and what factors may have influenced the author's point of view. Children also experiment with kennings and use them to write a poem. In Lesson 2 children consider the role of women in Viking society.

1: Writing about the Vikings. What do written sources tell us?

Lesson objectives
● To develop a chronologically secure knowledge and understanding of British, local and world history, establishing clear narratives within and across the periods they study.
● To understand how our knowledge of the past is constructed from a range of sources.
● To construct informed responses that involve thoughtful selection and organisation of relevant historical information.

Expected outcomes
● All children can describe some of the written sources we have for our knowledge about the Vikings.
● Most children can explain what these written sources tell us about the Vikings.
● Some children can rank these written sources in order of importance according to how much they tell us about the Vikings.

Resources
Photocopiable page 'Kennings' from the CD-ROM

Introduction
● Introduce this lesson's focus question: *Writing about the Vikings – What do written sources tell us?*
● See *Background knowledge* on page 117 for more information on written evidence from this period of Britain's history. Relay this information to the children.

Whole-class work
● Display photocopiable page 'Kennings' from the CD-ROM and read through the text together.
● After reading the first set of example phrases, ask the children to suggest more things the boy might do.
● After reading the first set of example kennings, ask the children to change their phrases into kennings, too. After reading the second set of example kennings, ask them to improve the kennings they wrote.
● Ask the children to suggest some more kennings to describe a tree.

Independent work
● Set children the task of composing at least ten kennings about a single person or object of their choice.
● Ask the children to improve and arrange their kennings to create a poem.

> **Differentiation**
> ● Support: use mixed ability pairings for paired work. During the independent activity, you might want to group children together and give them adult assistance.

Review
● Give children a few kennings to 'decode'; for example: *wave rider; ground whitener; howl maker.* Ask: *What do you think these kennings describe?* (ship, snow or frost, dog or wolf.)
● Give children a short length of time to write a kenning about a given person, animal or thing, for example, a farmer, a sheep, or a sword.

Lesson objectives

● To develop a chronologically secure knowledge and understanding of British, local and world history, establishing clear narratives within and across the periods they study.
● To understand how our knowledge of the past is constructed from a range of sources.
● To construct informed responses that involve thoughtful selection and organisation of relevant historical information.

Expected outcomes

● All children can recall some facts about the role of women in Viking society.
● Most children can say whether they think women were treated fairly in Viking society.
● Some children can use evidence to support their argument.

Resources

Photocopiable page 133 'Women in Viking society'; scissors; A3 paper; pens or pencils; glue (optional); digital cameras (optional)

2: Were women treated fairly in Viking society?

Introduction

● Introduce this lesson's focus question: *Were women treated fairly in Viking society?*
● Ask: *What do we mean by 'treated fairly'?* Give children a few minutes to discuss this question with a partner, and then share their ideas with the class. Reach agreement about the meaning of the phrase, perhaps writing a definition on the board.

Group work

● Organise the class into groups, giving each group a paper copy of photocopiable page 133 'Women in Viking society', a sheet of A3 paper, pens and some scissors.
● On the board, sketch a horizontal line with an arrow at either end. Label the left half of the line *Unfair* and the right half *Fair*. Ask groups to copy this diagram onto their A3 paper.
● Ask groups to discuss each fact about women in Viking society on the photocopiable page, cut it out, and place it in the appropriate place on the diagram. Next, ask them to record what they have done, for example, by sticking the cards down and/or by taking a digital photograph.

Differentiation

● Support: mixed-ability groups are recommended for the whole lesson.
● Challenge: during group work and whole-class work, children should explain their reasoning, both of their overall judgement, and of specific judgements they have made regarding particular facts about women.

Review

● Ask each group to show their diagram and say whether it suggests that, overall, women were treated fairly or unfairly in Viking society.
● Ask the class to take a vote on the answer to the focus question: *Were women treated fairly in Viking society?* Ask children to explain how they used the diagrams to help them make their final judgement.
● You might want to ask the following additional questions:
● *Do you think each fact on the cards is equally important when deciding whether women were treated fairly overall? If not, which facts do you think are more important than others? Why?*

Week 6 lesson plans

In Lesson 1 children explore the design of Viking longhouses. They then design their own longhouse, and make a model of it. This lesson is likely to require several sessions. In Lesson 2 children research the features of a Viking village and the role of children in Viking society. They use what they have found out to draw a diagram showing a typical day in the life of a child living in a Viking village, and compare it with a typical day in their own lives.

1: What were Viking houses like?

Lesson objective
● To develop a chronologically secure knowledge and understanding of British, local and world history, establishing clear narratives within and across the periods they study.

Expected outcomes
● All children can explain what a longhouse was.
● Most children can describe the features of a Viking longhouse.
● Some children can explain the reasons why a Viking longhouse had certain features.

Resources
Interactive activity 'Tour of a Viking longhouse' on the CD-ROM; materials for making a model of a Viking longhouse; computers or laptops (optional); internet access (optional)

Introduction
● Introduce this lesson's focus question: *What were Viking houses like?*
● Read out the following list of features, one at a time. Ask the children to say whether they think each one was a feature of Viking houses. Children could discuss their ideas briefly with a partner, before they express their opinion, perhaps using a show of hands, or using the thumbs up sign to mean 'This was a feature of Viking houses' and thumbs down to mean 'This wasn't a feature of Viking houses'.
● List of features (to read out in a random order):
  ● Features found in Viking houses: storage chests, sleeping platforms, sheepskin bedding, earthen floor, open fire, space for animals at one end of the house.
  ● Features *not* found in Viking houses: flat roof, chimney, glass window panes, stairs, wooden floor, cupboards.

Paired work
● Organise the class into pairs, each with access to interactive activity 'Tour of a Viking longhouse' from the CD-ROM.
● Give pairs some time to explore the interactive Viking longhouse.
● Ask pairs to go online and collect images of the interior and exterior of Viking longhouses, in order to create an 'ideas board' in preparation for creating their own longhouse design.

Group work
● Organise children into small groups (for example, by putting two pairs together to form a group of four).
● Give groups the task of designing a model of a longhouse. The designs should include a floor plan, an exterior view, and a list of materials and equipment they will use to make the model.
● You might want to provide children with a list of construction materials to choose from, or give them a completely free choice about the materials they will use. You might ask children to make their model within a particular range of dimensions, or allow them to choose the scale.
● Give groups enough time to make and evaluate their models.

Differentiation
● Support: use mixed-ability groupings for paired and group work.
● Challenge: children who are particularly skilled in design and technology, could research building techniques and materials used by the Vikings, and incorporate these into their design.

Review
● Ask: *Why did Viking houses that were built in different places use different building materials? Some Viking longhouses were covered in turf. Why do you think this was?*

Lesson objectives
● To develop a chronologically secure knowledge and understanding of British, local and world history, establishing clear narratives within and across the periods they study.
● To construct informed responses that involve thoughtful selection and organisation of relevant historical information.

Expected outcomes
● All children can describe some of the main features of daily life in a Viking village.
● Most children can say whether they would want to live in a Viking village, and explain why.
● Some children can demonstrate their understanding by creating an article about daily life in a Viking village.

Resources
Information bank on Viking daily life, internet access and/or suitable books; photocopiable page 'Daily life timeline' from the CD-ROM; materials for creating a class article, for example, wiki tools

2: Living like a Viking: would you want to live in a Viking village?

Introduction
● Introduce this lesson's focus question: *Living like a Viking: would you want to live in a Viking village?*
● Ask the children to imagine they have been transported back in time to live in a Viking village.
● Tell the children they will be using an information bank to find out what their day-to-day life would be like. Ask them to suggest what search terms might be useful for internet or index searches, and make a list of suggestions on the board (for example, *Viking village, Viking settlement, Viking children, Viking childhood, Viking daily life*).

Paired work
● Organise the class into pairs. Ask children to complete research using the information bank and/or internet access to discover and note what daily life for children was like in a Viking village.

Independent work
● Ask children to use what they have found out to draw a diagram (for example, a pie chart) showing a typical day in the life of a child living in a Viking village, and compare it with a typical day in their own lives. You may wish to supplement the information the children have found out for themselves by providing them with copies of photocopiable page 'Daily life timeline' from the CD-ROM.

Differentiation
● Support: use mixed-ability pairings.
● Challenge: children could collaborate on writing an article for the class Viking resource on daily life for children in a Viking village.

Review
● Ask: *What do you think would be the best thing about living in a Viking village? What do you think would be the worst thing? Why? What was the most surprising thing you learned about life for children in a Viking village? Why did you find this surprising? What does this tell you about the Vikings?*
● Ask: *Would you want to live in a Viking village? Why? Why not?* Invite individuals to give their answer to the question, explaining their reasoning. You might want to finish the lesson by holding a class vote.

Curriculum objective
● To develop a chronologically secure knowledge and understanding of British, local and world history, establishing clear narratives within and across the periods they study.

Resources
Teaching assistant (optional); sound recording equipment (optional)

Vikings quiz (1)

Revise

● Organise the class into pairs and/or groups of three. Ask each pair or three to write a question about the Vikings on one side of a sheet of paper and the answer on the other side. Encourage children to keep both question and answer secret.

● Take in all the questions. Divide the class into mixed-ability quiz teams and read out the questions one at a time.

Assess

● On the board write the following questions:
  1. Why did the Vikings come to Britain?
  2. How do we know about the Vikings?
  3. What do you know about Viking warriors?
  4. What was daily life like in a Viking village?
  5. What else do you know about the Vikings?

● Give children a set length of time (such as 20 minutes) to answer these questions. Emphasise the importance of working independently.

● To encourage children to attempt all five questions, remind them when it is time to move on to the next question.

● If any children struggle with reading or writing you could give them an alternative way of recording their answers (perhaps working with an adult and giving verbal responses which are recorded in an audio file).

Further practice

● Ask the children to incorporate what they know about the Vikings into a display in a public area in school.

Curriculum objectives
● To regularly address and sometimes devise historically valid questions about change, cause, similarity and difference, and significance.

Resources
Internet access

Viking research

Revise

● Revisit three or four of the focus questions from this chapter; for example:
  ● How did the design of longships help the Vikings?
  ● Were women treated fairly in Viking society?
  ● What were Viking houses like?

● Encourage children to explain and discuss answers to each focus question.

Assess

● Tell children that for the assessment they will each be writing their own question about the Vikings, and then researching the answer.

● On the board write four headings: Change, Cause, Similarity and difference, and Significance. Discuss the meaning of each heading, and give an example of an historical question that would fit into each category (for example:
  ● Change: How did Viking writing change over the centuries?;
  ● Cause: Why did so many Vikings leave Scandinavia during the dark ages?;
  ● Similarity and difference: In what ways were the Vikings and the Anglo-Saxons similar?;
  ● Significance: How important are the Vikings in the history of Britain?.

● Ask children to write a question about the Vikings that fits into one of these four categories. Emphasise the importance of working independently and writing their own question.

● Give children time to research the answer to their question and then present the answer in a format of your choice.

Further practice

● Ask children to devise and answer another question about the Vikings that belongs to a different category.

Viking battle tactics

Viking men learned to fight and use weapons when they were young through hunting and playing sports, but the Vikings did not have any professional armies. As Viking troops lacked training, tactics were fairly basic and discipline was not particularly good.

In a battle Viking troops would form a shield wall - a line of warriors, perhaps several men deep, all holding their shields in front of them so that they overlapped one another.

To start the battle a single spear would be thrown over the enemy line, followed by a hail of spears, arrows and other missiles. The leader would then start the charge, often using the 'boar's snout' formation: a wedge of warriors pointing towards the enemy.

One tactic Viking armies used was to attempt to kill their opponents' leader. With their leader dead, the opposing army would often scatter, and the battle would be over. However, this wasn't an easy job. A Viking leader was surrounded by a group of well-armed and skilled fighters known as *huscarls* ('household troops'), whose job was to protect him.

Some Viking leaders also used another type of specialist troops: berserkers. Berserkers believed they were given special powers by the Norse god of war, Odin. They wore no armour, and covered themselves in the skins of animals. (The word berserker comes from an Old Norse word meaning 'bear shirt'.)

Before battle berserkers worked themselves into an immense rage, howling like animals, and biting on the rim of their shields. During battle they would advance in a fearless and uncontrollable frenzy, cutting down everyone in their path, friend and foe alike. If they were wounded they did not seem to feel any pain, but just carried on fighting.

Discussion questions

1. a) What might have been the advantages of using berserker troops?
   b) And the disadvantages?
2. What sort of sports might be used for training in warfare?
3. a) Why do you think Viking armies would often scatter when their leader died?
   b) Would it have made any difference if Viking armies had been professionals?
   c) Why do you think this?

Messages

There is a new King in the far north, called Harald Finehair. He orders that your jarl (chieftain) and all the fighting men in the village go and serve in his army. One of the king's jarls now owns your land.

■ **What will you do?**

Fight

Surrender

Flee

King Harald's army has just attacked the village in the neighbouring valley. There are hundreds of men in Harald's army. The men of the village fought bravely, but were outnumbered, and eventually they surrendered. King Harald's men refused to accept their surrender, and killed them. They then set fire to all the buildings. Now they're on their way here.

■ **What will you do?**

Fight

Surrender

Flee

Name: _____   Date: _____

Women in Viking society

✂ -

Women were not allowed to cut their hair short or wear men's clothes.	Women were not allowed to go on raids.	Unmarried women were expected to obey their fathers.
Married women were expected to obey their husbands.	Viking women were usually in charge of the family finances.	Women took charge of the household when their husbands were away or if they died.
Women were allowed to divorce their husbands.	It was considered shameful for a man to harm a woman.	Women were allowed to inherit property.

The Vikings (2)

In this chapter children explore further aspects of Viking culture, including food, art, religion, sagas, and burial customs. They study the lives and actions of four historical figures who played an important part in the Viking and Anglo-Saxon struggle for the control of England: Alfred the Great, Athelstan, Ethelred the Unready and Cnut. The children round off the study by considering what happened to the Vikings and by constructing a timeline of Viking Britain.

Chapter at a glance

Curriculum objective

• The Viking and Anglo-Saxon struggle for the Kingdom of England to the time of Edward the Confessor.

Week	Lesson	Summary of activities	Expected outcomes
1	1	• Children explore the foods the Vikings ate. • They collaborate to plan and prepare a Viking feast.	• Can describe the Viking diet and say whether or not they would like to eat Viking food.
	2	• Children examine Viking art, comparing to Anglo-Saxon art. • They create their own design in a Viking style.	• Can compare Viking and Anglo-Saxon art and suggest possible reasons for the similarities.
2	1	• Children research Viking gods and compare them to the pagan gods of the Anglo-Saxons. • They discuss and explain the similarities.	• Can identify similarities between the Viking and Anglo-Saxon gods, and suggest reasons for them.
	2	• Children explore the role of sagas in Viking culture. • They dramatise a Viking saga.	• Can explain the role of sagas in Viking culture, and can retell the story of at least one saga.
3	1	• Children revise what they know about Maya burial customs. • They research Viking burial and draw up a list of similarities and differences.	• Can draw comparisons between Viking burial practices and those of the ancient Maya.
	2	• Children learn the story of Alfred and the burned cakes, and discuss the story's significance. • They read about King Alfred's achievements, and discuss why he was 'the Great'.	• Can explain who King Alfred was, the part he played in British history, and why he was given the title 'the Great'.
4	1	• Children study a map of Britain in AD878, transfer the area of the Danelaw onto a map of modern Britain. • They explore the meanings of Viking place names.	• Can explain the meaning of 'Danelaw'. • Can identify the areas of the country covered by the Danelaw.
	2	• Children research Athelstan and create a comic strip about his life.	• Can explain who Athelstan was and why he is an important figure in British history.
5	1	• Children role play members of the royal counsel who advise King Ethelred whether or not to pay the Danegeld.	• Can explain what the Danegeld was. • Can express and justify their opinion about whether Ethelred should have paid the Danegeld.
	2	• Children discuss the story of King Cnut and the tide. • They examine a timeline of King Cnut's life, selecting the most significant events.	• Can explain why King Cnut is still remembered today.
6	1	• Children discuss what happened to the Vikings, formulating and researching questions.	• Can explain what happened to the Vikings after Viking-Age Britain.
	2	• Children order significant events in Viking Britain and incorporate them into a timeline.	• Can create a timeline of Viking Britain.
Assess and review		• To review the half-term's work.	

Expected prior learning

● This chapter forms the second part of the study on Viking Britain – it is assumed that children have already studied the previous chapter.
● It is also expected that children have completed a study of the ancient Maya civilisation. In Week 3 Lesson 1 children are asked to compare Viking burial customs with Maya burial customs.

Overview of progression

● Children will build on their enquiry skills, using a variety of different methods to research what life was like in Viking Age Britain. They will respond to written, pictorial and video accounts of Viking life, and learn how various sources have contributed to our historical knowledge of the Vikings.
● Children will also develop their ability to draw comparisons, as they consider similarities and differences between Viking and Anglo-Saxon culture. Children will demonstrate their knowledge of the past in different ways, including taking part in discussions, writing articles, creating comic strips, filming videos, constructing timelines, annotating maps, writing notes, drawing up lists, and creating art.

Creative context

● The content of this chapter has strong links with the English curriculum, with children engaging in various activities across the domains of spoken language, reading and writing. These include taking part in discussions, applying research skills, exploring a role-play scenario, performing a reading of a play script, writing a comic strip, collaborating to write wiki articles, reading texts for information and creating a storyboard.
● Children undertake historical research online, which addresses several requirements of the computing curriculum, including using the internet safely and responsibly, using search engines effectively and evaluating online content. Children also have the option to create digital content in the form of a movie and wiki articles.
● Children plan and prepare a Viking feast, which links to work in design and technology.
● There are links to art and design with children creating a cartoon strip and an original three-dimensional artwork inspired by Viking designs.
● Children apply their geography skills when they superimpose the area of the Danelaw on a map of modern Britain and investigate Viking place names.

Background knowledge

● In the first lesson of this chapter children explore what the Vikings ate. As far as we know Vikings did not write down recipes. Certainly no Viking recipes have ever been found. However, scientists have been able to work out what Vikings ate from examining evidence found at Viking archaeological sites such as rubbish and human remains, and from knowing the types of food available in each region where the Vikings settled.
● Viking sagas were epic stories that played a central role in the transmission of Viking culture. Sagas included stories of real-life historical figures as well as mythical heroes and gods. Although sagas formed part of an oral tradition, Vikings living in Iceland wrote many of them down during the medieval period, which is why we know about them today.
● The term *Danelaw* refers to the part of Britain that was ruled by the Vikings during Anglo-Saxon times. It also refers to the system of law that was imposed there. Roughly speaking, the Danelaw covered the area to the north of a line between London and Chester, excluding the part of Northumbria east of the Pennines.

Week 1 lesson plans

This week children take a closer look at Viking culture. Lesson 1 will take two or more sessions to complete. The children investigate what the Vikings ate, before planning, preparing and holding a Viking feast. In Lesson 2 the children examine examples of Viking art, identifying common motifs and comparing it with Anglo-Saxon art. They create their own original design in a Viking style.

1: Would you want to eat Viking food?

Lesson objective
● To develop a chronologically secure knowledge and understanding of British, local and world history, establishing clear narratives within and across the periods they study.

Expected outcomes
● All children can describe what Vikings ate.
● Most children can say whether or not they would like to eat Viking food.
● Some children can compare the food the Vikings ate with the food eaten in another ancient culture.

Resources
Interactive activity 'What do you know about Viking food?' on the CD-ROM; computers with internet access; cooking equipment and ingredients; digital camera or camcorder (optional)

Introduction
● Introduce this lesson's focus question: *Would you want to eat Viking food?*
● Ask: *How do you think historians know about what the Vikings ate?* Give children a couple of minutes to discuss this question with a partner.
● Ask children to share their ideas with the class.
● See *Background knowledge* on page 135 for more information on how we know about the Vikings' diet.

Whole-class work
● Explore the interactive activity 'What do you know about Viking food?' on the CD-ROM. You could do this together as a class on the whiteboard, or children could work in pairs on computers.
● Explain that each Viking village was more or less self-sufficient in food, and that most people were involved in farming in some way. Ask the children what conclusions about Viking daily life they can draw from the information provided by the interactive text.
● Tell children they will be planning, preparing and eating a Viking feast.

Group work
● Ensure children have access to computers with internet access.
● Organise small groups of three or four and give each group the task of choosing a Viking recipe they would like to make for the feast. Entering the search term *Viking recipes* should bring up a broad range of Viking-age recipes. Children could also carry out more specific searches, for example for *Viking bread*, *Viking porridge* or *non-alcoholic mead*.
● Encourage groups to communicate with each other so that there will be a good range of foods at the feast.
● Give children time to research other aspects of the feast, such as what types of cutlery and crockery the Vikings used.

Whole-class work
● Allocate time for children to prepare the food and hold the feast. You may want to use a teaching assistant for this activity. Be aware of any food allergies or other dietary restrictions, and ensure health and safety guidelines are followed.
● Ask children to record the feast using a digital camera and/or camcorder.

Differentiation
● Challenge: children could compare the food the Vikings ate with the food eaten in another ancient culture they have studied, such as the Romans.

Review
● After the feast, take time to evaluate the palatability of the foods, and revisit the focus question, *Would you want to eat Viking food?*

2: Was Viking art similar to Anglo-Saxon art?

Introduction
● Introduce this lesson's focus question: *Was Viking art similar to Anglo-Saxon art?*
● Display the examples of Viking art. Ask the children to look for any recurring themes, forms, patterns or colours, and discuss these with a partner, and then discuss ideas together as a class.

Paired work
● Now show examples of Anglo-Saxon art (for example, children's own Anglo-Saxon-style artwork created during their study of the Anglo-Saxons).
● Ask pairs to discuss and record the similarities and differences between the art of the two cultures not just in terms of motifs, but also in terms of techniques and materials.
● Discuss ideas as a whole class.

Independent work
● Ask the children to copy one or more Viking motifs of their choice into their sketchbooks.
● Next, ask the children to draw a design for a Viking-style object that is decorated with original Viking-style motifs they have devised themselves. The object might be a weapon, such as a sword or a knife, or a piece of jewellery, such as a bangle.
● Finally, give children time to make the artworks they have designed.

Differentiation
● Challenge: children can research both ancient and contemporary Scandinavian styles in a particular area of design (for example, textiles, ceramics or furniture).

Review
● Give the children an opportunity to evaluate their own and others' works of art.
● The class could hold an exhibition of their Viking-style artworks.

Week 2 lesson plans

In this week's lessons the children explore Viking religion and mythology. In Lesson 1 children conduct research into Viking gods and goddesses, and compare them to the pagan deities of the Anglo-Saxons, drawing out and explaining the similarities between the two. They then collaborate to write an article on Viking gods and goddesses. In Lesson 2 children discuss the role of sagas in Viking culture. They watch a cartoon version of a Viking saga. They read and act out playscripts telling the stories of Viking sagas, and then retell summaries of these stories orally.

1: Were the Viking gods anything like the Anglo-Saxon gods?

Lesson objectives
● To develop a chronologically secure knowledge and understanding of British, local and world history, establishing clear narratives within and across the periods they study.
● To regularly address and sometimes devise historically valid questions about change, cause, similarity and difference, and significance.

Expected outcomes
● All children can name and describe some of the Viking gods and goddesses.
● Most children can identify similarities between Viking and Anglo-Saxon gods and goddesses.
● Some children can suggest possible reasons for the similarities between Viking and Anglo-Saxon gods and goddesses.

Resources
Computers with internet access and/or encyclopedia/reference books listing key Viking gods; materials for writing a class article, such as wiki tools

Introduction
● Introduce this lesson's focus question: *Were the Viking gods anything like the Anglo-Saxon gods?*
● Give the children, working with a partner or in a small group, a few minutes to discuss what they can remember about the Anglo-Saxon gods. You might want to prompt children by reminding them that some of the days of the week are named after Anglo-Saxon gods.
● Collate children's ideas on the board, writing the names and brief descriptions of the gods and goddesses they can remember.

Paired work
● Conduct a race to find information about Viking gods. This could be completed with internet access or using suitable books.
● Challenge pairs to find out and note the names of a given minimum number of Viking gods within a short period of time (such as six gods in five minutes).
● Collect the names the children have found and write them on the board. Discuss any similarities to the names of the Anglo-Saxon gods.
● This could also be completed as a whole-class challenge with individuals being called out and given a one-minute window for completing research.

Group work
● Organise the class into groups, asking each group to research information about a different god or goddess online and/or in books. If their Viking god has an Anglo-Saxon counterpart, ask them to compare and contrast the two.
● Ask the class to collaborate on writing an article for the class resource about Viking gods and goddesses that incorporates the information they have researched.
● Allow groups to decide for themselves how they will divide up the work between the individual members of the group, but emphasise the importance of distributing tasks fairly and also of taking into account group members' knowledge, skills and interests when deciding which tasks to allocate to whom.

Differentiation
● Support: use mixed-ability groups throughout the lesson.

Review
● Discuss with groups the information they have found out, drawing out the similarities between Anglo-Saxon and Viking gods and asking children to suggest the reason for these similarities.
● Discuss with the class the progress they have made on the collaborative article, deciding how and when they will complete it.

Lesson objective
● To develop a chronologically secure knowledge and understanding of British, local and world history, establishing clear narratives within and across the periods they study.

Expected outcomes
● All children can explain what a sage is.
● Most children can retell the story of one Viking saga in outline.
● Some children can retell the story of one of the Viking sagas in more detail.

Resources
A simplified retelling of a Viking saga in written form (such as photocopiable page 'Thor and the giants' on the CD-ROM) or in the form of a video (BBC School Radio has an animated series called Viking Sagas as part of their English resources); digital camera or camcorder

2: What were the Viking sagas?

Introduction
● Introduce this lesson's focus question: *What were the Viking sagas?*
● Discuss the role of sagas in Viking culture. Sagas were epic stories that played a central role in the transmission of Viking culture. They included stories of real-life historical figures as well as mythical heroes and gods. Although sagas formed part of an oral tradition, Vikings living in Iceland wrote many of them down during the medieval period, which is why we know about them today.

Whole-class work
● Ask the children to read or watch a simplified retelling of a Viking saga. Children could read photocopiable page 'Thor and the giants' from the CD-ROM, or watch a video, such as one of the animated cartoons on the BBC School Radio website (see *Resources*).
● Ask the children questions about the saga to test their comprehension of the story.

Group work
● Organise the class into groups and ask each group to retell the saga using drama. If you are using the photocopiable sheet, ensure each group has at least one copy to refer to.
● Give children plenty of time to devise and rehearse their dramatic retelling of the story. If possible, give each group an opportunity to review and feed back on one other group's performance, and then give children time to revise their work in the light of the feedback they have received.

Whole-class work
● Ask groups to perform their pieces in front of the whole class. You could ask one or two children to make a video recording of the performances.
● You could ask the most successful group to reprise their performance on a later date in front of a wider audience, such as the whole school and/or parents or carers.

> **Differentiation**
> ● Support: mixed-ability groups may work best for this lesson.

Review
● Review the expected outcomes for this lesson. Ask children to explain what a saga is. Ask the class to assess which groups managed to retell the story of one of the Viking sagas in outline and which groups managed to do so in more detail.

Week 3 lesson plans

In Lesson 1 children revise what they know about Maya burial customs. They research Viking burials and draw up a list of similarities and differences between the funeral customs of the two cultures. They create a list of objects that they would want to take with them to the afterlife if they were buried in the Viking fashion, and explain why they have chosen these things. In Lesson 2 the children investigate Alfred the Great. They watch a video clip telling the story of Alfred and the burned cakes. They read a text detailing Alfred's achievements and discuss why he was given the title 'the Great'. They add a page about King Alfred to the class wiki resource.

1: How did Viking burial compare to Maya burial?

Lesson objectives
• To develop a chronologically secure knowledge and understanding of British, local and world history, establishing clear narratives within and across the periods they study.
• To note connections, contrasts and trends over time.
• To regularly address and sometimes devise historically valid questions about change, cause, similarity and difference, and significance.

Expected outcomes
• All children can describe Viking burial practices.
• Most children can draw comparisons between Viking burial practices and those of the ancient Maya.
• Some children can suggest what Viking burial practices reveal about Viking culture.

Resources
Photocopiable page 'Viking burial' from the CD-ROM

Introduction
• Introduce this lesson's focus question: *How did Viking burial compare to Maya burial?*
• Give the children a couple of minutes to discuss with a partner what they can remember about Maya burial customs, and then share their ideas with the rest of the class.
• Establish some of the main features of Maya burial: people were buried with maize or a bead placed in their mouth; often covered with red dust; graves faced north or west or were located in caves; kings and other important were people buried in tombs, including in pyramids; and treasured possessions were buried with the dead person.

Paired work
• Organise the class into pairs, giving each pair a copy of photocopiable page 'Viking burial' from the CD-ROM.
• Give children time to study the photocopiable page and use the information it provides to draw up a list of similarities and differences between Viking and Maya burials.
• Discuss children's ideas. Through questioning, help them to draw out as many similarities and differences as possible between the burial practices of the two cultures. Create a class list of similarities and differences.

Independent work
• Ask children to create a list of objects that they would want to take with them to the afterlife if they were buried in the Viking fashion.
• Allow them a maximum number of objects, such as ten, and ask them to explain to a partner why they have chosen each object.

> **Differentiation**
> • Support: pair children with a more confident partner.
> • Challenge: ask children what Viking burial practices tell us about Viking culture.

Review
• Ask children to share the list of items they would choose to be buried with, and explain the reasoning behind their choices.
• Ask: *How similar were Viking and Maya burial customs? Were there more similarities than differences, or were there more differences than similarities? Can you explain any of the similarities or differences?*

Lesson objectives

● To develop a chronologically secure knowledge and understanding of British, local and world history, establishing clear narratives within and across the periods they study.
● To regularly address and sometimes devise historically valid questions about change, cause, similarity and difference, and significance.

Expected outcomes

● All children can explain who King Alfred was.
● Most children can explain why King Alfred was given the title 'the Great'.
● Some children can express their opinion about whether King Alfred deserves the title 'the Great' and support their opinion with evidence.

Resources

Map of Britain; timeline; a video clip about the story of Alfred and the cakes (source online); photocopiable page 149 'King Alfred the Great'; materials for creating a class article, such as wiki tools

2: King Alfred: why do we call him 'the Great'?

Introduction

● Introduce this lesson's focus question: *King Alfred: why do we call him 'the Great'?*
● Explain that King Alfred was an Anglo-Saxon King of Wessex during the Viking age, and that he is the only British monarch ever to be given the title 'the Great'.
● Ask children to locate Alfred's reign (871–899) on a timeline.
● Ask: *What do you already know about Alfred the Great?* Note children's ideas on the board. If anyone mentions the story of Alfred and the cakes, ask them to elaborate on what happened.
● Show children a short video clip telling the story of Alfred and the cakes (see *Resources*) or tell the story yourself. Ask questions, such as: *Why did King Alfred and his men have to go on the run?* (the Vikings had invaded his kingdom.) *What possible interpretations of the story are there?* (a literal story, a symbolic story – the cake is the kingdom, a psychological story.) *Do you think the story of Alfred and the burned cakes might be true? Why? Why not?*

Paired work

● Organise the class into pairs, giving each pair a copy of photocopiable page 149 'King Alfred the Great'.
● Ask pairs to discuss which of Alfred's actions might be described as 'great', and then share their ideas with the whole class.

Whole-class work

● Ask the class to collaborate on writing an article for the class resource about King Alfred the Great.
● Allow groups to decide for themselves how they will divide up the work between their members, but emphasise the importance of distributing tasks fairly and also of taking into account group members' knowledge, skills and/ or interests when deciding which tasks to allocate to whom.

> ### Differentiation
> ● Challenge: children could write about whether or not King Alfred deserves the title 'the Great', supporting their opinion with evidence.

Review

● Ask any children who have written about whether or not King Alfred deserves the title 'the Great' to share what they have written, and if necessary, to explain their viewpoint further. If possible, have at least one speaker from each side of the argument. Take a class vote on whether or not King Alfred deserves the title 'the Great'.

Lesson objective
● To develop a chronologically secure knowledge and understanding of British, local and world history, establishing clear narratives within and across the periods they study.

Expected outcomes
● All children can explain the meaning of the term *Danelaw* and identify place names of Viking origin.
● Most children can work out the meaning of Viking place names.
● Some children understand that some place names are of partial Viking origin and can research the meanings of these combination words.

Resources
Photocopiable page 150 'Map of Britain in AD878'; photocopiable page 'Viking place names' on the CD-ROM; maps of Britain (enough for pairs); photocopiable page 'Wordbank of Anglo-Saxon place names' on the CD-ROM (optional); maps of the local area (optional)

Week 4 lesson plans

In Lesson 1 children discuss the meaning of the term *Danelaw* and study a map of Britain in AD878. They use a modern map to explore Viking place names. In Lesson 2 children compile a list of facts about Athelstan, considering which of these might count as reasons why he is considered an important figure in the history of Britain. Finally, they create a comic strip about Athelstan.

1: What was the Danelaw?

Introduction
● Introduce this lesson's focus question: *What was the Danelaw?*
● Give children a couple of minutes to discuss the meaning of the word *Danelaw* with a partner, and then share their ideas with the rest of the class.
● See *Background knowledge* on page 135 for more information on Danelaw and relay this to the children.

Whole-class work
● Ask: *Where was the Danelaw?* Ask a volunteer to show on a map of Britain whereabouts they think the Danelaw was.
● Explain that the boundaries of the Danelaw changed over time, as Vikings and Anglo-Saxons fought for control of the country. Display photocopiable page 150 'Map of Britain in AD878'.

Independent work
● Give each child a copy of the photocopiable map. Ask them to transfer the area of the Danelaw onto a map of modern Britain.

Whole-class work
● Display photocopiable page 'Viking place names' from the CD-ROM. On the whiteboard write a place name of Viking origin. Ask the children to work out its meaning.
● Explain that many place names are a mixture of Viking and Anglo-Saxon words. You may want to display a copy of the wordbank of Anglo-Saxon place names from Year 5 Chapter 1.

Paired work
● Divide the class into pairs, giving each pair a map of Britain (and a map of the local area if appropriate). Also give each pair a copy of the list of Viking place names. Challenge pairs to find ten place names that are partly or completely of Viking origin. Can they find place names that are different from those other pairs on their table have found?
● Ask pairs to work out and write down full or partial meanings of as many of the place names as possible.

Differentiation
● Challenge: ask children to find the full meanings of place names only part of which are Viking in origin. Ask them to identify not only the meaning but also the linguistic origin of the other part(s) of each place name.

Review
● By combining two or more elements from the wordbank of Viking place names, give the children some made-up Viking place names to translate.

Lesson objectives

- To develop a chronologically secure knowledge and understanding of British, local and world history, establishing clear narratives within and across the periods they study.
- To regularly address and sometimes devise historically valid questions about change, cause, similarity and difference, and significance.

Expected outcomes

- All children can explain who Athelstan was.
- Most children can recount the important events of Athelstan's life.
- Some children can explain why Athelstan is an important figure in British history.

Resources

Information bank on Athelstan (such as books and/or internet access); example of a comic strip; materials for creating a comic strip (paper-based or digital)

2: Who was Athelstan and why is he important?

Introduction

- Introduce this lesson's focus question: *Who was Athelstan and why is he important?*
- Ask children if they already know anything about Athelstan, making a note on the board of anything the children tell you about him.

Paired work

- Organise the class into pairs, giving each access to an information bank on Athelstan. Suitable search terms include 'Athelstan' and 'Aethelstan'.
- Give children time to research Athelstan and make notes about what they find out, in particular noting facts they think might count as reasons why Athelstan is considered an important figure in British history.

Whole-class work

- Ask pairs to share what they have found out about Athelstan.
- Ask children to suggest the reasons why Athelstan is considered an important figure in British history. (For example, he took York from the Danes, after which he became the first Anglo-Saxon ruler of the whole of England, so historians class him as the first true King of England; he defeated an invasion by the Scots and Vikings at the Battle of Brunaburh; and he built alliances overseas by marrying several of his sisters to various European kings.)
- Display an example comic strip.
- Ask children working in pairs or small groups, to discuss and make notes on the features of a comic strip and then share their ideas with the rest of the class.

Independent work

- Give children the task of creating a comic strip about the life of Athelstan that is suitable for a younger class. Depending on the resources available, children could create a paper-based or a digital comic strip.

> **Differentiation**
> - Support: use mixed-ability pairings.

Review

- Ask children to review and comment on each other's comic strips, both as works in progress and when completed. Give children the chance to share their completed comic strips with their chosen audience.

Week 5 lesson plans

In Lesson 1 the children read and discuss a text about Ethelred the Unready. They take part in a role-play scenario, in which they play members of the royal counsel, the Witan, who advise the king. The king's advisers meet to advise him what to do after the Anglo-Saxons' defeat to the Vikings at the Battle of Maldon. In Lesson 2 children learn about the story of King Cnut and the tide. They examine a timeline of King Cnut's life, identify the most significant events in it, and discuss why he is still remembered today. Over several sessions, they work in groups to make a short film of Cnut's life.

1: Should Ethelred have paid the Danegeld?

Lesson objectives
● To develop a chronologically secure knowledge and understanding of British, local and world history, establishing clear narratives within and across the periods they study.
● To develop the appropriate use of historical terms.
● To construct informed responses that involve thoughtful selection and organisation of relevant historical information.

Expected outcomes
● All children can explain what the Danegeld was.
● Most children can express their opinion about whether Ethelred should have paid the Danegeld.
● Some children can justify their opinion.

Resources
Photocopiable page 'Biography of Ethelred II: The Unready' from the CD-ROM

Introduction
● Introduce this lesson's focus question: *Should Ethelred have paid the Danegeld?*
● Distribute or display photocopiable page 'Biography of Ethelred II: The Unready' from the CD-ROM.
● Work through the questions together.

Whole-class work
● Present the role-play scenario. The children are members of the royal council, the Witan, who advise the King.
● The Year is 991. King Ethelred is 20 years old. Viking forces claim victory over the Anglo-Saxons at the Battle of Maldon. Should the king
   a) continue the armed struggle against the Vikings,
   b) surrender to the Vikings, or
   c) buy them off? What will you advise him to do?

Group work
● Organise the class into groups. Give each group time to discuss the options, and decide what they think the king should do.
● Ask a spokesperson from each group to present their case to the class. Hold a whole-class vote. The king will follow the course of action recommended by the greatest number of advisors.
● Explain what happens next, depending on the course of action children chose.
   ● Fight: The Anglo-Saxon army suffers a crushing defeat, Ethelred is killed, and the Vikings take control of England.
   ● Surrender: The Vikings take control of England. Ethelred is put in prison, where he dies.
   ● Pay: A huge payment of silver stops the Vikings from invading for a while. To raise the money the king imposes a new tax, which makes him very unpopular. It's not long before the Vikings are back, this time demanding an even larger payment…
● Explain what happened in reality (Ethelred paid the Danegeld, but the Vikings kept on returning, demanding larger and larger amounts of money). Ethelred's decision affected the way he has been portrayed ever since. His nickname 'the Unready' derives from the Old English word unræd, which means 'bad counsel', suggesting that he was poorly advised.

Review
● Revisit the focus question, *Should Ethelred have paid the Danegeld?*, asking children to express and justify their opinion.

Lesson objectives
● To develop a chronologically secure knowledge and understanding of British, local and world history, establishing clear narratives within and across the periods they study.
● To regularly address and sometimes devise historically valid questions about change, cause, similarity and difference, and significance.

Expected outcomes
● All children can tell and explain the story of Cnut and the tide.
● Most children can explain the significance of King Cnut in the history of Britain.
● Some children can tell the story of Cnut's life effectively in film.

Resources
The story of King Cnut, for example video clip: 'Cnut making a point' extract from the BBC series 'Blood of the Vikings' or *Horrible Histories* 'Movie Pitch: The King Cnut Project'; photocopiable page 'King Cnut timeline' from the CD-ROM; examples of storyboards; film-making equipment (optional); film editing software (optional)

2: Why is King Cnut remembered today?

Introduction
● Introduce this lesson's focus question: *Why is King Cnut remembered today?*
● Ask: *What do you already know about King Cnut?* Give children a minute or two to talk with a partner. Share ideas.

Whole-class work
● Tell the story of King Cnut and the tide. This is a visually appealing story if you can act it out briefly using a willing teaching assistant (or see suggestions in *Resources*).
● Ask: *What point or points do you think the story about King Cnut and the tide is trying to make? Do you think the story is true? Why? Why not?* Remind them of the work they did on the story of King Alfred and the cakes.

Paired work
● Organise the class into pairs, and distribute photocopiable page 'King Cnut timeline' from the CD-ROM.
● Ask them to read through the timeline and select between six and eight events from Cnut's life they judge to be most important. Ask pairs to discuss their work with other pairs.

Group work
● Organise the class into groups of four or six children, giving each group the task of creating a short film about King Cnut, relating the most important events in his life.
● The film could be live action with children acting out the parts, or it could be a puppet play. Some children might be able to use simple stop-motion techniques; for example, using building blocks.
● Whatever sort of film they will be making, ask all groups to start the planning process by creating a storyboard. Show some example storyboards.
● Give children time to plan, rehearse, film and edit their films, before showing them to a selected audience.

Differentiation
● Support: mixed-ability groupings are recommended for most groups; however, you may want to group the most confident children together for the film-making activity.

Review
● Ask: *Why do you think King Cnut is still remembered today?* Establish that King Cnut is remembered only in part for his achievements as a king, and that the principle reason he is still remembered today is because of the story about him and the tide. Draw out the fact that a good story can ensure someone is remembered for a very long time. Explain that the story need not necessarily be true.

Week 6 lesson plans

In this week's lessons the children wrap up their study of the Vikings by finding out what happened to them, and considering their legacy. In Lesson 1 children discuss what happened to the Vikings, then conduct further research. In Lesson 2 children order significant events from Viking Britain and incorporate them into a timeline.

Lesson objectives
● To develop a chronologically secure knowledge and understanding of British, local and world history, establishing clear narratives within and across the periods they study.
● To regularly address and sometimes devise historically valid questions about change, cause, similarity and difference, and significance.

Expected outcomes
● All children can say when the Viking age came to an end.
● Most children can explain what happened to the Vikings after the Viking age ended.
● Some children can describe the legacy of the Vikings.

Resources
Information bank on Viking Britain (such as books and/or internet access); materials for creating a collaborative article, such as wiki tools

1: What happened to the Vikings?

Introduction
● Introduce this lesson's focus question: *What happened to the Vikings?*. Discuss the meaning of the word *legacy*.
● On the board write three questions based on the expected outcomes: *When did the Viking age come to an end? What happened to the Vikings? What legacy did the Vikings leave behind?*
● Give children, working in pairs, a couple of minutes to discuss each of these questions in turn.
● Ask pairs to share their ideas with the class, but do not correct any misconceptions at this stage.

Group work
● Ask the pairs from the introductory activity to group together in fours or sixes.
● Ask each group to use books and/or the internet to find out the answers to the questions written on the board, making notes about what they discover.

Whole-class work
● Discuss the answers to the questions. *When did the Viking age come to an end?* (The Viking age ended officially when the Norsemen stopped raiding. The final Viking raid on Britain was the attempted invasion of King Harald of Norway in 1066.) *What happened to the Vikings?* (After the Viking age came to an end nothing happened to the Vikings; they carried on living their lives in their homelands and in the lands where they had settled, such as Britain. Over time, Vikings living in Britain, through intermarriage with non-Vikings, gradually blended into the general population.) *What legacy did the Vikings leave behind?* (Many modern-day words derive from the old Norse language; the Vikings set up a legal system that was the foundation for today's legal system; and it was as a result of Viking extortion that English kings started taxing the people.)

Independent work or Paired work
● Ask individuals or pairs within each group to write an article for the class resource with the title of one of the three questions. Allocate the question *What legacy did the Vikings leave behind?* to the more confident members of each group.

Review
● Ask individuals and pairs to share what they have written so far, inviting the rest of the class to provide constructive feedback.
● Ask: *How valuable is the Vikings' legacy to Britain? Is it more valuable or less valuable than the legacy of the Romans/the Anglo-Saxons?*

Lesson objectives
● To develop a chronologically secure knowledge and understanding of British, local and world history, establishing clear narratives within and across the periods they study.
● To note connections, contrasts and trends over time and develop the appropriate use of historical terms.

Expected outcomes
● All children can describe some of the key events in Viking Britain.
● Most children can describe and order the key events in Viking Britain.
● Some children can describe, order, and recall the dates of the key events in Viking Britain.

Resources
Photocopiable page 151 'Key events in Viking Britain'; interactive activity 'Timeline maker' on the CD-ROM; information bank on Viking Britain (for example, books and/or internet access); materials for creating a collaborative article, such as wiki tools (optional)

2: What does a timeline of Viking Britain look like?

Introduction
● Introduce this lesson's focus question: *What does a timeline of Viking Britain look like?*
● Organise the class into pairs or small groups. Give each pair or group a paper copy of photocopiable page 151 'Key events in Viking Britain'. Ask the children to order the events from earliest to latest, adding years in pencil where they think they know them.

Group work
● In each group assign one individual or pair to work with interactive activity 'Timeline maker' on the CD-ROM to create a timeline of Viking-age Britain.
● Ask the rest of the group to work in pairs or individually to write a sentence or two describing an event from the photocopiable page, use books and/or the internet to find out the date of the event, and then pass on their notes to the pair using the timeline tool.
● Once a group has entered all the listed events on their timeline, ask them to find more events from the Viking period (AD793 to 1066) to add to the timeline.
● Encourage group members to swap roles at intervals so that everyone gets a chance to use the timeline tool.

Differentiation
● Support: children might find it helpful to cut up and reorder the PCP.
● Challenge: children can write an article for the class wiki resource on one or more of the events featured in the timeline.

Review
● Ask the children to share the dates they have found out for the events on the photocopiable, and check to see if their original order was correct.
● Ask the children to report back on any additional events they added to the timeline.
● Review the timelines and choose the most complete one to print out for display.

Curriculum objectives
● To regularly address and sometimes devise historically valid questions about change, cause, similarity and difference, and significance.

Resources
Interactive activity 'Vikings quiz' on the CD-ROM; audio recording equipment (optional)

Vikings quiz (2)

Revise
● Introduce the interactive activity 'Vikings quiz' from the CD-ROM.
● Organise the class into pairs, giving each pair access to the quiz, and give children time to answer the questions.
● Alternatively, attempt the quiz questions as a whole class, using the whiteboard.

Assess
● On the board write the following names: *Alfred the Great, Cnut, Athelstan*, and *Ethelred the Unready*.
● Ask children to choose one of these historical figures to write about. You could either ask them simply to write as much as they know about the figure they choose, or you could provide them with a question to answer; for example, *why is he an important figure in the history of Britain?*
● Give the children a set length of time (such as 25 minutes) to complete the task. Emphasise the importance of working independently. Any children who finish writing about their chosen figure should start writing about a second one.
● If any children struggle with writing you could give them an alternative way of recording what they know (for example, through a conversation with an adult that is recorded as an audio file).

Further practice
● Ask children to write additional quiz questions for the Viking quiz, and quiz each other or a parallel class.

Curriculum objective
● To develop the appropriate use of historical terms.

Resources
Multiple sets of cards, each card featuring an historical term from the Vikings study card; scissors

Viking historical terms

Revise
● Organise the class into groups, giving each group a set of historical term cards, for example: tactics, berserker, raid, longship, archaeological evidence, artefact, kenning, longhouse, quern, saga, Odin, Valhalla, Midgard, Asgard, Danelaw, alliance, succession, heir, royal counsel, Witan, and Danegeld.
● Ask each group of children to work together collaboratively to sort the cards into groups.
● Discuss with children the criteria they have used for sorting the cards.

Assess
● Introduce the assessment task. Children should choose six of the words from the cards. Each word must belong to a different group from the sorting activity, unless there are fewer than six groups, in which case children must choose at least one word from each group. For each word children must write a definition and then use the word in context, in a sentence or short paragraph.
● Demonstrate the task, choosing one of the words from the cards. Encourage children to help you write the definition and suggest a sentence or short paragraph in which to put the word in context. Tell children this word is now 'off limits'.
● Give the children a set length of time (for example, 25 minutes) to complete the task. Emphasise the importance of working independently.

Further practice
● Challenge children to create an illustrated dictionary of historical terms suitable for use throughout Key Stages 1 and 2.

King Alfred the Great

Alfred's childhood

Alfred was born in Wantage in today's Oxfordshire in AD849. He was the lively youngest son of Aethelwulf, the king of the Anglo-Saxon kingdom of Wessex. One story tells how Alfred's mother promised a poetry book to the first of her children who could memorise it. Alfred quickly learned every poem and won the book.

Alfred the warrior prince

By AD866, his fourth brother, Aethelred, was the King of Wessex. Alfred helped him defend Wessex against their great threat – the Vikings. In AD871, a large Viking army arrived in Wessex. Even though the Anglo-Saxons won the Battle of Ashdown on the Berkshire Downs, the Vikings kept attacking. By the end of the year, Aethelred had been killed and Alfred was king.

Alfred's escape

To stop the Vikings raiding, Alfred reluctantly agreed to pay them money every year. However, this changed in AD878 when the Viking leader, Gunthrum, decided to attack Wessex. In January, as the Saxons were enjoying Christmas in their homes, the Vikings struck. Many Saxons were killed but Alfred and a few of his followers escaped and hid in the marshes of Somerset. It was here that Alfred was said to have burned the cakes of a peasant woman.

Alfred's victory

In the marshes, Alfred built a fort and secretly began to gather up his Saxon troops. By spring the Saxons had crushed the Vikings at the Battle of Edington in Wiltshire. Exhausted and beaten, Gunthrum agreed to convert to Christianity and to allow the English to rule the South and the Vikings the North.

Alfred the defender

Alfred did not want to risk another Viking invasion so he built new forts around towns, called *burhs*. He also improved the army and built larger ships to stop coastal raids.

Alfred the lawmaker

Alfred believed that law and order were very important for his people. He established a code of laws based on the Old Testament and on laws used by other Anglo-Saxon leaders. He liked to keep an eye on the judgements that were being made, to check that his people were being treated fairly.

Alfred the educator

Alfred believed education should play a large part in his kingdom. He translated Latin texts into old English and encouraged other teachers to do the same.

Map of Britain in AD878

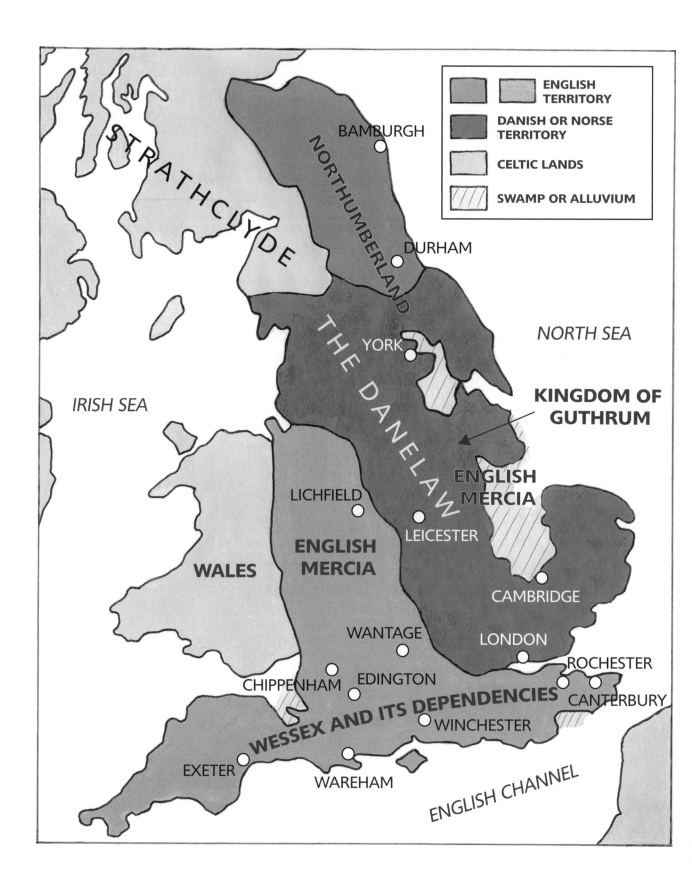

STRATHCLYDE

NORTHUMBERLAND

BAMBURGH

DURHAM

NORTH SEA

IRISH SEA

THE DANELAW

YORK

KINGDOM OF GUTHRUM

ENGLISH MERCIA

LICHFIELD

LEICESTER

WALES

ENGLISH MERCIA

CAMBRIDGE

WANTAGE

LONDON

ROCHESTER

CHIPPENHAM

EDINGTON

WESSEX AND ITS DEPENDENCIES

CANTERBURY

WINCHESTER

EXETER

WAREHAM

ENGLISH CHANNEL

Legend:

ENGLISH TERRITORY

DANISH OR NORSE TERRITORY

CELTIC LANDS

SWAMP OR ALLUVIUM

Key events in Viking Britain

✂

King Athelstan defeats the Vikings and Scots at Brunaburh.	Alfred becomes King of Wessex.	Vikings attack the monastery of Iona, Scotland.
King Alfred agrees a treaty with the Vikings to divide England.	Erik Bloodaxe, the last Viking king in England, is forced out of York.	Cnut becomes King of England.
King Aethelred defeats the Viking army at the Battle of Ashdown.	York is captured by a Viking army.	Vikings attack the monastery at Lindisfarne, Northumbria.

Medicine (1)

In this chapter the children study medicine from the Anglo-Saxons to the present. They begin the study by investigating some early theories of disease and some medical treatments used in the past. They examine changes in hospitals, medical equipment, dental care, and the way mental illness is treated. They also look at the history of several diseases: the plague, scurvy and smallpox. Finally, they consider the role of women in the history of medicine.

Chapter at a glance

Curriculum objectives

• A study of an aspect or theme in British history that extends pupils' chronological knowledge beyond 1066: changes in an aspect of social history (medicine from the Anglo-Saxons to the present).

Week	Lesson	Summary of activities	Expected outcomes
1	1	• Children research early theories of disease. • They create a poster about one theory.	• Can describe some early theories of disease.
	2	• Children investigate some of the more unusual medical treatments from the past. • They suggest which treatments might have been the most dangerous and why.	• Can describe some early medical treatments and explain why they were dangerous.
2	1	• Children read about the development of hospitals. • They arrange pictures of hospitals in chronological order. • They draw a hospital of the future.	• Can draw comparisons between the earliest hospitals in Britain and modern-day hospitals.
	2	• Children compare medical equipment from the past millennium. • They research one item and write about how it has changed.	• Can identify some of the ways in which medical equipment has changed since Anglo-Saxon times.
3	1	• Children learn about the history of dental care. • They write and perform a play sketch or a rap.	• Can describe some of the changes in dental care over the centuries.
	2	• Children order a text about the history of the treatment of mental illness. • They write the diary of a monk working in Bedlam the Middle Ages.	• Can describe some of the ways in which mental illness was treated in the past.
4	1	• Children learn about the Great Plague of 1665. • They play the role of villagers in Eyam, and hold a class debate on whether to isolate the village.	• Can explain the main factors behind the rampant spread and high mortality rate of the plague.
	2	• Children read and discuss a text about scurvy. • They carry out an experiment to compare the Vitamin C content of various juices.	• Can describe the symptoms and causes of scurvy, and explain why it was once such a problem for sailors.
5	1	• Children read about the history of smallpox. • They write and answer quiz questions about smallpox.	• Can explain why smallpox was such a feared disease.
	2	• Children learn about Edward Jenner and vaccination, and then write a comic strip retelling the story.	• Can describe the part Edward Jenner played in the fight against smallpox.
6	1	• Children look at a timeline of women in medicine. • They write a biography of one of the women.	• Can describe various roles of women in the history of medicine.
	2	• Children learn about Florence Nightingale. • They create a dance retelling her story.	• Can describe the contribution Florence Nightingale made to medicine.
Assess and review		• To review the half-term's work.	

Expected prior learning
● Children do not need any prior knowledge about the history of medicine in order to study this chapter.

Overview of progression
● In this chapter the children will address historically valid questions about change, cause, similarity and difference, and significance. They will respond to written, pictorial and video accounts of medical history. They will also develop their ability to draw comparisons, as they consider similarities and differences between aspects of medicine in the past and the same aspects of medicine today.
● Children will demonstrate their knowledge of the past in different ways, including writing posters, reports, play sketches, raps, diaries, quizzes, comic strips and biographies, creating dances, drawing pictures, taking part in debates and conducting experiments.

Creative context
● The content of this chapter has strong links with the English curriculum, with children engaging in various activities across the domains of spoken language, reading and writing. These include taking part in discussions and debates, applying research skills, exploring a role-play scenario, writing and performing a rap or a play sketch, reading texts for information, and writing reports, diaries, quiz questions, comic strips and biographies.
● Children apply their skills of scientific enquiry when they carry out an experiment to compare the Vitamin C content of various juices.
● Children undertake historical research online, which address several requirements of the computing curriculum, including using the internet safely and responsibly, using search engines effectively, and evaluating online content.
● Children apply skills developed in design and technology to design a hospital of the future and to investigate the design of medical equipment.
● There are links to art and design with children creating a comic strip about Edward Jenner and a poster about an early theory of disease.
● Children create a dance telling the story of Florence Nightingale, which links to the PE curriculum.

Background knowledge
● Here are instructions for making the cornstarch-iodine indicator solution used in Week 4 (see page 161): Gradually and thoroughly mix two tablespoons of cornstarch with 500ml of water. Filter the water and cornstarch mixture through three or four coffee filter papers at once. Repeat this process until the liquid is clear. Add tincture of iodine to the cornstarch solution one drop at a time, stirring as you do so, until the solution turns a deep, dark blue. Pour the indicator solution into a watertight, non-breakable container, and label it clearly.
● This recipe makes enough indicator solution for about 50 tests. If you will be testing many varieties of juice and/or dividing the class into several groups, you may want to make double the quantity.
● The indicator solution is safe for children to use without wearing gloves, but iodine is toxic, and children will need to follow the usual safety rules for doing practical work in science.
● When the experiment is finished, the indicator solution is safe to pour down the drain, although you may want to check with your school leadership first.

Week 1 lesson plans

In Lesson 1 children research two early theories of disease: the miasma theory and the humoral theory, and create a poster explaining one of these theories. In Lesson 2 children investigate some of the more unusual medical treatments from the past. They consider which treatments might have been the most dangerous and suggest why. They choose one historical medical treatment to research further and then write a report about it.

1: What did people used to think caused disease?

Lesson objectives
● To develop a chronologically secure knowledge and understanding of British, local and world history, establishing clear narratives within and across the periods they study.
● To regularly address and sometimes devise historically valid questions about change, cause, similarity and difference, and significance.

Expected outcomes
● All children know that for most of history people did not understand what caused disease.
● Most children can name and describe some early theories of disease.
● Some children can explain one of the early theories of disease in detail.

Resources
Computers with internet access; materials for creating posters

Introduction
● Introduce this lesson's focus question: *What did people used to think caused disease?*
● Give children a few minutes to discuss what they know about the causes of disease. Discuss ideas together.
● Establish that many different factors, often acting together, contribute to disease. These include micro-organisms such as bacteria and viruses, other environmental factors such as toxins, lifestyle factors such as diet and exercise, and genetic factors. Explain that our current understanding of the causes of disease is relatively recent, and that it is still developing.

Paired work
● Organise the class into pairs, giving each pair access to the internet.
● Write the following questions on the board: *What was the miasma theory of disease (also called miasmatism)? What was the humoral theory of disease (also called humorism)?*
● Explain to children they will be using the internet to find the answers to the questions on the board. Remind them of the need to get information from credible websites, and briefly revise how to assess online sources for credibility. You might like to suggest the following search terms: *theories of disease, miasma,* and *four humours.*
● Give children time to use the internet to find the answers to the questions.

Whole-class work
● Ask children to share what they have found out. If there is disagreement over any facts relating to the two theories of disease, ask children how they could judge which piece of information is more likely to be correct.
● Discuss the implications of these theories for doctors' treatments and patients' health.

Group work
● Organise the class into groups. Ask each group to work together to create a poster about one of the historical theories of disease.

Review
● Ask: *Why do you think people attributed some diseases to 'foul air'?* (Foul smells were often associated with unsanitary conditions, where disease was rife.)

Lesson objectives
● To develop a chronologically secure knowledge and understanding of British, local and world history, establishing clear narratives within and across the periods they study.
● To regularly address and sometimes devise historically valid questions about change, cause, similarity and difference, and significance.

Expected outcomes
● All children can describe some early medical treatments.
● Most children can explain why some of these treatments were dangerous.
● Some children can explain how modern medical treatments are tested for safety.

Resources
Photocopiable page 167 'True or false?'; information bank on medical science such as books and/or the internet (optional)

2: Kill or cure: why were early medical treatments often so dangerous?

Introduction
● Introduce this lesson's focus question: *Kill or cure: why were early medical treatments often so dangerous?*
● Ask children whether they know about any historical medical treatments (for example, from their research during the previous lesson). For each example children give, ask: *Is this treatment dangerous? If so, how dangerous is it? Why is it dangerous?*

Paired work
● Organise the class into pairs, giving each pair a copy of photocopiable page 167 'True or false?'.
● Ask pairs to read the historical medical treatments described on the photocopiable page and decide, through discussion, which treatments they think are genuine, and which are not.
● You might want to ask pairs to team up with other pairs to compare ideas and refine their answers.

Whole-class work
● Ask children to tell you which treatments they think are genuine and to explain why.
● Tell children that all the treatments on the photocopiable page *are* genuine.
● Review all the treatments, discussing the likely efficacy of each treatment. Ask children to suggest which treatments might have been the most dangerous and why.

Independent work
● Ask children to write a report on one (or more) of the treatments from the photocopiable page, giving their report the title 'Why this treatment is dangerous'.
● Pose questions to help children focus on the dangerous elements of some of the cures (arsenic, corpses) as opposed to the simply ineffective elements.
● If appropriate, allow access to books and/or the internet for further research.

Differentiation
● Challenge: let children research how modern medical treatments are tested for safety; you could provide them with some search terms, such as *drug trials*, *clinical trials*, and *double-blind trials*.

Review
● Ask a few children to share their reports.
● If any children have researched how modern medical treatments are tested for safety, ask them to share what they have found out with the rest of the class.

Week 2 lesson plans

In Lesson 1 the children read about the development of hospitals. They describe and discuss the differences between the earliest hospitals and modern-day hospitals. They arrange pictures of historical hospital wards in chronological order, and draw an annotated picture of a hospital of the future, explaining how the future hospital's features are an improvement on those of a modern-day hospital. In Lesson 2 the children investigate examples of medical equipment from the past millennium. They research one item of historical medical equipment and its modern equivalent. They write a report about how it has changed and developed.

Lesson objectives
● To develop a chronologically secure knowledge and understanding of British, local and world history, establishing clear narratives within and across the periods they study.
● To note connections, contrasts and trends over time.
● To regularly address and sometimes devise historically valid questions about change, cause, similarity and difference, and significance.

Expected outcomes
● All children can draw comparisons between the earliest hospitals in Britain and modern-day hospitals.
● Most children can arrange pictures of hospitals in chronological order.
● Some children can use pictures of hospitals from various eras to draw conclusions about medicine in the past.

Resources
Photocopiable page 'A history of hospitals' from the CD-ROM; media resource 'Hospitals through the ages' on the CD-ROM; interactive tool 'Timeline maker' on the CD-ROM; drawing materials (paper-based or digital)

1: Were early hospitals anything like modern hospitals?

Introduction
● Introduce this lesson's focus question: *Were early hospitals anything like modern hospitals?*
● Ask: *What are modern hospitals like?* Ask pairs of children to list the features of a modern hospital. Discuss children's ideas.

Paired work
● Organise the class into pairs again, giving each pair a copy of photocopiable page 'History of hospitals' on the CD-ROM. Ask children to read the text.
● Ask questions about the text, such as: *Which ancient civilisations had hospitals? What was one difference between early Christian hospitals and hospitals in the Islamic empire? What changes were there to hospitals during the Middle Ages? What differences are there between early hospitals and modern-day hospitals, or hospitals in the 19th and 20th centuries?*
● Ask: *What differences are there between early hospitals and modern-day hospitals?*

Group work
● Organise the class into groups. Then display media resource 'Hospitals through the ages' on the CD-ROM.
● Ask children to work together in their group to arrange the pictures of hospital wards in chronological order. Ask groups to share and explain their ordering with the rest of the class.
● Reveal the correct order of the pictures which can be seen on screen 2.

Independent work
● Challenge children to draw a picture of a hospital of the future. Ask them to annotate the picture, explaining how the future hospital's features are an improvement on those of a modern-day hospital.

Review
● Ask children to share and discuss their pictures with the rest of the class. Ask them to describe the features they imagine a hospital of the future might have, and how they are an improvement on those of a modern-day hospital.

Lesson objectives

● To develop a chronologically secure knowledge and understanding of British, local and world history, establishing clear narratives within and across the periods they study.
● To note connections, contrasts and trends over time.
● To regularly address and sometimes devise historically valid questions about change, cause, similarity and difference, and significance.

Expected outcomes

● All children can identify and describe examples of old medical equipment.
● Most children can describe some of the ways in which medical equipment has changed since Anglo-Saxon times.
● Some children can explain the medical advances behind the development of specific pieces of medical equipment.

Resources

Media resource 'Medical equipment through the ages' on the CD-ROM; information bank on medical science such as books and/or the internet (optional)

2: How has medical equipment changed since Anglo-Saxon times?

Introduction

● Introduce this lesson's focus question: How has medical equipment changed since Anglo-Saxon times?
● Display the image showing multiple pieces of medical equipment from the media resource 'Medical equipment through the ages' on the CD-ROM. Give children a few minutes, working with a partner, to talk about what each piece of equipment might be.

Group work

● Organise the class into groups. Give each access to the media resource or display the separate images of the medical equipment.
● Ask group members to work together to do the following, encouraging them to discuss their reasoning with you as well as the other members of the group:
   ● Quickly sketch each piece of equipment.
   ● Label with a name and/or description of what it did.
   ● Arrange the pictures in chronological order.
● Bring the class back together to share ideas and to give the correct answers.
● Then discuss differences between these instruments and those used today.

Independent work

● Ask individuals to select one instrument and write a report about how it has changed and/or developed. If appropriate, allow further research using books and/or internet access.

Differentiation

● Challenge: children could find out about the development of medical equipment in the recent past (for example, over the last few decades or years) by devising a questionnaire to give to health professionals connected to the school.

Review

● Select some individuals to read out their reports. Ask: *What factors or events led to changes being made to this piece of medical equipment? In what ways is the modern version an improvement on previous versions?*

Week 3 lesson plans

In Lesson I the children write and answer questions on a text about the history of dental care and discuss the changes in dental care over the centuries. They then write and perform a play sketch about a visit to the dentist in another period of history, or a rap about the history of dental care. In Lesson 2 children order a cut-up text about the history of the treatment of mental illness. They discuss what it might have been like to work in an early mental hospital such as Bedlam, or to spend time as one of its patients. Children write the diary of a doctor or nurse working in Bedlam during the middle ages.

I: When barbers pulled teeth: how has dental care changed over the centuries?

Introduction
● Introduce this lesson's focus question: *When barbers pulled teeth: how has dental care changed over the centuries?*

Independent work
● Give out copies of the photocopiable page 'A history of dental care' from the CD-ROM. Ask children to read the text and then write questions about the text for a friend to answer. You could ask some children to write more questions.
● Ask selected children to read out a question they have written, challenging the class to answer it.
● Ask: *In what ways has dental care changed over the centuries?* Give children time to discuss this question with the person sitting next to them before asking the class for their ideas.

Paired work
● Ask children to work with a partner to write one of the following:
  ● a play sketch about a visit to a dentist in another period of history (featuring just two characters – the dentist and the patient)
  ● a rap about the history of dental care.

Group work
● Put pairs together to form groups of six or eight.
● Ask one pair at a time to perform their sketch or rap to the rest of the group and get constructive feedback.
● Encourage pairs to make changes to their sketch or rap in the light of this feedback.

Differentiation
● Support: children who struggle with reading and/or writing may need individual or group support when reading the text on the photocopiable page and writing questions on it.

Review
● Ask pairs to perform their revised sketches and raps in front of the whole class.
● One or more children could record the performances on video.

Lesson objectives
● To develop a chronologically secure knowledge and understanding of British, local and world history, establishing clear narratives within and across the periods they study.
● To note connections, contrasts and trends over time.
● To regularly address and sometimes devise historically valid questions about change, cause, similarity and difference, and significance.

Expected outcomes
● All children can read and answer questions about the history of dental care.
● Most children can describe some of the changes in dental care over the centuries.
● Some children can explain the reasons for some of the changes in dental care over the centuries.

Resources
Photocopiable page 'A history of dental care' from the CD-ROM; video recording equipment (optional)

2: How was mental illness treated in the past?

Introduction
● Introduce this lesson's focus question: *How was mental illness treated in the past?*

Paired work
● Organise the class into pairs, giving each pair a copy of the photocopiable page 168 'How was mental illness treated in the past?' and a pair of scissors. You could also give each pair a sheet of plain paper and some glue so that they can stick the text down in the correct order.
● Ask pairs to cut up the photocopiable page along the lines, read the text, and put the paragraphs in order.

Whole-class work
● Discuss the correct order of the text with the class. The correct order is: D, E, A, F, C, B.
● Ask questions about the content of the text.
● Ask: *What might it have been like to work in an early mental hospital like Bedlam?*
● Display an example of a diary extract, such as that on photocopiable page 'A Victorian girl's diary' from the CD-ROM. Ask the children to describe the features of a diary.

Independent work
● Ask children to write an extract from the diary of a monk working in Bedlam during the middle ages.
● Some children may want to find out more about Bedlam before writing their diary entries, so make sure suitable information is available.

Differentiation
● Support: children who struggle with writing may need adult support during the independent work.
● Challenge: more confident children to do research in order to compare modern treatments for mental illness with treatments used in the past.

Review
● If any children did additional research into Bedlam before writing their diaries, ask them to share what they found out.
● Ask selected children to read out their diary extracts. Ask: *If an inmate were relating the same events, what do you think they would say about them?*

Week 4 lesson plans

In Lesson 1 the children read and discuss a text about the Great Plague of 1665. They play the role of villagers in Eyam, and hold a class debate on whether to isolate the village. In Lesson 2 the children read and discuss a text about scurvy. They carry out an experiment to compare the Vitamin C content of various juices, and record their results in the form of a graph.

1: Why did the plague kill so many people?

Introduction
● Introduce this lesson's focus question: *Why did the plague kill so many people?*

Paired work
● Organise the class into pairs, giving each pair a copy of photocopiable page 'The Great Plague' from the CD-ROM. Allow time to read and discuss the text.
● Ask: *Why did the plague spread so fast? Why do you think it was so deadly? Can you explain the thinking behind each of the efforts to control the plague? Why might killing cats and dogs have made the plague spread more rapidly?*

Group work
● Remind the children about the village of Eyam, referred to in the text.
● Divide the class into six groups, giving each group a different character card from photocopiable page 'The village of Eyam: should you stay or should you go?' from the CD-ROM. Groups should discuss the arguments their character could use in order to support their position. The group with the card for Anna Olds should write an equal number of arguments for both leaving and staying.

Whole-class work
● Conduct a class debate, with a spokesperson from each group presenting their arguments.
● After the debate, reveal what actually happened. William and his wife Catherine persuaded the villagers to isolate the village. The plague took hold and in just over a year, three quarters of the residents died. William held church services outdoors to stop the spread of germs and Catherine nursed the sick. Their plan succeeded; the plague stopped at Eyam and did not go any further. William survived, but Catherine died after catching the plague from one of her patients. The village still holds an annual remembrance on 'Plague Sunday'.

> ### Differentiation
> ● Challenge: during the debate, one or two children could keep notes summarising the arguments on each side, and provide a quick recap before the vote.

Review
● Complete the debate by asking children to vote for the point of view that was supported by the most compelling arguments. Ask: *Which way did you vote? Did you find the decision about which way to vote difficult to make? Why? Why not?*

Lesson objectives
● To develop a chronologically secure knowledge and understanding of British, local and world history, establishing clear narratives within and across the periods they study.
● To note connections, contrasts and trends over time.
● To regularly address and sometimes devise historically valid questions about change, cause, similarity and difference, and significance.
● To construct informed responses that involve thoughtful selection and organisation of relevant historical information.

Expected outcomes
● All children can describe what happened during the Great Plague.
● Most children can explain the main factors behind the rapid spread and high mortality rate of the plague.
● Some children can put forward a compelling argument in support of their point of view in a debate about the plague.

Resources
Photocopiable page 'The Great Plague' on the CD-ROM; photocopiable page 'The village of Eyam: should you stay or should you go?' from the CD-ROM

Lesson objectives
● To develop a chronologically secure knowledge and understanding of British, local and world history, establishing clear narratives within and across the periods they study.
● To note connections, contrasts and trends over time.
● To regularly address and sometimes devise historically valid questions about change, cause, similarity and difference, and significance.

Expected outcomes
● All children can describe the symptoms and cause of scurvy.
● Most children can explain why scurvy was once such a problem for sailors.
● Some children can describe the symptoms, cause and history of another disease caused by a vitamin deficiency.

Resources
Photocopiable page 'Scurvy' from the CD-ROM; corn starch and iodine indicator solution (see *Preparation*); variety of juices; measuring spoons; plastic vials; pipettes; graphing materials (paper-based or digital)

2: What was scurvy and why don't sailors suffer from it today?

Preparation
● Make a cornstarch-iodine indicator solution (approximately 50 tests) using the instructions in *Background knowledge* on page 153.

Introduction
● Introduce this lesson's focus question: *What was scurvy and why don't sailors suffer from it today?*
● Give children a few minutes to discuss the focus question with a partner and then ask them to share their ideas with the class.

Paired work
● Organise the class into pairs, giving each pair a copy of photocopiable pages 'Scurvy' from the CD-ROM.
● Ask children to read the text and discuss the questions with their partner, before discussing them as a class.

Whole-class work
● Demonstrate the following experiment.
● Decant 10ml of indicator solution into a clean plastic vial. Using a clean pipette, drop one drop at a time of one of the juices into the vial, swirling the solution around after adding each drop. Ask children to keep count of the number of drops you add.
● Explain that if the colour of the indicator solution changes, it indicates the presence of vitamin C.
● Continue adding at drop at a time of the juice until the indicator solution becomes colourless. Record the number of drops added. The fewer drops added before the solution becomes colourless, the higher the vitamin C content.
● Tell children they will do this experiment on several types of juice. Emphasise the importance of using a fresh batch of indicator solution each time. Ask: *What will you do to ensure the test is fair?*

Group work
● Divide the class into groups to carry out the experiment. When groups have completed the experiment, ask them to draw a bar chart of their results.

> **Differentiation**
> ● Challenge: more confident learners can research the symptoms, cause and history of another disease caused by a vitamin deficiency: rickets.

Review
● Discuss results with the class. Ask: *Which juice has the highest vitamin C content? Are everyone's test results the same? If not, what might be the reasons for the differences? Do we need to check any of our data? How could we do this?*
● Tell the children that scurvy was a result of a vitamin deficiency and discuss why this was a problem for sailors.

Week 5 lesson plans

This week's lessons centre on smallpox, responsible for many millions of deaths over the course of recorded history. In Lesson 1 the children read and discuss a text about the history of smallpox. They consider the reasons why the disease was so feared. They write and answer quiz questions about smallpox. In Lesson 2 the children read and order a text telling the story of Edward Jenner and vaccination, and then write a comic strip retelling the story.

1: What was so scary about smallpox?

Lesson objectives
● To develop a chronologically secure knowledge and understanding of British, local and world history, establishing clear narratives within and across the periods they study.
● To regularly address and sometimes devise historically valid questions about change, cause, similarity and difference, and significance.

Expected outcomes
● All children can explain what smallpox was.
● Most children can explain why smallpox was such a feared disease.
● Some children can explain why the campaign to inoculate people against smallpox met with resistance, and why inoculation is still controversial.

Resources
Photocopiable page 'A history of smallpox' from the CD-ROM; computers with internet access

Introduction
● Introduce this lesson's focus question: *What was so scary about smallpox?*
● Ask: *Have you heard of smallpox before? What are the symptoms of the disease? What causes smallpox?* Discuss children's ideas.
● Tell children that smallpox is caused by a virus called *variola*. Explain that smallpox was one of the most feared diseases throughout recorded history, but that a prolonged campaign of vaccination eventually eradicated it.

Paired work
● Organise the class into pairs, giving each pair a copy of photocopiable page 'A history of smallpox' from the CD-ROM.
● Ask them to read the text.

Whole-class work
● Ask children questions about the text; for example:
  ● *What reminder of the disease were survivors usually left with?* (Scars.)
  ● *Which civilisation first developed a form of inoculation against smallpox?* (Ancient China.)
  ● *When?* (10th century.)
  ● *What was this form of inoculation called?* (Variolation.)
  ● *In the late 18th century Edward Jenner developed a safer and more effective form of inoculation against smallpox. What was this called?* (Vaccination.)
  ● *In what year was smallpox finally eradicated?* (1979.)
● Finally ask: *Why do you think smallpox was such a feared disease?*

Paired work
● Ask each pair to write a set of quiz questions about smallpox. They could use just the information in the text they have read, or they could do some further research to find out more facts about the disease.

> **Differentiation**
> ● Challenge: ask children to find out why the campaign to inoculate people against smallpox met with resistance, and why inoculation is still a controversial topic today.

Review
● Ask pairs to swap quizzes and attempt to answer each other's questions.
● If you have time you could ask each pair to pose one of their questions to the whole class.

Lesson objectives
● To develop a chronologically secure knowledge and understanding of British, local and world history, establishing clear narratives within and across the periods they study.
● To regularly address and sometimes devise historically valid questions about change, cause, similarity and difference, and significance.

Expected outcomes
● All children can explain what Edward Jenner is famous for.
● Most children can describe the part Edward Jenner played in the fight against smallpox.
● Some children can describe the global campaign to eradicate smallpox.

Resources
Photocopiable page 169 'Edward Jenner and vaccination'; scissors; example of a comic strip; materials for making a comic strip (paper-based or digital)

2: What part did Edward Jenner play in the fight against smallpox?

Introduction
● Introduce this lesson's focus question: *What part did Edward Jenner play in the fight against smallpox?*
● Remind children that Edward Jenner was mentioned in the text they read in the previous lesson. Ask them if they can remember what part he played in the fight against smallpox.
● Establish that Edward Jenner was the doctor who developed a safer and more effective technique of inoculation against smallpox, which he called vaccination.

Paired work
● Organise the class into pairs, giving each pair a copy of photocopiable page 169 'Edward Jenner and vaccination' and a pair of scissors. Ask children to read the text, cut along the lines, and arrange the paragraphs in the correct order. (The correct order is E, C, G, D, A, F, B.)
● Ask children questions about the text, such as:
    ● *What link did Edward Jenner spot between cowpox and smallpox?* (Milkmaids often got cowpox but did not get smallpox.)
    ● *What was the vaccine Jenner used?* (Pus from cowpox blisters.)
    ● *How did Edward Jenner introduce the vaccine into James Phipps' body?* (Through a scratch on his arm.)
    ● *How did Edward Jenner test whether the vaccination had worked?* (He deliberately tried to infect James I with smallpox.)
● Revise briefly the features of a comic strip, displaying and discussing an example comic strip.

Independent work
● Ask children to create a comic strip retelling the story of Edward Jenner and vaccination. Suggest that they create one cell of the comic strip for each paragraph of text from the photocopiable page. Children could use paper-based or digital media to create their comic strip.
● Consider making children's comic strips available to a wider audience; for example, by uploading them to the school learning platform.

Differentiation
● Support: during the independent work, provide a more extensive word list, or a storyboard.
● Challenge: children could find out about the global campaign to eradicate smallpox.

Review
● Ask any children who did the extension activity to describe the global campaign to eradicate smallpox. Ask: *What organisations were involved in the campaign? When did the campaign take place? What methods did it use? What problems did it encounter? Was it successful?*

Week 6 lesson plans

In this week's lessons the children investigate the role women have played in the history of medicine. In Lesson 1 children explore a timeline of women in medicine. They choose one of the women featured on the timeline to research further, and work in groups to write a biography of her life for a display. In Lesson 2 children learn about Florence Nightingale. They then create and perform a dance retelling her story.

1: What part have women played in the history of medicine?

Lesson objectives
● To develop a chronologically secure knowledge and understanding of British, local and world history, establishing clear narratives within and across the periods they study.
● To note connections, contrasts and trends over time.
● To regularly address and sometimes devise historically valid questions about change, cause, similarity and difference, and significance.

Expected outcomes
● All children can describe various roles women have played in the history of medicine.
● Most children can describe the way women's roles in medicine have changed over the centuries.
● Some children can explain the factors affecting the roles of women in medicine.

Resources
Photocopiable page 'Timeline of women in medicine' from the CD-ROM; computers with access to the internet; writing materials (paper-based or digital with a facility to print); display materials

Introduction
● Introduce this lesson's focus question: *What part have women played in the history of medicine?*
● Give children a few minutes, working in pairs, to discuss and make notes on the topic 'Women in the history of medicine'. Ask them to keep their notes to hand, as they will be using them again at the end of the lesson.
● Discuss what children already know about women in the history of medicine. Their knowledge may be fairly limited.

Paired work
● Organise the class into pairs, giving each pair a copy of the photocopiable page 'Timeline of women in medicine'.
● Give pairs time to read and discuss the text and then write questions about it for the rest of the class to answer.

Whole-class work
● Ask each pair to choose one of their questions to put to the rest of the class. Discuss answers.
● Ask children to choose one of the women featured in the timeline to research further (apart from Florence Nightingale, who will be the subject of the following lesson).

Group work
● Organise the class into groups, depending on which woman they want to research.
● Ask each group to collaborate to write a biography of their chosen woman's life for a classroom or corridor display.

Differentiation
● Support: children will be choosing their groups for group work, but if possible, ensure each group is mixed ability.
● Challenge: more able group members, as part of their research, can investigate the factors affecting the changing roles of women in medicine.

Review
● Give children a few minutes, working in the same pairs as during the introduction, to add new information to their earlier notes.
● Ask: *What have you learned?*

Lesson objectives
● To develop a chronologically secure knowledge and understanding of British, local and world history, establishing clear narratives within and across the periods they study.
● To note connections, contrasts and trends over time.
● To regularly address and sometimes devise historically valid questions about change, cause, similarity and difference, and significance.

Expected outcomes
● All children know some facts about Florence Nightingale.
● Most children can describe how Florence Nightingale improved treatment at the hospital in Scutari.
● Some children can describe the wider contribution to medicine made by the work of Florence Nightingale.

Resources
A video clip about the story of Florence Nightingale (source online), PE kit, hall time, music (optional)

2: The lady with the lamp: what changes did Florence Nightingale bring to medicine?

Introduction
● Introduce this lesson's focus question: *The Lady with the Lamp: what changes did Florence Nightingale bring to medicine?*
● Give children a few minutes to discuss with a partner what they already know about Florence Nightingale, before asking them to share their ideas with the class.

Whole-class work
● Draw out key information about the work of Florence Nightingale, for example by hot seating in character as Florence or watching a video clip (see *Resources*).
● Ask questions to test children's understanding, such as:
  ● *What was different about Florence Nightingale's approach to training nurses?* (She taught them cleanliness and hygiene; organisation and tidiness.)
  ● *What changes did Florence Nightingale make to the hospital at Scutari?* (Thorough cleaning, including sheets.)
  ● *What was Florence's nickname?* (The Lady with the Lamp.)
  ● *How did she get it?* (Caring for the wounded at night.)
  ● *What reward did Florence and her nurses get for their efforts at Scutari?* (Soldiers' health improved.)
  ● *When Florence got back home, what did she do with the trust fund that the British public had set up for her?* (She founded the first nurses' training school.)

Group work
● Tell children they will be working in groups to create a dance that tells the story of Florence Nightingale.
● You could divide the story up into sections, giving each group a different section to tell in their dance (for example, Florence's childhood, training the nurses, arriving at the hospital at Scutari, transforming the hospital, and tending to the sick soldiers). You could then link each group's dance in order to tell the whole story.
● Consider whether you will use music in the dance, and if so, how many pieces and who will choose it.
● Give children time to go through the process of creating, reviewing, revising and rehearsing their dance(s), before giving them the opportunity to perform the dance(s) to an audience, such as parents and/or the rest of the school.

Review
● Finally, ask: *What changes did Florence Nightingale make to the hospital at Scutari? Why did she make these changes? What were the effects of these changes? What wider contribution did Florence Nightingale make to the practice of medicine?*

Medicine today and in the past

Revise
● Working in groups, ask children to make a list of the aspects of the history of medicine they have investigated so far.
● Discuss ideas as a class and write a complete list on the board (for example, theories of disease, medical treatments, hospitals, medical equipment, dental care, mental illness, plague, scurvy, smallpox, Edward Jenner and vaccination, the role of women in medicine, and Florence Nightingale). Leave the list on the board for reference during the assessment activity.

Assess
● Revise the term *mind map* and show an example. Ideally, the mind map should be one drawn by members of the class.
● Tell the children they will be creating a mind map. On the board write: *How was medicine in history different from medicine today?*
● Give the children a set length of time (for example, 25 minutes) to complete the task. Emphasise the importance of working independently. Encourage the children to work fast and to include as much breadth *and* depth of information as they can.
● Ask any children who struggle with writing to write the main headings only (go for breadth rather than depth). They could communicate details to you verbally later.

Further practice
● Ask the children to use the interactive timeline tool to begin to create a timeline of the history of medicine, incorporating events they have learned about so far.

History of medicine vocabulary

Revise
● Organise the class into groups, giving each group a set of historical term cards for example, miasmatism, humorism, middle ages, bubonic plague, pneumonic plague, epidemic, The Great Plague, scurvy, mortality, smallpox, virus, variola, inoculation, variolation, vaccination, cowpox, hygiene, gangrene.
● Ask each group of children to work together collaboratively to sort the cards into groups.
● Discuss with children the criteria they have used for sorting the cards.

Assess
● Introduce the assessment task. Children should choose six of the words from the cards. Each word must belong to a different group from the sorting activity, unless there are fewer than six groups, in which case children must choose at least one word from each group. For each word children must write a definition and then use the word in context, in a sentence or short paragraph.
● Demonstrate the task, choosing one of the words from the cards. Encourage children to help you write the definition and suggest a sentence or short paragraph in which to put the word in context. Tell children this word is now 'off limits'.
● Give the children a set length of time (for example, 25 minutes) to complete the task. Emphasise the importance of working independently.

Further practice
● Challenge children to create a card game that involves matching historical and/or medical terms with their definitions.

Name: _____ Date: _____

True or false?

- Which of these medical treatments were really used in the past?
- Circle T for true or F for false.

1. Treating warts by cutting a mouse in half and placing it on the affected area.   T / F

2. Treating stuttering by cutting off half the tongue.   T / F

3. Trying to prevent catching the Black Death by inhaling farts collected in a jar.   T / F

4. Trying to lose weight by swallowing tapeworm eggs.   T / F

5. Treating coughs by drinking syrup of snails.   T / F

6. Treating gut pain by blowing tobacco smoke up the patient's bottom.   T / F

7. Treating headaches by drilling a hole in the skull.   T / F

8. Treating almost anything by applying leeches to the patient's body to drink their blood.   T / F

9. Treating mental illness by inserting a metal rod into the patient's brain through the eye socket.   T / F

10. Treating rapier wounds with a powder made of earthworms, pigs' brains, rust and bits of mummified corpses.   T / F

11. Treating malaria using arsenic.   T / F

12. Treating eye infections by dripping bat's blood into the patient's eyes.   T / F

I know different types of medical treatment that was used in the past.

How did you do?

How was mental illness treated in the past?

A. The first asylums (hospitals for the mentally ill) were founded in the Middle Ages. The regime in early asylums, including London's Bethlehem Hospital (known as 'Bedlam'), was a combination of punishment and religious devotion – chains, manacles, locks and stocks appear in the hospital inventory from this time.

B. By the 1980s and 1990s, new technologies had been developed which seemed to offer a new biological approach to treatment. These included specially targeted antidepressant drugs, and brain-scanning techniques such as magnetic resonance imaging (MRI).

C. By the early 20th century, asylums had become increasingly cut off from the outside world. Conditions were crowded and unpleasant – sometimes even abusive. Patients became test subjects for new and dangerous 'treatments' like lobotomy (having a section of brain cut using a sharp instrument inserted through the eye socket) and ECT (electric shock 'therapy').

D. Even the basic idea of a 'mental illness' is problematic. Who decides what behaviour is 'normal' and what behaviour is abnormal, or even sick? If people, including doctors, can't agree on how to define mental illness, how can they agree on the best way to treat it?

E. In ancient times people who behaved strangely were thought to be possessed by demons. Some demons, it was believed, could only be driven out by torture or death. Early doctors thought mental illness was caused by an excess of one of the four bodily fluids or 'humours'. They believed medicine could not do much to help – nature had to take its course.

F. The Victorian era prided itself on notions of 'improvement'. Despite few advances in medical knowledge regarding mental illness, the 19th century saw a concerted effort to try to cure sufferers. The number of asylums increased, as did the number of doctors dedicated to specialist practice in psychiatry. Critics said that the claims of cures in asylums were exaggerated.

Name: _____   Date: _____

Edward Jenner and vaccination

A. A few weeks later, Dr Jenner took pus from a smallpox victim and tried to give James the disease. James did not become ill. This suggested Dr Jenner's theory had been correct. Dr Jenner repeated the experiment on other children, including his own 11-month-old son, always with the same result.

B. Before long, however, everyone could see how effective vaccination was at protecting people against smallpox, and the practice of vaccination spread. People stopped ridiculing Dr Jenner. He became famous and well respected, and spent most of his time researching improvements to the vaccine.

C. Cowpox was a mild disease, unlike the deadly smallpox, but Dr Jenner wondered whether the two diseases might be related. He theorised that catching cowpox gave milkmaids immunity against smallpox.

D. On 14 May 1796, Dr Jenner took pus from a cowpox blister on the hand of milkmaid Sarah Nelmes, and rubbed it into a scratch he had made on James' arm. James developed some of the symptoms of cowpox, but soon recovered.

E. Edward Jenner was an English doctor and scientist who wanted to find a cure for smallpox. He noticed that very few milkmaids caught smallpox and wondered why. Cows sometimes caught a disease called cowpox, and milkmaids often caught cowpox from infected cows.

F. Dr Jenner published his results in 1798, naming his new technique 'vaccination', from the Latin 'vacca' for cow. At first, many people doubted the effectiveness of vaccination, and made fun of Dr Jenner. A cartoon of 1802, for example, showed people growing cows' heads after being vaccinated.

G. In order to test his theory, Dr Jenner needed to carry out an experiment on a human subject. His subject needed to be someone young who had not had either cowpox or smallpox. He chose eight-year-old James Phipps, the son of his gardener.

Medicine (2)

This chapter focuses on developments in medicine over the last century and a half. Children begin by learning about the germ theory of disease. They look into the development of various medical techniques and technologies. They study cholera, polio and influenza, and they investigate the setting up of the National Health Service in 1948. Finally, they devise and answer historically valid questions about further aspects of the history of medicine.

Chapter at a glance

Curriculum objectives

• A study of an aspect or theme in British history that extends pupils' chronological knowledge beyond 1066: changes in an aspect of social history (medicine from the Anglo-Saxons to the present).

Week	Lesson	Summary of activities	Expected outcomes
1	1	• Children watch and discuss video clips on the development of germ theory. • They about a contributor to the theory.	• Can describe the germ theory of disease and explain the part played in its development by Ignaz Semmelweis and Louis Pasteur.
	2	• Children read about the origins of cholera. • They draw a timeline showing British cholera epidemics.	• Can describe the major contributing factors to cholera outbreaks in Britain in the 19th century.
2	1	• Children learn about John Snow and the Broad Street cholera outbreak using an online interactive.	• Can describe the contribution made by John Snow to the development of medicine.
	2	• Children learn about developments in surgery. • They fill in a table comparing and contrasting surgery in the past with surgery today.	• Can describe some surgical tools and techniques. • Can compare and contrast early surgery with modern surgery.
3	1	• Children arrange anaesthetic developments in chronological order and match each development with the advantages it brought.	• Can order anaesthetic developments on a timeline and explain the advantages associated with each development.
	2	• The children read about Joseph Lister and antiseptic surgery. • They plan and carry out an experiment on the effect of hand cleaners on bacterial growth.	• Can explain the impact of Joseph Lister's pioneering work in antiseptic surgery.
4	1	• Children read about the development of medical imaging technologies. • They look at X-ray art and create their own X-ray-style artwork.	• Can describe the historical development of medical imaging technologies.
	2	• Children watch and discuss a slide show about the 1918–19 flu pandemic. • They take part in a role-play based on the pandemic.	• Can explain some of the effects of the flu pandemic in 1918–19.
5	1	• Children learn about Alexander Fleming and the discovery of penicillin. • They hold a debate on 'the greatest medical discovery of all time'.	• Can tell the story of Alexander Fleming's discovery of penicillin and explain its significance.
	2	• Children learn about the history of polio. • They research the history of one of the other diseases vaccinated against in the UK's childhood immunisation programme.	• Can describe the historical background of polio, and at least one other disease children are routinely vaccinated against.
6	1	• Children examine a variety of primary sources related to the setting up of the NHS.	• Can explain the historical background to the setting up of the NHS in 1948, and explain the reasons behind it.
	2	• Children research another area of medical history of their choice. • They present the results of their research in a whole-class outcome.	• Can devise historically valid questions about the history of medicine. • Can research answers to their questions, evaluating the sources they use for reliability.
Assess and review		• To review the half-term's work.	

■SCHOLASTIC
www.scholastic.co.uk

Expected prior learning
● It is expected that children will have already studied the proceeding chapter.

Overview of progression
● This chapter, in conjunction with the previous chapter, provides children with knowledge and understanding of an aspect of British history that extends their chronological knowledge beyond 1066.
● In this chapter the children continue to address historically valid questions about change, cause, similarity and difference, and significance. They have the opportunity to note connections, contrasts and trends over time and develop the appropriate use of historical and medical terms.
● Children demonstrate their knowledge of the past in different ways, including taking part in discussions, debates and role-play scenarios, writing articles, constructing timelines, drawing bar charts, filling in tables, and creating slide shows.

Creative context
● The content of this chapter has strong links with the English curriculum. Children take part in discussions and debates, construct persuasive arguments, apply research skills, explore a role-play scenario, read texts for information and write articles.
● Children apply their skills of scientific enquiry by deciding which pieces of evidence support a theory. They also devise and carry out a fair test, recording results and drawing conclusions.
● Children undertake historical research online, which addresses several requirements of the computing curriculum, including using the internet safely and responsibly, using search engines effectively and evaluating online content.
● Children apply skills developed in art and design to create X-ray-style art.

Background knowledge
● The germ theory of disease states that many diseases are caused by micro-organisms (germs), and that different germs cause different diseases. The germ theory was developed during the mid to late 19th century and it eventually replaced existing theories of disease, radically changing the practice of medicine. Once the germ theory was accepted, work could begin on identifying disease-causing germs and developing life-saving treatments.
● In 1928 microbiologist Alexander Fleming observed that mould that had accidentally grown in a petri dish containing a colony of bacteria had killed the bacteria around it. He found the active substance in the mould and called it 'penicillin'. Penicillin was the first antibiotic – a group of drugs that have saved countless lives.
● The First World War was one of the deadliest conflicts in human history – over 16 million people were killed. However, the influenza pandemic that began during the last few months of the war killed more than three times as many people. The 'Spanish flu' as it was known was one of the worst pandemics in recorded history. Over 40 per cent of the worldwide population was infected and more than 50 million people died. Some estimates put the death toll as high as 100 million. In the UK alone around a quarter of a million people died.

Week 1 lesson plans

In Lesson 1 the children watch video clips on the development of germ theory. They research the work of a contributor to the theory, and write an article on their chosen scientist's contribution. In Lesson 2 children read and answer questions on a text about the cholera epidemics of the 19th century. They learn what causes cholera and discuss reasons why the disease spread so quickly in Victorian cities. They construct a timeline of British cholera epidemics.

1: Who came up with the germ theory of disease?

Lesson objectives
● To develop a chronologically secure knowledge and understanding of British, local and world history, establishing clear narratives within and across the periods they study.
● To regularly address and sometimes devise historically valid questions about change, cause, similarity and difference, and significance.

Expected outcomes
● All children can describe the germ theory of disease.
● Most children can explain the part Ignaz Semmelweis and Louis Pasteur played in the development of the theory.
● Some children can explain the effect on medicine of the acceptance of the germ theory of disease.

Resources
100 Greatest Discoveries: Theory on Germs and 100 Greatest Discoveries: Germ Theory Origins from www.science.howstuffworks.com (source online); information bank on Semmelweis and Pasteur (such as books and/or internet access)

Introduction
● Introduce this lesson's focus question: *Who came up with the germ theory of disease?*
● Explain that the work of several scientists contributed to the development of the germ theory of disease.

Whole-class work
● Show children the film about 'theory on germs' (see *Resources*). Ask questions about the clip. For example: *What observation did Semmelweis make about the deaths from child-bed fever?* (There were more deaths on the ward led by physicians than the ward led by midwives.) *What theory did he come up with to explain his observation?* (Physicians had more contact with dead bodies. Their hands were transmitting disease-causing agents from dead bodies to live patients.) *What test did he conduct?* (His student physicians washed their hands in chlorine solution.) *What were the results?* (Deaths reduced dramatically.)
● Show children the film clip about Germ Theory Origins (see *Resources*). Ask questions about the clip. For example:
    ● *Why was Louis Pasteur particularly dedicated to finding a way of preventing infectious diseases?* (Three of his children had died of typhoid.)
    ● *What was happening to France's wine?* (It was getting spoiled.) *What did Pasteur do to help preserve the wine?* (Heating.)
    ● *What is the name given to the process he invented?* (Pasteurisation.)
    ● *What is the central idea of the germ theory?* (One micro-organism causes one disease.) *How is it different from the theories that came before?*

Paired work
● Organise the class into pairs with access to an information bank.
● Ask children to research and make notes about the work of Semmelweis or Pasteur, or the work of one of the other contributors to the development of the germ theory (Agostino Bassi, John Snow and Robert Koch).

Independent work
● Ask children to use their notes to write an article about their chosen scientist's work.

Differentiation
● Challenge: ask children to research the effect on medicine of the acceptance of the germ theory.

Review
● Ask children to share what they found out about the work of the contributors to germ theory. If children have done the extension activity, ask: *What effect did the acceptance of the germ theory of disease have on medicine?*

Lesson objectives
● To develop a chronologically secure knowledge and understanding of British, local and world history, establishing clear narratives within and across the periods they study.
● To regularly address and sometimes devise historically valid questions about change, cause, similarity and difference, and significance.

Expected outcomes
● All children can explain what cholera is.
● Most children can describe the major contributing factors to cholera outbreaks in the 19th century and draw a timeline of cholera outbreaks.
● Some children can describe the work of Joseph Bazalgette, and how it helped to end the cholera outbreaks in London.

Resources
Photocopiable pages 'Origins of cholera' and 'Origins of cholera: question sheet' from the CD-ROM; interactive activity 'Timeline maker' on the CD-ROM or materials for creating a timeline on paper

2: What were the causes of cholera?

Introduction
● Introduce this lesson's focus question: *What were the causes of cholera?*
● Ask: *What do you know about cholera?* Ask children to discuss the question with a partner before sharing their ideas with the class.
● Explain that cholera is a bacterial infection that affects the gut. The symptoms include severe diarrhoea and vomiting which, if left untreated, can lead to death within hours. Cholera is spread by drinking or eating contaminated water or food. For this reason cholera is still a risk in countries without clean water supplies or proper sewage disposal.
● Ask: *What do you know about living conditions in British cities in Victorian times? How might these conditions have contributed to the spread of cholera?*

Paired work
● Organise the class into pairs, giving each pair photocopiable pages 'Origins of cholera' and 'Origins of cholera: question sheet' from the CD-ROM.
● Ask children to read the text and work with their partner to answer the questions. As children are working, discuss their answers to the questions and ask them more questions to both test and facilitate their understanding of the text.
● The final question on the photocopiable sheet asks children to use the data in the text to construct a timeline of cholera outbreaks in Britain. You might want to encourage children to use the interactive activity 'Timeline maker' on the CD-ROM for this activity, or alternatively, to create a timeline on paper.

Differentiation
● Challenge: ask children to find out more about Joseph Bazalgette's work, how it was linked to the cholera epidemics in London, and how it helped to end them.

Review
● Ask: *Why does cholera no longer exist in this country? Whereabouts in the world does it still exist? Why?*
● For homework you could ask children to find out about charities working to eliminate waterborne diseases, such as WaterAid UK, Just a Drop or The Water Project, and ask them to suggest ways the class could raise funds to support their work.

Week 2 lesson plans

In Lesson 1 children continue their investigation into cholera. They learn about John Snow and the Soho cholera outbreak of 1854. In Lesson 2 children read and discuss a text about developments in surgery over the ages. They consider images to find out about surgical instruments from the past. Finally, they compare and contrast surgery in the past with surgery today.

1: How did John Snow advance medical knowledge?

Lesson objectives
● To develop a chronologically secure knowledge and understanding of British, local and world history, establishing clear narratives within and across the periods they study.
● To note connections, contrasts and trends over time.
● To develop the appropriate use of historical terms.
● To regularly address and sometimes devise historically valid questions about change, cause, similarity and difference, and significance.

Expected outcomes
● All children can explain who John Snow was.
● Most children can describe the contribution made by John Snow to the development of medicine.
● Some children can explain the relationship between modern methods of disease control and prevention and the methods John Snow used.

Resources
The story of John Snow (for example, for hot-seating in character); online interactive 'Tracking down the source of disease: The Broad Street cholera epidemic of 1854' at www.sciencemuseum.org.uk; computers

Introduction
● Introduce this lesson's focus question: *How did John Snow advance medical knowledge?*
● On the board write the word *epidemiology*. Ask children what they think it means. Children may notice the link with the word *epidemic* from the previous lesson. Explain that *epidemiology* is the branch of medicine that studies the causes and spread of epidemics and aims to control and prevent them.

Whole-class work
● Before showing the Science Museum interactive resource, give children information about John Snow and the London cholera outbreak of 1854, for example by hot-seating in role as John Snow.
● Establish that John Snow, a doctor, was determined to find the cause of the cholera outbreak. He felt that miasma could not be the cause, as victims' lungs were not affected. He questioned victims in Soho and marked his data on a map (victims' homes, water sources used). He pinpointed the source of the outbreak to one water well on Broad Street. When the well was closed, the number of cases fell dramatically. The well on Broad Street had become contaminated by a leaking cesspool.
● Now display the online interactive (see *Resources*). Read the introductory text together, and then click 'Start investigation'. Demonstrate moving the cursor around the map to find features you can interact with. Click on the brewery and read the text together.

Paired work
● Ask the children to discuss in pairs whether the evidence John Snow observes at the brewery supports his theory that cholera is waterborne.
● If you have class computer access, children can complete the interactive in their pairs, following in the footsteps of John Snow to track down the source of the disease.
● Otherwise, continue to display the resource for the whole class.

Differentiation
● Challenge: children could find out about modern epidemiological methods and how they relate to the methods John Snow developed.

Review
● Review the lesson's focus question. Ask: *How did John Snow advance medical knowledge?* First, he showed that cholera was a water-borne disease. This contradicted the miasma theory of disease and contributed to the development of the germ theory. Second, he developed techniques that are still used in epidemiology today.

Lesson objectives
● To develop a chronologically secure knowledge and understanding of British, local and world history, establishing clear narratives within and across the periods they study.
● To note connections, contrasts and trends over time.
● To develop the appropriate use of historical terms.
● To regularly address and sometimes devise historically valid questions about change, cause, similarity and difference, and significance.

Expected outcomes
● All children can describe some surgical tools and techniques used in the past.
● Most children can compare and contrast early surgery with modern surgery.
● Some children can evaluate the risks associated with early surgery.

Resources
Information bank on surgery through the ages (including media resource 'Medical equipment through the ages' on the CD-ROM); photocopiable page 185 'Surgery then and now'

2: Would you let a surgeon from the past operate on you?

Introduction
● Introduce this lesson's focus question: *Would you let a surgeon from the past operate on you?*
● Ask children what they know about surgery today. Ask: *Do patients feel any pain during their operation? Why not? What do surgeons do to stop the patient from getting an infection?*
● Ask children whether they know anything about surgery in the past, and discuss their ideas.

Whole-class work
● Provide an information bank on surgery in the past that includes information on pain relief, infection prevention, instruments used and surgeons' training and qualifications. Depending on the resources available, you could either concentrate on a particular period of history (for example, Tudor times), or take a broader overview of the history of surgery.
● Ask questions based on the information in order to prepare the class for the independent work.

Independent work
● Give out copies of photocopiable page 185 'Surgery then and now'. Discuss how to complete the table, and give children time to do so, working independently.

Differentiation
● Support: during whole-class work, you might want to group less confident learners together and give them adult support.
● Challenge: during independent work, ask children to evaluate the risks associated with various aspects of early surgery.

Review
● Discuss the focus question together: *Would you let a surgeon from the past operate on you?* Ask children to explain their reasoning. You may wish to use the following additional questions: *What has struck you most about surgery in the past? Why?*

Week 3 lesson plans

In Lesson 1 children arrange anaesthetic developments in chronological order and match each development with the advantages it brought. They then record this information on a timeline. They answer quiz questions about the history of anaesthesia. In Lesson 2 children learn about Joseph Lister and antiseptic surgery. They plan and carry out an experiment to investigate the effect of various hand-cleaning substances on bacterial growth.

1: When were anaesthetics developed?

Lesson objective
● To develop a chronologically secure knowledge and understanding of British, local and world history, establishing clear narratives within and across the periods they study.

Expected outcomes
● All children can explain what anaesthetics are and name some anaesthetics.
● Most children can order anaesthetic developments on a timeline.
● Some children can explain the advantages associated with each new development in anaesthetics.

Resources
Photocopiable page 186 'The history of anaesthetics'; interactive activity 'Timeline maker' on the CD-ROM OR materials for creating a paper-based timeline; scissors; internet access (optional)

Introduction
● Introduce this lesson's focus question: *When were anaesthetics developed?*
● Ask: *What are anaesthetics? What is the difference between a local and a general anaesthetic? How are modern anaesthetics given to patients?*
● Explain that people have been experimenting with anaesthesia since ancient times, but it took a long time to develop effective anaesthetics.

Group work
● Organise the class into groups, giving each group a copy of the photocopiable page 186 'The history of anaesthetics' and a couple of pairs of scissors.
● Ask each group to cut out the cards, discussing the content of each numbered 'development' card and trying to match it with the correct lettered 'notes' card, while arranging the pairs of cards in chronological order.
● Finally, ask children to assign a date card to each pair of cards.
● Discuss each group's answers with them, and then provide them with the correct answers: 3D and 6A (both 'since antiquity'); 4F 1799; 1C 1846; 5B 1847; 2E 1848.
● Ask each group to create a timeline of anaesthetic developments. Children could use the interactive activity 'Timeline maker' on the CD-ROM, or create a timeline on paper.
● If time and internet access allows, ask children to research other developments in anaesthetics since 1848, and add these to the timeline.

> **Differentiation**
> ● Support: use mixed ability groups throughout the lesson.

Review
● Ask children to hide their timelines and the cards from the photocopiable page.
● Give the class a quiz about the development of anaesthetics. Children could answer the questions individually, in pairs, or in groups.
● You may wish to use the following additional questions: *How did you decide which development was first? Why did you decide to put [development a] after [development b]? What made you decide to put this 'notes' card here?*

Lesson objectives
- To develop a chronologically secure knowledge and understanding of British, local and world history, establishing clear narratives within and across the periods they study.
- To note connections, contrasts and trends over time.
- To develop the appropriate use of historical terms.
- To regularly address and sometimes devise historically valid questions about change, cause, similarity and difference, and significance.

Expected outcomes
- All children can describe Joseph Lister's pioneering work in the development of antiseptic surgery.
- Most children can explain the impact of Joseph Lister's work.
- Some children can draw conclusions from an experiment investigating the effects of different hand cleaning substances on the growth of bacteria.

Resources
Photocopiable page 'Getting to know Joseph Lister' on the CD-ROM; about 30 plastic petri dishes; agar; water; saucepan and hob- or microwave-proof container and microwave; cotton wool buds; sticky tape; sticky labels; paper towels; variety of hand soaps, hand washes and hand gels

2: Why is Joseph Lister remembered today?

Preparation
- The content described here will require two sessions to complete, and several days for the results to become apparent.
- Before the lesson, make sure you know how to conduct an experiment on bacterial growth, including how to prepare agar jelly. There are plenty of online resources available. You may want to consider bookmarking or downloading resources to help you explain the process.

Introduction
- Introduce the focus question: *Why is Joseph Lister remembered today?*
- Ask: *Have you ever heard of Joseph Lister? Do you know what he is remembered for?*

Whole-class work
- Before the beginning the experiment, give children information about Joseph Lister and antiseptic surgery, for example, by distributing and discussing photocopiable page 'Getting to know Joseph Lister' from the CD-ROM.
- Ask:
  - *What observation did Joseph Lister make?* (He noticed that more patients died after surgery in Glasgow than in Edinburgh.)
  - *What theory did he advance to explain this observation?* (That it was caused by a lack of cleanliness.)
  - *Which other scientist inspired him?* (Louis Pasteur.)
  - *Which technique of Pasteur's did he decide to try out?* (Using chemicals to kill micro-organisms.)
  - *Was Lister's theory correct?* (Yes.)
  - *How do you know?* (Because the number of deaths from infection reduced dramatically.)
- Show the children a range of hand washes, soaps and gels. Tell them you want them to devise an experiment to find out which substance is the most effective at killing bacteria on your hands.
- Explain how scientists use petri dishes filled with agar jelly to conduct experiments on bacterial growth. If you have bookmarked or downloaded any online resources, share them with the children, if copyright terms allow.

Group work
- Ask groups to plan their experiment. Discuss each group's plan with them before allowing them to start work. In particular, make sure children have a clear idea of what they will do to ensure their test is fair.
- Carry out the experiment in a separate session. (You or the children will need to start this session by making agar jelly.)
- Several days later, once the bacteria have had a chance to grow, ask children to collect results and draw conclusions.

Review
- Ask groups to share their results and conclusions with the rest of the class and relate back to Joseph Lister.

Week 4 lesson plans

In Lesson 1 children discuss the current use of medical imaging technologies. They read and answer questions about a text detailing the development of these technologies. They look at the work of X-ray artists and create their own X-ray-style artwork. In Lesson 2 children watch and discuss a slide show about the 1918–19 flu pandemic and its effects on Britain. They take part in a role-playing activity based on the pandemic, improvising, rehearsing and performing a short play sketch.

1: How long have we been able to see inside the body?

Lesson objective
● To develop a chronologically secure knowledge and understanding of British, local and world history, establishing clear narratives within and across the periods they study.

Expected outcomes
● All children can explain the purpose of medical imaging technologies.
● Most children can describe the historical development of medical imaging technologies.
● Some children can explain how one of these technologies works.

Resources
Photocopiable page 'A history of medical imaging technologies' from the CD-ROM; examples of X-ray art (Hugh Turvey and Nick Veasey are two X-ray artists worth exploring, but do not give the class free access to their images as not all of them are suitable for children); materials for creating X-ray-style art (paper-based or digital)

Introduction
● Introduce this lesson's focus question: *How long have we been able to see inside the body?* Ask children to make an educated guess of the answer to the question. (Since 1895.)
● Ask: *Why might a doctor want to look inside a patient's body? How do doctors look inside patients' bodies?* Briefly discuss the current use of imaging technologies such as X-rays, MRI (magnetic resonance imaging) and ultrasound. Explain that techniques that are used to produce pictures of the inside of the body are collectively known as medical imaging technologies.
● Share the expected outcomes with the class.

Paired work
● Organise the class into pairs, giving each pair a copy of photocopiable page 'A history of medical imaging technologies' from the CD-ROM.
● Ask children to read the text and talk through the discussion questions with their partner.

Whole-class work
● Explain that some people use X-rays to create art.
● Display and discuss the examples of X-ray art you have collected.

Independent work
● Ask children to create their own images in the style of X-ray art. They could use paper-based materials, such as pastel crayons, metallic pens or paper cut-outs on black paper, or they could use a digital drawing program.

Differentiation
● Support: during paired work, children may benefit from working with a more confident partner, or from working in a larger group with adult assistance.
● Challenge: ask children to research how one of the technologies mentioned on the photocopiable page works.

Review
● Ask children to show their X-ray-style artwork to the class and describe the techniques they used.
● If any children have done research into how one of the imaging technologies works, encourage them to share what they have found out.

Lesson objectives
● To develop a chronologically secure knowledge and understanding of British, local and world history, establishing clear narratives within and across the periods they study.
● To note connections, contrasts and trends over time.
● To develop the appropriate use of historical terms.
● To regularly address and sometimes devise historically valid questions about change, cause, similarity and difference, and significance.

Expected outcomes
● All children can explain what happened during the flu pandemic in 1918-19.
● Most children can describe some of the short-term effects of the pandemic.
● Some children can suggest what some of the longer-term effects of the pandemic might have been.

Resources
Interactive activity 'The flu pandemic of 1918–1919' on the CD-ROM; photocopiable page 187 'Flu pandemic role-playing cards'

2: The flu pandemic of 1918–19: how did it affect Britain?

Introduction
● Introduce this lesson's focus question: *The flu pandemic of 1918-19: how did it affect Britain?*
● Ask: *What is a pandemic?* Establish that a pandemic is like an epidemic but larger; an outbreak of disease that has spread across several continents, or even across the world.
● Ask: *Do you know anything about the flu pandemic of 1918–19?*
● Share the expected outcomes with the class.

Whole-class work
● Display the interactive activity 'The flu pandemic of 1918–1919' on the CD-ROM.
● Ask children questions about the slide show, such as:
  ● *What is the flu virus of 1918 also known as?* (Spanish flu.)
  ● *What were the likely first breeding grounds for the flu virus?* (The trenches of the first World .)
  ● *How many people did the flu kill?* (Between 50 and 100 million. Over 40% of the world's population were infected. A quarter of a million died in the UK.)
  ● *How does that compare with the number of people killed in the First World War?* (Over three times greater.)
  ● *Why do you think the authorities were reluctant to put reports of the flu on the front page of newspapers?* (To keep people calm.)
  ● *How were public services affected by the flu?* (For example, hospitals were overstretched, and rubbish and bodies began piling up.)
  ● *In what form did the flu find its way onto the school playground?* (In a skipping game.)

Group work
● Organise the class into six groups. Give each group a role-playing card from photocopiable page 187 'Flu pandemic role-playing cards'.
● Give groups time to discuss the characters and situation on the card and devise a short, unscripted play sketch to explore the scene and what happens next.
● Ask groups to perform their sketches in front of the class, providing each other with constructive feedback.
● Give groups time to revise and rehearse their sketches in light of the feedback received.

Differentiation
● Challenge: during discussion, children should suggest what the longer-term effects of the flu pandemic might have been, and explain their reasoning.

Review
● Finally, arrange for children to perform their sketches in front of an audience, such as a parallel class.

Week 5 lesson plans

In Lesson 1 children learn about Alexander Fleming and the discovery of penicillin. They hold a game-show-style debate in which each group investigates an important medical discovery. In Lesson 2 children learn about the history of polio. In groups they research one of the other diseases vaccinated against in the childhood immunisation programme in the UK, and prepare a slide show describing the history of the disease.

1: Why did the discovery of penicillin make Alexander Fleming famous?

Lesson objectives
● To develop a chronologically secure knowledge and understanding of British, local and world history, establishing clear narratives within and across the periods they study.
● To regularly address and sometimes devise historically valid questions about change, cause, similarity and difference, and significance.

Expected outcomes
● All children can retell the story of Alexander Fleming's discovery of penicillin.
● Most children can explain the significance of the discovery.
● Some children can put forward a compelling argument in support of their group's point of view in a class debate.

Resources
The story of Alexander Fleming (for hotseating in character); information bank on specific medical discoveries (for example, penicillin, vaccination, germ theory, X-rays, blood circulation, DNA and tissue culture)

Introduction
● Introduce this lesson's focus question: *Why did the discovery of penicillin make Alexander Fleming famous?*

Whole-class work
● Begin by giving the children information about Alexander Fleming, for example, by hot seating in role as Fleming.
● Establish that, in 1928, microbiologist Alexander Fleming observed that a mould that had accidentally grown in a petri dish containing a colony of bacteria had killed the bacteria around it. He found the active substance in the mould and called it 'penicillin'. Penicillin was the first antibiotic – a group of drugs that have saved countless lives.

Group work
● Tell the class they will be holding a game-show-style debate, in which each group will investigate an important medical discovery, explaining why it deserves the title of 'Greatest medical discovery of all time'.
● Divide the class into groups, giving each group an important medical discovery. Examples: (already studied): penicillin, vaccination, germ theory, and X-rays, (not already studied): blood circulation, DNA and tissue culture
● Give groups access to the information bank, asking them to research and make notes about the discovery and how it advanced medicine, and then make a list of arguments they could use to support the assertion that it is the greatest medical discovery of all time.

Whole-class work
● Hold a game-show-style debate, with each group explaining why their discovery deserves the title of 'Greatest medical discovery of all time'.
● As teacher, play the part of sneering, cynical game show host who is difficult to convince.

Review
● Ask the class to vote for the breakthrough that was supported by the most compelling arguments. You may wish to use the following additional questions: *Which way did you vote? Did you find the decision about which way to vote difficult to make? Why? Why not?*

Lesson objectives

● To develop a chronologically secure knowledge and understanding of British, local and world history, establishing clear narratives within and across the periods they study.
● To regularly address and sometimes devise historically valid questions about change, cause, similarity and difference, and significance.

Expected outcomes

● All children can explain the cause and symptoms of polio.
● Most children can describe the historical background of polio, and explain why babies are vaccinated against it.
● Some children can describe the history of one of the other diseases babies are vaccinated against.

Resources

Information bank on diphtheria, tetanus, whooping cough, meningitis, measles and mumps; presentation software; interactive activity 'Timeline maker' on the CD-ROM (optional)

2: Why are babies vaccinated against polio?

Introduction

● Introduce this lesson's focus question: *Why are babies vaccinated against polio?*
● Ask: *What do you know about polio?*
● Explain that polio (full name: poliomyelitis) is caused by a virus. It is transmitted through person-to-person contact. Its effects include muscle weakness and temporary or permanent paralysis in one or more parts of the body.
● Polio has been present throughout history but major outbreaks in Victorian times coincided with industrialisation. It remains incurable but has been eradicated from the UK, US and much of Europe.
● In the UK, the polio vaccine is part of the 5-in-1 vaccine that babies are given. Discuss the reasons why babies are still vaccinated against the disease.

Group work

● Organise the class into six groups, giving each access to slide show software and the information bank.
● Give each group the name of one of the other diseases that children in this country are routinely vaccinated against: diphtheria, tetanus, whooping cough, meningitis, measles and mumps.
● Ask each group to research the disease they have been given and create a slide show about the history of the disease. You may want to revise the features of the slide show software children will be using.
● You could some ask members of each group to create a timeline of the disease using the interactive activity 'Timeline maker' on the CD-ROM.

Differentiation
● Support: use mixed-ability groups.

Review

● Give each group an opportunity to share their slide show with the rest of the class, receive feedback, and answer questions.
● Ask: *How does the history of the disease you have researched compare with the history of polio? Why are children in this country routinely vaccinated against it?*

Week 6 lesson plans

In Lesson 1 children examine a variety of primary sources related to the setting up of the National Health Service. They draw their own conclusions from the evidence and discuss their ideas with others. In Lesson 2 children make notes about what else they would like to find out about the history of medicine that they have not already covered in the study. They turn these notes into historically relevant questions and research the answers, evaluating their sources for reliability. They present the results of their research in a whole-class outcome.

1: Why and when was the National Health Service set up?

Introduction
- Introduce this lesson's focus question: *Why and when was the National Health Service set up?*
- Give children a couple of minutes to discuss the focus question with a partner and then share their ideas with the class. Do not correct any misconceptions at this stage.

Whole-class work
- On the board write the phrase *primary sources*. Give children a couple of minutes to discuss with a partner what this phrase means. Establish that *primary sources* are sources of evidence about the past that were created at the time in question.
- Ask: *What sorts of primary sources do you think might still exist about the setting up of the National Health Service?*

Paired work
- Display or give children access to the different primary sources about the early NHS (see *Resources*).
- Organise the class into pairs, asking each pair to examine the primary sources and discuss and make notes on what each source tells them about the setting up of the NHS. Ask them to consider which pieces of information are facts and which are opinions.

Group work
- Ask pairs to get together with another group and explain their ideas to each other.

Review
- Ask pairs to share the conclusions they have drawn. Focus discussion around any sources that have been interpreted differently by different groups.
- Ask: *What were the reasons behind the setting up of the National Health Service? What effects did the setting up of the NHS have on medicine in the UK? Were any of these effects unexpected?*

Lesson objectives
- To develop a chronologically secure knowledge and understanding of British, local and world history, establishing clear narratives within and across the periods they study.
- To regularly address and sometimes devise historically valid questions about change, cause, similarity and difference, and significance.
- To understand how our knowledge of the past is constructed from a range of sources.

Expected outcomes
- All children can state when the National Health Service was set up.
- Most children can explain why the National Health Service was set up.
- Some children can describe some of the effects of the National Health Service being set up.

Resources
Various different kinds of primary source about the early NHS such as Government poster about the introduction of the NHS; a newspaper or magazine article about the new NHS; audio, video or transcript of an interview with a medical professional about the new NHS (interview to have been conducted at the time, not as reminiscence)

■SCHOLASTIC
www.scholastic.co.uk

Lesson objectives

● To develop a chronologically secure knowledge and understanding of British, local and world history, establishing clear narratives within and across the periods they study.
● To regularly address and sometimes devise historically valid questions about change, cause, similarity and difference, and significance.
● To construct informed responses that involve thoughtful selection and organisation of relevant historical information.

Expected outcomes

● All children can devise historically valid questions about the history of medicine.
● Most children can research answers to their questions, evaluating the sources they use for reliability.
● Some children can curate research results.

Resources

Information bank on the history of medicine (for example, books and/ or internet access); other resources will vary

2: What else would we like to find out about the history of medicine?

Introduction

● Introduce this lesson's focus question: *What else would we like to find out about the history of medicine?*
● Revise or explain the term *curate* (to organise or manage; used especially for organising exhibits in an art gallery or museum).

Paired work

● Ask: *What questions would you like to ask about the history of medicine?* Organise the class into pairs and give children time to discuss and write down their questions.

Whole-class work

● Ask pairs to share their questions, creating a class list. Help children to adapt their questions if necessary so that they are specific and cover one of the historical concepts of change, cause, similarity and difference, and significance. The questions in the list need to be distinct from one another, so encourage children to offer only questions that are not yet covered by questions already on the board.
● For those researching online, revise effective internet search techniques, e-safety considerations and how to evaluate the reliability of online sources of information.
● Discuss possible ways of presenting research results and agree on a common presentation approach all pairs will use in order to create a whole-class outcome.

Paired work or Independent work

● Ask individuals or pairs to choose a question from the list to research, and make or collect appropriate notes that will help them answer their question.
● When they have found out the answer to their question they should present it using the agreed method.

Differentiation
● Challenge: set children the task of collecting and curating the results of everyone's research.

Review

● Ask selected pairs or individuals to collect research results together to create the whole-class outcome.
● Review the collated outcome with the class, asking for constructive feedback, and reaching agreement on ways in which it could be improved. Set a group of children the task of implementing the agreed changes.
● Share the outcome with an audience of the children's choice.

Curriculum objective
● To note connections, contrasts and trends over time.

Resources
Interactive activity 'History of medicine quiz' on the CD-ROM; laptops or tablets (optional)

Developments in medicine

Revise
● Introduce the interactive activity 'History of medicine quiz' on the CD-ROM.
● Organise the class into pairs, giving each pair a laptop or tablet with access to the quiz, and give children time to answer the questions.
● Alternatively, attempt the quiz questions as a whole class, using the whiteboard.

Assess
● On the board write the question: *In what ways has medicine changed over the course of history?*
● Give the children a set length of time (such as 25 minutes) to answer the question as fully as they can.
● Tell the children it is important that they work independently for this task, because you need a record of what they know, not what someone else knows.
● If you have any children who really struggle with writing you might want to assess what they know through a one-to-one conversation conducted with a teaching assistant, or which you conduct yourself later.

Further practice
● Ask teams or pairs to write additional questions for the quiz, providing multiple-choice answers to choose from. The rest of the class could then have a go at answering the questions.

Curriculum objective
● To regularly address and sometimes devise historically valid questions about change, cause, similarity and difference, and significance.

Resources
Teaching assistant (optional); audio recording equipment (optional); internet access or reference books

Medical discoveries

Revise
● Ask: *What medical discoveries have you learned about?*
● Organise the class into pairs, asking each pair to make a list of all the medical discoveries they have learned about over the course of the entire study (chapters 3 and 4).
● Compile a list on the board of all the children's suggestions and give them clues about any discoveries you have studied but they have overlooked.

Assess
● On the board write: *Which of these discoveries was the most important?*
● Give the children a set length of time (such as 20 minutes) to write an answer to the question, answering as fully as they can, providing an explanation of their reasoning. Emphasise the importance of working independently.
● If you have any children who struggle with writing you might want to give them an alternative way of recording their ideas (for example, by explaining their answer to a teaching assistant who makes an audio recording of it).

Further practice
● Ask children, working in pairs or groups, to attempt to sort the medical discoveries listed on the board in order of importance. Allow access to the internet or reference books in order to find out more about the impact of each discovery.

■ SCHOLASTIC
www.scholastic.co.uk

Name: _____   Date: _____

Surgery then and now

Aspect of surgery	In the past	Today
Surgeons' training and qualifications		
Type of pain relief given		
Effectiveness of pain relief		
Instruments and techniques used		
Risk factors for infection		
Measures taken to prevent infection		
Chances of surviving the operation		

Name: _____   Date: _____

The history of anaesthetics

✂

1. Ether	**A.** Administered by drinking Often mixed with other substances Not very effective Danger of poisoning	Since antiquity
2. Anaesthetic inhaler	**B.** Vapour inhaled from a handkerchief or through a mask Presented less of a fire risk than ether, but was more toxic	Since antiquity
3. Acupuncture	**C.** Vapour inhaled from a handkerchief or through a mask Stronger and longer-lasting than nitrous oxide Highly flammable, so danger of fire	1799
4. Nitrous oxide	**D.** Needles inserted into the body Developed in ancient China Used as a local anaesthetic Effective for some but not all kinds of pain	1846
5. Chloroform	**E.** Invented by John Snow Controlled the dose of chloroform patients received, improving safety	1847
6. Alcohol	**F.** Inhaled Also known as laughing gas First effective general anaesthetic Not very strong or long-lasting	1848

Flu pandemic role-playing cards

Scenario: School's out!	Scenario: Too many patients
Where? Outside the gates of a school	*Where?* A city hospital
Who? Sisters Lillian Grimes and Maude Evans and their children	*Who?* People in charge of running the hospital (the chief administrator, and representatives from the staff)
Background: Lillian's husband has been killed in the war. Maude's is still fighting. Lillian and Maude both work full time at the munitions factory.	*Background:* The hospital is already short-staffed. It normally admits between 10 and 30 patients per day.
What happens? Lillian and Maude bring their children to school one morning. The headmaster tells them that, due to the influenza, the school will be closed until further notice.	*What happens?* There is a sudden influx of patients – over 200 in the last 48 hours. The people who run the hospital meet to discuss how to deal with the crisis.
Scenario: Cut off	**Scenario: On the Western Front**
Where? A remote village in Scotland	*Where?* France
Who? Residents of the village	*Who?* Leaders of British troops
Background: Due to the pandemic, trains are not running and the village store is closed. The nearest town is a five-hour drive away and no one in the village owns a car.	Background: You are ready to launch an assault on the enemy, but get reports that huge numbers of troops have been struck down by a mystery illness, and many are dying.
What happens? Residents are running out of food.	*What happens?* You call a meeting to discuss what to do.
Scenario: Law and order?	**Scenario: Piling up**
Where? London's police headquarters	*Where?* Council offices
Who? The chief of police and leading police officers	*Who?* Town councillors
Background: Due to the pandemic, nearly 1500 police officers have called in sick.	*Background:* As a result of the pandemic, there are not enough people to dig graves and bury bodies fast enough, so corpses are piling up.
What happens? The chief of police meet with leading police officers to discuss how to deal with the crisis.	*What happens?* The leader of the town council calls a council meeting to discuss how to deal with the crisis.

The Battle of Britain

In this chapter the children investigate a significant turning point in British history: the Battle of Britain. They begin the study by gaining an overview of the battle, finding out where it fits on a timeline, and exploring the main events leading up to the battle and of the battle itself. They then look at the people and things that played a part in the Battle of Britain. Finally, they evaluate its significance.

Chapter at a glance

Curriculum objectives

• A study of an aspect or theme in British history that extends pupils' chronological knowledge beyond 1066: a significant turning point in British history: The Battle of Britain.

Week	Lesson	Summary of activities	Expected outcomes
1	1	• Children listen to Winston Churchill's speech of June 1940. • They highlight points from an overview of the Battle of Britain.	• Can give a general description of the Battle of Britain, and show where it fits on a timeline.
	2	• Children examine and evaluate the reliability of sources of evidence about the Battle of Britain.	• Can identify some of the main sources of evidence we have for the Battle of Britain, explaining their relevance.
2	1	• Children order events leading up to the Battle of Britain, place them on a timeline, and answer quiz questions about them.	• Can describe, order, and discuss the significance of the events leading up to the Battle of Britain.
	2	• Children research and complete fact sheets about the commanders of the Battle of Britain. • They write a biography of one of them.	• Can name and describe the roles of the Allied and German commanders of the Battle of Britain.
3	1	• Children write an account of an air battle from the point of view of a fighter pilot.	• Can explain the significance of Churchill's famous quote, explaining why 'so many' owe 'so much' to 'so few'.
	2	• Children read about and summarise the events of the Battle of Britain, and then create a timeline.	• Can describe and order the main events in the Battle of Britain.
4	1	• Children create Top Trumps® style cards for the aircraft in the Battle of Britain and then play games with them. • They answer quiz questions about the aircraft.	• Can identify and compare the principle aircraft in the Battle of Britain.
	2	• Children examine the strategy behind the Blitz and evaluate its success.	• Can explain the objectives of the Blitz, and evaluate its success.
5	1	• Children research roles played by people on the ground during the Battle of Britain. • They dramatise these roles.	• Can identify some of the roles played by people on the ground in the Battle of Britain.
	2	• Children read about and discuss air-raid shelters. • They build a model of a shelter.	• Can describe what life was like in air-raid shelters.
6	1	• Children view a video clip about radar. • They play a game simulating air raids with and without radar.	• Can explain the part played by radar in the Battle of Britain.
	2	• Children investigate German occupation of the Channel Islands. • They write a fictional eyewitness account.	• Can evaluate the significance of the Battle of Britain.
Assess and review		• To review the half-term's work.	

Expected prior learning
● Children are not expected to have any prior knowledge of the Battle of Britain or the Second World War.
● They need to be familiar with different types of evidence used by historians to develop theories about the past.

Overview of progression
● In this chapter children use timelines to help them establish a clear chronological narrative of the Battle of Britain. They respond to various accounts of the battle, and examine a range of sources. They address and devise historically valid questions – in particular, about cause and significance.
● Children demonstrate their knowledge of the past in different ways, including constructing timelines, taking part in discussions, writing and answering quiz questions, playing games, ordering events, creating dramatisations, making films, designing models, and writing summaries, fact sheets, biographies, accounts and reports.

Creative context
● The content of this chapter has strong links with the English curriculum. Children take part in discussions, apply research skills, write and perform a dramatisation, read texts for information, learn RAF terms and slang from the war years, and write scripts, summaries, quizzes, biographies, reports, and imaginary eyewitness accounts.
● Children apply skills developed in design and technology to design and make Top Trumps® style playing cards, create props and costumes for a dramatisation, and design and build a model of an air-raid shelter.
● Children undertake historical research online, which addresses several requirements of the computing curriculum, including using the internet safely and responsibly, using search engines effectively and evaluating online content.
● There are links to PE, with children playing an invasion and defence game simulating an air raid.

Background knowledge
● The Battle of Britain was the battle for air superiority over the skies of Britain between the RAF and the German air force, the Luftwaffe, during the Second World War. It took place from 10 July to 31 October 1940.
● Sir Winston Churchill was Prime Minister at the time. He famously said, in a speech he made in August 1940, that 'never in the field of human conflict was so much owed by so many to so few'. By the 'few' he meant the airmen of the Royal Air Force – bomber crews as well as fighter pilots. The RAF Roll of Honour for the Battle of Britain recognises 2927 airmen, of whom 574 came from countries other than the United Kingdom, including Poland, New Zealand, Canada and Czechoslovakia.
● The Blitz was a period of sustained bombing of Britain by Germany, which started on 7 September 1940. Although the Blitz started during the Battle of Britain it carried on for months afterwards, until 21 May 1941. During the Blitz there were major air raids on 16 British cities. London suffered the greatest number of attacks, with 71 in total, 57 of which were on consecutive nights from 7 September 1940.

Week I lesson plans

In Lesson I children listen to and discuss Winston Churchill's 'finest hour' speech from June 1940. They read and discuss a text giving a brief overview of the Battle of Britain. They write a summary of the battle and add it to a timeline. In Lesson 2 children summarise different categories of historical sources. They evaluate the reliability of various source of evidence about the Battle of Britain, and discuss what each source tells us.

I: What was the Battle of Britain and when did it happen?

Lesson objective
● To develop a chronologically secure knowledge and understanding of British, local and world history, establishing clear narratives within and across the periods they study.

Expected outcomes
● All children can give a general description of the Battle of Britain.
● Most children can place the Battle of Britain and Second World War on a timeline.
● Some children can identify other important events of the war and add them to the timeline.

Resources
A3 paper; highlighter pens; Winston Churchill's speech from 18 June 1940 (source online); photocopiable page 'The Battle of Britain' from the CD-ROM; highlighter pens; interactive activity 'Timeline maker' on the CD-ROM or materials for making a paper-based timeline

Introduction
● Introduce this lesson's focus question: *What was the Battle of Britain and when did it happen?*
● Organise the class into pairs, giving each pair a sheet of A3 paper.
● Ask pairs to sketch a timeline that includes the Second World War and the Battle of Britain, writing a sentence or two explaining what the Battle of Britain was.
● Ask children to share their ideas with the class.
● Briefly confirm what the Battle of Britain was and when it took place (see *Background knowledge* on page 189).

Whole-class work
● Listen to Winston Churchill's speech from 18 June 1940 in which he coined the phrase 'the Battle of Britain'.
● Draw out the following points: *What event happened just before this speech?* (Germany had successfully invaded France.) *What message was Churchill giving to the British people?* (That the outcome of the war and the future of the whole of the western world depended on them.) *Churchill made a pointed reference to the United States. What did he say, and why?* (He said that if Germany won the war the whole world, 'including the United States' would 'sink into the abyss of a new dark age'. Churchill wanted to persuade the USA to get involved in the war.) *Churchill ended the speech on a positive and uplifting note. How?* (He imagined a future in which people remembered the Battle of Britain as the British people's 'finest hour'.)

Paired work
● Organise the class into pairs, giving each pair photocopiable page 'The Battle of Britain' from the CD-ROM.
● Give pairs time to read the text, and work together to highlight the most important words/phrases/facts.

Independent work
● Ask each child to create a timeline (for example, of the 20th century), marking on the Battle of Britain and Second World War. (They may need to research dates.) Children could use the interactive activity 'Timeline maker' on the CD-ROM, or create a timeline on paper.

Differentiation
● Support: children could input only the most important dates.
● Challenge: children can research other important events of Second World War and add them to the timeline.

Review
● Ask each child to write a summary of the Battle of Britain to add to their timeline, based on the sections of the text they highlighted during paired work.

Lesson objectives
● To develop a chronologically secure knowledge and understanding of British, local and world history, establishing clear narratives within and across the periods they study.
● To understand how our knowledge of the past is constructed from a range of sources.

Expected outcomes
● All children can identify and classify some of the main sources of evidence we have for the Battle of Britain.
● Most children can explain what each source tells us about the battle.
● Some children can evaluate the reliability of those sources.

Resources
Primary and secondary sources from the Battle of Britain (see *Lesson plan* for examples)

2: How do we know about the Battle of Britain?

Introduction
● Introduce this lesson's focus question: *How do we know about the Battle of Britain?*
● On the board write *How do we know about the past?* Ask the children, working with a partner or in small groups, to discuss the question, noting down as many answers as they can think of.

Whole-class work
● Discuss the children's notes, revising the term 'historical source' and asking the children to explain the difference between a primary and secondary source.
● List on the board the major categories of historical sources – documents, video recordings, audio recordings, buildings, images (such as photographs), artefacts (made objects), and oral testimony (eyewitness accounts which may be recorded in written or audio form).
● Display an equal number of primary and secondary sources. If possible, try to include an example of the following types of source: documents, video recordings, audio recordings, images artefacts and oral testimony (eyewitness accounts which may be recorded in written or audio form). For example:
Primary sources:
  ● a video clip of newsreel footage
  ● an artefact relating to the Battle of Britain, such as a medal won by a Battle of Britain pilot
  ● a photograph from the time (such as showing pilots preparing to fly, or damage caused by the battle).
Secondary sources:
  ● a modern newspaper article (such as from the 50th anniversary of the battle)
  ● an excerpt from a modern children's history book
  ● an audio clip or written transcript of an oral testimony (such as a recent(ish) interview with someone who fought in the Battle of Britain).

Paired work
● Working in pairs, ask children to examine the sources. They should write notes for each source, assigning it to the appropriate category from the board, identifying it as a primary or secondary source, suggesting what it tells us about the Battle of Britain, and evaluating its reliability as a source of evidence. Encourage pairs to discuss all aspects of the exercise.
● Ask pairs who finish to discuss their ideas with other pairs, amending or adding to their original notes afterwards, if they wish.

Differentiation
● Support: use mixed-ability pairs and groups throughout the lesson.

Review
● At the end of the lesson discuss the children's paired work. Ask: *Which category would you think is most reliable? Why? Which source do you think is most unreliable? Why?*

Week 2 lesson plans

In Lesson 1 children order events leading up to the Battle of Britain and place them on a timeline. They answer quiz questions about the events leading up to the Battle of Britain. In Lesson 2 children research the commanders on both sides of the Battle of Britain, and discover the part each played in the battle. They complete a fact sheet about the commanders, and then choose one of the commanders to research further and write a biography about.

Lesson objectives
● To develop a chronologically secure knowledge and understanding of British, local and world history, establishing clear narratives within and across the periods they study.
● To regularly address and sometimes devise historically valid questions about change, cause, similarity and difference, and significance.

Expected outcomes
● All children can describe some of the key events leading up to the Battle of Britain.
● Most children can create a timeline of the events leading up to the Battle of Britain.
● Some children can suggest which events contributed most significantly to the battle and explain their thinking.

Resources
Photocopiable page 203 'Events leading up to the Battle of Britain'; scissors; photocopiable page 'Outline of key events' from the CD-ROM; interactive activity 'Timeline maker' on the CD-ROM (optional)

1: The background to the battle: what events led up to the Battle of Britain?

Introduction
● Introduce this lesson's focus question: *The background to the battle: what events led up to the Battle of Britain?*

Paired work or Group work
● Organise the class into pairs or small groups. Give each pair or group a copy of photocopiable page 203 'Events leading up to the Battle of Britain', photocopiable page 'Outline of key events' on the CD-ROM, and one or more pairs of scissors.
● Ask children to read the photocopiable page 'Outline of key events' from the CD-ROM carefully.
● The children then need to cut out the event cards from the photocopiable page 203 'Events leading up to the Battle of Britain' and arrange them in chronological order, using the information on photocopiable page 'Outline of key events' to help them.
● The correct order of the cards is: D, G, B, E, A, I, H, C, and F.
● Once children have put the events in order, ask them to write a date on each card. For each event they should aim to write both the month and the year, and wherever relevant and possible, the day(s) of the month as well.
● Finally, ask children to create a timeline of the events leading up to the Battle of Britain. They could do this by drawing a timeline on paper and sticking the cards onto it, or by using the interactive activity 'Timeline maker' from the CD-ROM.

Differentiation
● Challenge: ask children to tell you which events they think contributed most significantly to the Battle of Britain, and why.

Review
● Ask children to hide their timelines.
● Give children a quiz about the events leading up to the Battle of Britain.
● You may wish to use the following additional questions: *Could the Battle of Britain have been averted? If so, when and how?*

Lesson objective
● To develop a chronologically secure knowledge and understanding of British, local and world history, establishing clear narratives within and across the periods they study.

Expected outcomes
● All children can name the Allied and German commanders of the Battle of Britain.
● Most children can describe the roles of each commander.
● Some children can write an interesting and informative biography of one of the commanders.

Resources
Photocopiable page 204 'Battle of Britain commanders'; example of a short (ione-page) biography of a historical figure (online or paper based); information bank and/or internet access about the Second World War

2: The commanders of the Battle of Britain: who was who?

Introduction
● Introduce this lesson's focus question: *The commanders of the Battle of Britain: who was who?*
● Ask: *What were the names of the commanders of the Battle of Britain?* Give children a couple of minutes to discuss this question with a partner, before taking ideas from the whole class. Do not correct any misconceptions at this stage.

Paired work
● Organise the class into pairs, giving each pair two copies of photocopiable page 204 'Battle of Britain commanders', and numerous history books about the Second World War or internet access.
● Write on the board the names of the commanders you want the children to find out about. They should find out about Winston Churchill, Hugh Dowding, Adolf Hitler and Hermann Goering.
● Ask children to research the commanders on both sides of photocopiable page 204 'Battle of Britain' using to oragnise their notes.

Independent work
● Ask children to choose one of the commanders to find out more about, in preparation for writing a short biography about him.
● Give children time to do their research and write their biographies.
● Share the biographies with a wider audience; for example, through a class blog or school learning platform.

Differentiation
● Support: ask pairs to concentrate on finding out about two or three commanders only.
● Challenge: when children have completed the paired work, provide them with additional sheets and ask them to find out about other notable commanders such as Quintin Brand, Keith Park and Hugo Sperrle.

Review
● Ask children to share what they have found out about who the commanders were, what each commander's role was in the battle, and any other information they have found out.
● Revise the features of a short biography, referring to the example you have chosen.

Week 3 lesson plans

In Lesson I children consider a fighter pilot's account of the Battle of Britain. They learn some RAF terms and slang from Second World War. They write an account of an air battle from the point of view of a fighter pilot, incorporating some of the words they have learned. In Lesson 2 children work in small groups to look in detail at one particular event or series of events from the Battle of Britain. Each group writes and presents a summary of their research to the rest of the class. The class works together to create a timeline of the Battle of Britain.

Lesson objectives
● To develop a chronologically secure knowledge and understanding of British, local and world history, establishing clear narratives within and across the periods they study.
● To regularly address and sometimes devise historically valid questions about change, cause, similarity and difference, and significance.

Expected outcomes
● All children can explain who 'the few' were.
● Most children can explain why so many owed 'the few' so much.
● Some children can write an account of an air battle from the point of view of a fighter pilot, incorporating RAF terms and slang.

Resources
Battle of Britain 'The Few' poster (source online); photocopiable page 'Hurricane versus Messerschmitt' from the CD-ROM; photocopiable page 'RAF terms and slang' from the CD-ROM

I: Who were 'the few' and why do so many owe them so much?

Introduction
● Introduce this lesson's focus question: *Who were 'the few' and why do so many owe them so much?*
● Display the Battle of Britain 'The Few' poster.
● Ask: *Who does the quote on the poster come from? Who did Churchill mean by 'The Few'? Why did so many people owe them so much?* Give children time to discuss each question with a partner before sharing their ideas with the class.

Whole-class work
● Provide children with photocopiable page 'Hurricane versus Messerschmitt' from the CD-ROM which gives a first-person account of the Battle of Britain. They can also read and discuss photocopiable page 'RAF terms and slang' from the CD-ROM.

Independent work
● Ask children to write an account of an air battle from the point of view of a fighter pilot, incorporating some of the RAF terms and slang on the photocopiable page. It could be written in the form of either a diary or a letter to a loved one.

Differentiation
● Support: children can highlight just six words that they would like to include in their letter or diary.
● Challenge: children can be more descriptive. Ask them to include about what they see and how they feel.

Review
● Ask: *What is the famous quote from Winston Churchill's speech? What did 'the few' airmen do? What did the many owe to the few? Who were the many?*

Lesson objectives
● To develop a chronologically secure knowledge and understanding of British, local and world history, establishing clear narratives within and across the periods they study.

Expected outcomes
● All children can describe some of the main events of the Battle of Britain.
● Most children can order the main events in the Battle of Britain and place them on a timeline.
● Some children can write a summary of the entire Battle of Britain.

Resources
One of the timelines created in Week 2 Lesson 1 or materials for creating a new timeline (such as. interactive activity 'Timeline maker' on the CD-ROM or paper and pens); group computer and internet access

2: Battle of Britain timeline: what happened when?

Introduction
● Introduce this lesson's focus question: *Battle of Britain timeline: what happened when?*
● Ask children, working individually, to write answers to the following questions:
  ● *When did the Battle of Britain begin?*
  ● *How long did the Battle of Britain last?*
  ● *What were some of the main events in the Battle of Britain?*

Paired or group work
● Divide the class into 12 groups, giving each group access to the internet.
● Assign each group a different key event from the following list:
  ● Germany advances through Europe
  ● Churchill becomes Prime Minister
  ● Britain retreats from France
  ● Churchill decides to fight on
  ● Hitler plans the invasion of Britain
  ● Germany bombs British towns and cities
  ● Germany bombs British coastal airfields
  ● Germany attacks RAF fighter command
  ● Britain bombs Berlin
  ● Germany bombs London
  ● Battle of Britain day
  ● Hitler postpones the invasion of Britain.
● Ask each group to work together to write a summary of their event to present to the rest of the class at the end of the lesson.
● Tell the children that it is important that they find out the date that the event occurred. Distribute a small piece of paper to each group and ask them to write the name of their event along with the date.

Whole-class work
● Ask a child from each group to stand up and form a line in front the class. Then work together to organise the children in the order of events.
● In chronological order, ask each group to present their summary to the rest of the class.
● Ask the class to work together to create a timeline of the Battle of Britain. Children could extend and add to one of the timelines created in Week 2 Lesson 1 (showing the events leading up to the battle). Alternatively, they could create a new timeline, either on paper or using the interactive activity 'Timeline maker' on the CD-ROM.

Differentiation
● Challenge: ask children to write a summary of the entire battle.

Review
● Revisit the questions from the introduction to this lesson, asking children to write down their answers. Compare their answers now with the answers they gave earlier. Ask: *What have you learned?*

Week 4 lesson plans

In Lesson 1 children create Top Trumps® style cards for the principle aircraft in the Battle of Britain and use them to play games. They then answer quiz questions about the aircraft in the Battle of Britain. In Lesson 2 children watch and discuss a documentary film from October 1940 about the London Blitz. They suggest what the Luftwaffe's objectives behind the Blitz might have been, and then put these objectives in order of importance. They discuss which, if any, of its objectives the Blitz achieved, and evaluate its overall success.

1: Which aircraft fought in the Battle of Britain?

Lesson objectives
● To develop a chronologically secure knowledge and understanding of British, local and world history, establishing clear narratives within and across the periods they study.
● To regularly address and sometimes devise historically valid questions about change, cause, similarity and difference, and significance.

Expected outcomes
● All children can name some of the principle aircraft in the Battle of Britain.
● Most children can compare and describe the aircraft.
● Some children can identify the aircraft from their pictures.

Resources
Photocopiable page 205 'Aircraft card game'; information bank on Battle of Britain aircraft as listed on the photocopiable page (for example www.raf.mod.uk); scissors

Introduction
● Introduce this lesson's focus question: *Which aircraft fought in the Battle of Britain?*
● Ask children if they can name any of the aircraft that fought in the Battle of Britain. Make a note on the board of children's suggestions.

Whole-class work
● Tell children they will be making and playing a card game that will help them to learn about the aircraft of the Battle of Britain.
● Explain how to play a Top Trumps® style game. You could show an example pack and ask for volunteers to help you play a demonstration round.
● Distribute multiple copies of photocopiable page 205 'Aircraft card game' and talk through the completed card.

Group work
● Organise the class into groups of three or four. Give each group access to the information bank.
● Ask each group to make a set of 12 Top Trumps® cards, filling in the details using the information bank.
● Ask them to cut out the cards and spend ten minutes playing the game.

> **Differentiation**
> ● Support: use mixed ability groups.
> ● Challenge: children can research and make a set of 'aircraft spotting cards' as used during Second World War for spotting friendly and enemy plane silhouettes.

Review
● Give the class a quiz about the aircraft of the Battle of Britain. Providing multiple-choice answers will make the quiz accessible for most children.
● Revisit the lesson's focus question, asking children to complete (and if necessary correct) the list of aircraft written on the board from the beginning of the lesson.

Lesson objectives
● To develop a chronologically secure knowledge and understanding of British, local and world history, establishing clear narratives within and across the periods they study.
● To regularly address and sometimes devise historically valid questions about change, cause, similarity and difference, and significance.

Expected outcomes
● All children can explain what the Blitz was.
● Most children can explain the objectives of the Blitz.
● Some children can evaluate whether or not the Blitz was successful.

Resources
Video clip about the London Blitz: 'London can take it' (source online)

2: What was the strategy behind the Blitz?

Introduction
● Ask: *What was the Blitz?* Establish that the Blitz was the bombing of Britain by Germany during the Second World War. It took place between September 1940 and May 1941. There were major aerial raids on 16 British cities. London suffered by far the greatest number of attacks (71 altogether) including 57 consecutive nights starting on 7 September 1940.
● Introduce this lesson's focus question: *What was the strategy behind the Blitz?* Discuss the meaning of the word *strategy*.

Whole-class work
● Watch a documentary film from October 1940 about the London Blitz: 'London Can Take It' (See *Resources*).
● Ask questions about the purpose of the film, such as: *Which audience do you think the film was made for?* (The people and government of the United States.) *Why do you think the film was made?* (To persuade the US to join Britain in the war against Germany.)
● Ask questions about the content of the film, such as:
  ● *What problems did Londoners have to deal with during the Blitz?* (Working very long hours – doing their normal jobs by day and defending the city at night; being made homeless; being killed, injured or bereaved; having their sleep disturbed by air raids.)
  ● *How might they have felt?* (Exhausted, terrified, traumatised.)
  ● *The documentary maker claims that no one showed signs of fear during the raids. How likely is this to be true?* (Highly unlikely.)
  ● *If it is not true, why do you think the documentary maker claims it?* (To emphasise the fact that the British people's morale was not broken, and they were not about to surrender.)

Group work
● Organise the class into groups. Write another version of the focus question on the board: *What were the objectives of the Blitz?* Ask each group to list as many possible objectives as they can think of.
● Ask each group to discuss the relative importance of each objective they have listed and order them from most to least important.

Review
● Ask groups to share their ideas with the class. Compile a class list of Blitz objectives.
● Ask groups to assess the success of the Blitz in terms of how many of its objectives it achieved. Ask: *Was the Blitz successful?*
● You may wish to use the following additional questions: *Do you think London could have continued to 'take it' if the Blitz had carried on much longer? What do you think German documentaries about the Blitz might have focused on?*

Week 5 lesson plans

In Lesson 1 children research some of the roles played by people on the ground during the Battle of Britain. They write scripts and prepare props and costumes for a dramatised presentation, which they record in the form of a video. This lesson will take several sessions to complete. In Lesson 2 children read and discuss a text about air-raid shelters and explore what life in the shelters was like. They build a model of an Anderson shelter.

Lesson objective
● To develop a chronologically secure knowledge and understanding of British, local and world history, establishing clear narratives within and across the periods they study.

Expected outcomes
● All children can identify some of the roles played by people on the ground in the Battle of Britain.
● Most children can explain in detail one of the roles played by people on the ground.
● Some children can create an effective dramatised presentation about the role they have researched.

Resources
Information bank on the role of ground support during the Battle of Britain (see lesson notes for list of individual services) and/or internet access; various materials for making props and costumes; video recording equipment

1: What part did people on the ground play in the Battle of Britain?

Introduction
● Introduce this lesson's focus question: *What part did people on the ground play in the Battle of Britain?*
● Ask children if they can remember any of the jobs Londoners did at night during the Blitz, from the documentary they watched during the previous lesson.
● Briefly discuss various roles in the battle on the ground, both military and civilian, such as radar operator, anti-aircraft gunner, barrage balloon controller, aircraft spotter, air-raid warden, ambulance driver and firefighter.

Group work
● Divide the class into groups and allow access to the information bank you have gathered, or internet access.
● Assign each group a separate service to research. These could include the RAF's Anti-Aircraft Command, the ATS (Auxiliary Territorial Service), the Royal Observer Corps, the ARP (Air Raid Precaution Service), the AFS (Auxiliary Fire Service), the ATA (Air Transport Auxiliary), the WAAF (Women's Auxiliary Air Force), and Local Defence Volunteers (LDV; later named the Home Guard).
● Let children find out about the service, making notes about how its members contributed to the Battle of Britain.

Whole-class work
● Give children the task of using the notes they have collected in order to put together a short dramatised presentation, explaining the role they have researched. Discuss what they may need to create for the presentation (such as scripts, props and costumes). This is likely to form the end of the first session.

Group work
● In subsequent sessions, give groups time to plan and rehearse their presentations.
● Arrange for the presentations to be filmed. The filming could be approached as a whole-class activity, or each group's presentation could be recorded separately and then edited together.
● Arrange for the completed video presentation to be shared with a wider audience.

Differentiation
● Support: children should focus on one particular detail.
● Challenge: children can conduct additional research.

Review
● Show the completed video presentation to the class, asking children to review and give feedback on each group's section. Ask: *Which sections of the presentation were most effective? Why?*

2: What was life in the shelters like?

Lesson objective
● To develop a chronologically secure knowledge and understanding of British, local and world history, establishing clear narratives within and across the periods they study.

Expected outcomes
● All children can name and describe the various types of air-raid shelters and explain how and why they were used.
● Most children can describe what life was like in air-raid shelters.
● Some children can make an accurate model of an air-raid shelter.

Resources
Photocopiable page 'Air-raid shelters' from the CD-ROM; a first-person account of life in an air-raid shelter (optional); images of the interior and exterior of Anderson shelters (source online); materials and equipment for making a model Anderson shelter

Introduction
● Introduce this lesson's focus question: *What was life in the shelters like?*
● Ask: *If you had been a child living in London during the Blitz, how much time might you have spent in an air-raid shelter?* (On nights when there were air raids, you might have spent most of the hours of darkness in an air-raid shelter. In London, there was an air raid almost every night.) *What do you think life would have been like in the shelters?* (Conditions were cramped; private shelters were typically very small and public shelters were often crowded.)

Paired work
● Organise the class into pairs, giving each pair a copy of the photocopiable page 'Air-raid shelters' from the CD-ROM. Ask them to read the text and talk through the discussion questions with their partner.

Whole-class work
● Ask for children's feedback on the discussion questions.
● Now give children access to a first-person account of life in an air-raid shelter (ideally an Anderson shelter). Alternatively, put yourself in the hot-seat as someone who used an Anderson shelter as a child, and allow children to question you about what it was like.

Group work
● Tell groups that they will be constructing a model of an Anderson shelter.
● Show the children images which shows the exterior and interior of Anderson shelters.
● Ask each group to design and build a model of an Anderson shelter, carefully considering the contents of the shelter as well as the building itself.

Differentiation
● Support: use mixed ability groupings.
● Challenge: children can research a different type of shelter and make a model of it instead of the Anderson shelter.

Review
● Ask: *What advantages did each type of shelter have? What were its disadvantages? Given the choice, which shelter would you have used, and why?*

Week 6 lesson plans

In Lesson 1 children view a video clip explaining how radar works. They play a game simulating an air raid, first without radar and then with radar, compare the outcomes of the two games and discuss how radar made a difference. In Lesson 2 children discuss what might have happened next if the RAF had lost the Battle of Britain. They investigate the German occupation of the Channel Islands and use this information to suggest what might have happened if the Germans had invaded the mainland of Britain. They write an eyewitness account of the invasion and occupation.

1: What part did radar play in the Battle of Britain?

Introduction

● Introduce this lesson's focus question: *What part did radar play in the Battle of Britain?*
● Ask: *What is radar and how does it work?* Give children, working in pairs, a couple of minutes to discuss this question, and then ask them to share their ideas with the class.

Whole-class work

● Show them a clip explaining how radar works (see *Resources*).
● Tell children that radar technology was kept secret during the war, and ask: *Why do you think this war.*

Group work

● Display and discuss the photocopiable page 'Air-raid game' on the CD-ROM.
● Go outside to play the air-raid game, taking with you the equipment listed on the photocopiable page.
● Remember to ask each group to play the game twice – the first time without using radar and the second time using radar.

Differentiation

● Challenge: ask children to write a report on radar and the part it played in the Battle of Britain. They will need to research information for their report (in books and/or online).

Review

● Ask children to compare the two rounds of the game they played, and explain what difference radar made to the outcome.
● Ask: *What difference do you think radar made to the Battle of Britain?*

Lesson objectives

● To develop a chronologically secure knowledge and understanding of British, local and world history, establishing clear narratives within and across the periods they study.
● To develop the appropriate use of historical terms.
● To construct informed responses that involve thoughtful selection and organisation of relevant historical information.

Expected outcomes

● All children can explain what radar is and how it works.
● Most children can explain the part played by radar in the Battle of Britain.
● Some children can write a detailed report about radar and the part it played in the Battle of Britain.

Resources

Video clip about how radar works (for example, from howstuffworks); photocopiable page 'Air-raid game' from the CD-ROM; buckets; soft balls; beanbags; blindfolds; whistle; teaching assistant (optional); information on radar and the Battle of Britain (optional)

Lesson objectives
● To develop a chronologically secure knowledge and understanding of British, local and world history, establishing clear narratives within and across the periods they study.
● To develop the appropriate use of historical terms.
● To construct informed responses that involve thoughtful selection and organisation of relevant historical information.

Expected outcomes
● All children can suggest what might have happened if the RAF had lost the Battle of Britain.
● Most children can suggest what some of the longer-term consequences might have been.
● Some children can evaluate the significance of the Battle of Britain within the wider context of British history as a whole.

Resources
Photocopiable page 'Channel Island character cards' from the CD-ROM

2: Why is the Battle of Britain considered a turning point in British History?

Introduction
● Introduce this lesson's focus question: *Why is the battle of Britain considered a turning point in British history?*
● Ask: *What is meant by a turning point in history?*

Group work
● Organise the class into groups.
● Ask: *What might have happened next if the RAF had lost the Battle of Britain?*
● Give groups a few minutes to discuss this question, and then share their ideas with the rest of the class.

Whole-class work
● Explain that the Channel Islands of Jersey and Guernsey, which are part of the British Isles, were occupied by Germany from 30 June 1940 until the end of the war in Europe on 9 May 1945.
● Read and discuss photocopiable page 'Channel Island character cards' from the CD-ROM.

Independent work
● Ask children to imagine that is the autumn of 1940. The RAF has lost the Battle of Britain, and the Germans have invaded the mainland.
● Can they suggest people who might have an interesting story to tell about the invasion and occupation?
● Ask children to choose one of these characters, and write an eyewitness account of the invasion and occupation from their point of view.

Differentiation
● Support: provide an information bank to support children's account writing.
● Challenge: ask children to consider the significance of the Battle of Britain to British history as a whole.

Review
● Ask selected children to share their written accounts with the class. Review the focus question: *Why is the Battle of Britain considered a turning point in British history?* Draw out the fact that had the Luftwaffe won the Battle of Britain, Hitler would probably have gone ahead with his plans to invade Britain. The British would not have surrendered without a fight, and many thousands of people would probably have been killed – civilians as well as military personnel. If the invasion had been successful, the whole of Britain could have ended up under Nazi rule.

Curriculum objective
● To develop a chronologically secure knowledge and understanding of British, local and world history, establishing clear narratives within and across the periods they study.

Resources
Interactive activity 'Battle of Britain quiz' on the CD-ROM; computers/laptops (optional)

Battle of Britain quiz

Revise
● Introduce the interactive activity 'Battle of Britain quiz' from the CD-ROM.
● Organise the class into pairs, giving each pair access to the quiz, and give children time to answer the questions.
● Alternatively, attempt the quiz questions as a whole class, using the whiteboard.

Assess
● On the board write the title 'The Battle of Britain'. Underneath draw a table with six columns. Label the columns: *What?*, *When?*, *Where?*, *Why?*, *Who?* and *Significance.*
● Give the children a set length of time (for example, 20 minutes) to copy the table and fill it in, including as much detail as they can.
● Tell the children it is important that they work independently for this task, because you need a record of what they know, not what someone else knows.
● If you have any children who really struggle with writing you might want to assess what they know through a one-to-one conversation conducted with a teaching assistant, or which you conduct yourself later.

Further practice
● Ask children to create an introduction to the Battle of Britain, to be used with the next class that studies the topic.

Curriculum objectives
● To regularly address and sometimes devise historically valid questions about change, cause, similarity and difference, and significance.

Resources
Audio recording equipment (optional)

Who's who?

Revise
● Organise the class into pairs or small groups.
● Ask: *Who played a part in the Battle of Britain?*
● Give pairs or groups a few minutes to list as many answers to the question as they can, and then discuss suggestions as a whole class.

Assess
● Write the following questions on the board:
  ● What part did each of these play in the Battle of Britain?
  a) Winston Churchill b) airmen of the RAF c) volunteers on the ground.
  ● Which person or group of people do you think made the greatest contribution? Explain your reasoning.
● Give the children a set length of time (for example, 25 minutes) to write answers to the questions, answering as fully as they can. Emphasise the importance of working independently.
● If you have any children who struggle with writing you might want to give them an alternative way of recording what they know (such as explaining their answer to a teaching assistant who makes an audio recording of it).

Further practice
● Ask children to write an answer to the question: *Could the battle of Britain have been avoided? If not, why not? If so, how?*

Name: _____   Date: _____

Events leading up to the Battle of Britain

A Germany invades Denmark and Norway.	**B** Russia signs a pact with Germany.	**C** France signs an armistice with Germany.
D Germany invades Poland.	**E** Russia invades Finland.	**F** Hitler prepares to invade Britain.
G Britain and France declare war on Germany.	**H** British and French troops are rescued from Dunkirk.	**I** Germany invades France, Belgium and Holland.

Battle of Britain Commanders

Name: _____

Nationality: _____

Post held: _____

_____

Role in the Battle of Britain: _____

_____

_____

_____

_____

Name: _____

Nationality: _____

Post held: _____

_____

Role in the Battle of Britain: _____

_____

_____

_____

_____

Name: _____ Date: _____

Aircraft card game

Hawker Hurricane (British)

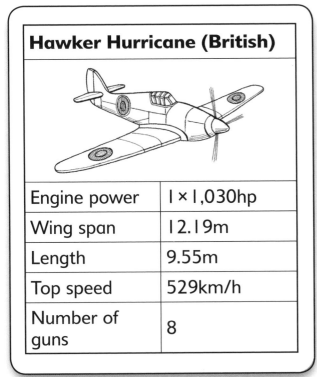

Engine power	1 × 1,030hp
Wing span	12.19m
Length	9.55m
Top speed	529km/h
Number of guns	8

Engine power	hp
Wing span	m
Length	m
Top speed	km/h
Number of guns	

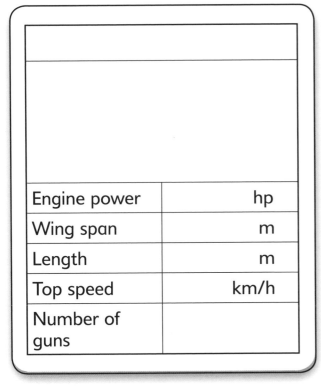

Engine power	hp
Wing span	m
Length	m
Top speed	km/h
Number of guns	

Engine power	hp
Wing span	m
Length	m
Top speed	km/h
Number of guns	

Other aircraft of the Battle of Britain:

British: Supermarine Spitfire, Gloster Gladiator, Boulton Paul Defiant, Bristol Beaufighter, Bristol Blenheim

German: Dornier 17, Heinkel 111, Junkers Ju87, Junkers 88, Messerschmitt 109, Messerschmitt 110

Early Islamic civilisation

In this chapter children investigate a non-European society that contrasts with British history: the Golden Age of Islam. They explore religious beliefs, social structure, and the importance of writing in early Islamic society. They consider the reasons why Baghdad was the centre of early Islamic civilisation, find out about daily life in the city, and investigate the role of its House of Wisdom. Children examine early Islamic scholarship, art, and architecture. Finally, they devise and answer their own questions about early Islamic civilisation.

Chapter at a glance

Curriculum objectives

• A study of a non-European society that provides contrasts with British history: early Islamic civilisation, including a study of Baghdad circa AD900.

Week	Lesson	Summary of activities	Expected outcomes
1	1	• Children locate and record the Golden Age of Islam on a map of the world and on a timeline.	• Can identify the location and time frame of the Golden Age of Islam.
	2	• Children learn about writing in early Islamic civilisation. • They examine Arabic script.	• Can evaluate the role and significance of writing in the rise of early Islamic civilisation.
2	1	• Children compare Islamic beliefs to Viking beliefs. • They research one of the pillars of Islam and create a slide show about it.	• Can compare and contrast Islamic beliefs with Viking beliefs.
	2	• Children read about early Islamic social structure and draw a diagram about it.	• Can explain in simple terms the social structure of early Islamic civilisation.
3	1	• Children discuss the factors influencing the location of settlements. • They read about early Baghdad and create a map of the city.	• Can explain why Baghdad was the centre of early Islamic civilisation.
	2	• Children research everyday life in early Baghdad and compare it with Viking life. • They write a diary entry for a citizen of early Baghdad.	• Can compare and contrast daily life in Baghdad around AD900 with life in a Viking village.
4	1	• Children find out more about the work carried out at Baghdad's House of Wisdom. • They write a report on its significance.	• Can explain the significance of Baghdad's House of Wisdom.
	2	• Children learn to read and write Arabic numerals, and then play a game of bingo using Arabic numerals.	• Can describe some of the contributions to mathematics made by early Islamic scholars.
5	1	• Children research three early Islamic scientists. • They debate which made the greatest contribution to science.	• Can describe some of the contributions to science made by early Islamic scholars.
	2	• Children examine examples of Islamic art. They create their own original tile design in an Islamic style.	• Can describe some forms of Islamic art, in terms of both media and motifs.
6	1	• Children look at Islamic architecture. • They design and make a model of Baghdad's House of Wisdom.	• Can describe early Islamic architecture.
	2	• Children devise relevant questions about early Islamic civilisation, and then research answers, evaluating their sources for reliability. • They present their findings to an audience.	• Can devise historically valid questions about early Islamic civilisation. • Can research answers and evaluate the sources.
Assess and review		• To review the half-term's work.	

Expected prior learning
● Children do not need any prior knowledge of early Islamic civilisation.
● It is assumed that children are familiar with Viking culture (for example, from studying the first two Year 6 chapters in this book).

Overview of progression
● In this chapter children continue to develop a chronologically secure knowledge and understanding of world history. They regularly address historically valid questions, and in the final lesson they devise their own. Through their work in this final lesson they construct informed responses that involve thoughtful selection and organisation of relevant historical information.
● Children demonstrate their knowledge of the past in different ways, including constructing timelines, drawing maps, taking part in discussions, writing and answering quiz questions, constructing information tables, making models, creating artwork, drawing diagrams, holding debates, and writing reports and diary entries.

Creative context
● The content of this chapter has strong links with the English curriculum. Children take part in discussions and debates, apply research skills, read texts for information, and write quizzes, reports and diary entries.
● There are also strong links with geography. Children locate the early Islamic civilisation on a map of the world and on a map of the Middle East, southern Europe and northern Africa; they explore the factors influencing the location of settlements, and they draw a map of early Baghdad.
● The work in this chapter links to art and design through children designing and making a bookmark featuring Arabic script, and an Islamic-style tile.
● Children apply skills developed in design and technology to design and make a model of Baghdad's House of Wisdom.
● Children also get a chance to apply their mathematical skills. They learn to read and write numbers using Arabic numerals and explore symmetry in Islamic art.
● Children undertake historical research online, which addresses several requirements of the computing curriculum, including using the internet safely and responsibly, using search engines effectively and evaluating online content. They also create digital content in the form of a slide show.
● There are links to RE, with children exploring the origins of the Islamic faith and learning about some important Islamic beliefs and practices.

Background knowledge
● Early Islamic civilisation is often referred to as the Golden Age of Islam. It begins with the founding of Islam by the prophet Muhammad in the mid 7th century, and ends with the conquest of Baghdad by the Mongols in the mid 13th century.
● The early Muslim empire was a caliphate (a state led by a ruler called a caliph). For over 500 years the Muslim empire was ruled by the Abbasid dynasty. During the time of the Abbasid Caliphate the capital of the empire was Baghdad.
● The Muslim Empire was a major intellectual centre for science, philosophy, medicine and education. In Baghdad, the caliph established the House of Wisdom where scholars, both Muslim and non-Muslim, gathered to translate the world's knowledge into Arabic as well as to make original contributions to a wide range of fields of knowledge.
● The Arabs learned the secret of paper making from the Chinese. They improved upon Chinese techniques and devised a method of mass production. This aided the transmission of knowledge, both religious and secular, throughout the Muslim world, and the expansion of the empire.

Week 1 lesson plans

Lesson 1 begins with an introduction to the Golden Age of Islam. Children mark the position of the Golden Age civilisation on a world map and timeline. They collect questions about the Golden Age of Islam, and choose one to research for homework. In Lesson 2 children explore the role and significance of writing in early Islamic civilisation. They are introduced to the Arabic alphabet and write their name in Arabic script.

1: When and where was the Golden Age of Islam?

Lesson objective
● To develop a chronologically secure knowledge and understanding of British, local and world history, establishing clear narratives within and across the periods they study.

Expected outcomes
● All children can describe the Golden Age of Islam.
● Most children can locate the Golden Age of Islam on a timeline and a map of the world.
● Some children can explain why this period in the history of Islam is known as the Golden Age.

Resources
Globes, atlases or online maps of the world; computers with internet access; coloured pencils or pens; blank timelines; outline map of the Middle East, southern Europe and northern Africa (optional)

Introduction
● On the left-hand side of the board write the words *Golden Age*. Ask: *What is a golden age?* Give children a few minutes to talk about this with a partner and then discuss ideas as a class. On the right-hand side of the board write the word *Islam*. Ask: *What is Islam?* Repeat the discussion process. Finally, join the words to create the phrase *Golden Age of Islam*. Ask: *What do you think historians mean when they talk about this?*
● Introduce this lesson's focus question: *When and where was the Golden Age of Islam?*
● Organise the class into groups, giving each group an outline world map and a timeline. Ask each group to talk about where and when they think the Golden Age of Islam took place, and to mark this on the world map and on the timeline.
● Ask groups to share their ideas, but do not correct any misconceptions.

Paired work
● Organise the class into pairs, giving each pair access to a globe, atlas or online map of the world, access to the internet, a fresh outline map of the world, and a fresh timeline.
● Ask pairs to search the internet for information on the Golden Age of Islam, and then mark the civilisation on the map and the timeline. Useful search terms include *Golden Age of Islam*, and *Abbasid Caliphate*. The following websites are useful: www.1001inventions.com and www.muslimheritage.com.
● Ask any pairs who finish to write three questions about the Golden Age of Islam which they would like to find out the answers to.

> **Differentiation**
> ● Support: children can work with a more confident partner.
> ● Challenge: ask children explain why this period called the Golden Age, and provide evidence to support their explanation.

Review
● Review the focus question.
● Question any children who have taken on the challenge activity, asking them to provide evidence to support their explanation.
● Ask any pairs who wrote questions about the Golden Age of Islam to share them. Write selected questions on the board.
● Ask children to choose one of the questions on the board to research for homework.

2: Why was writing so important for early Islamic civilisation?

Introduction
● Introduce this lesson's focus question: *Why was writing so important for early Islamic civilisation?*

Paired work
● Organise the class into pairs, giving each pair a copy of the photocopiable page 221 'The role of writing in early Islamic civilisation'.
● Ask pairs to read the text, discuss the questions with their partner and then write down their answers.

Whole-class work
● Discuss the answers to the questions from the sheet:
  ● *Why did the spread of Islam go hand-in-hand with the spread of literacy?* (Because one of the duties of a Muslim is to read and study the holy text of Islam, the Qur'an.)
  ● *What inspired the Caliphs of the Abbasid dynasty to set up the House of Wisdom in Baghdad?* (The fact that the Qur'an stresses the value of knowledge and scholarship.)
  ● *What technological developments allowed early Islamic civilisation to produce more books than ever before?* (Learning the secret of papermaking from the Chinese, improving papermaking techniques, and inventing assembly-line methods of hand-copying manuscripts.)
  ● *What social factors might have made producing a lot of books profitable?* (Because Muslims were expected to read the Qur'an, more people learned to read. Because more people could read, and because the Qur'an stresses the value of knowledge, there would have been a bigger demand for books.)
● Display a chart showing the Arabic alphabet, such as the one listed in *Resources*. Clicking on each letter in this chart gives a link to a short video clip showing how to write the letter and pronounce its name.
● Discuss the characteristics of Arabic script, such as the fact that it is written right to left, and that most letters change their shape depending on where they appear in the word.
● Direct the children to your chosen translation site, and show them how to change a name written in English into the Arabic alphabet.

Independent work
● Give each child access to the internet.
● Ask them to use the translation site to find out what their name looks like in Arabic script.
● Ask children to copy the Arabic script version of their name carefully onto paper.
● As a homework activity, children could create a bookmark decorated with their name in Arabic script.

Differentiation
● Support: group less confident learners together for the comprehension activity; ask them to answer the questions orally rather than in writing.
● Challenge: ask children to explain the role of writing in early Islamic civilisation.

Review
● Ask: *How does the role of writing in early Islamic civilisation compare with the role of writing in today's western civilisation?*

Week 2 lesson plans

In Lesson 1 children read about Islamic beliefs and compare them with Viking beliefs. They also research one of the pillars of Islam and create a slide show about it. In Lesson 2 children read a text about early Islamic social structure and write and answer quiz questions about what they have read. They draw a diagram showing early Islamic social structure.

1: How do Islamic beliefs compare with Viking beliefs?

Lesson objectives
● To develop a chronologically secure knowledge and understanding of British, local and world history, establishing clear narratives within and across the periods they study.
● To regularly address and sometimes devise historically valid questions about change, cause, similarity and difference, and significance.

Expected outcomes
● All children can explain some of the main beliefs of Islam.
● Most children can compare Islamic beliefs with Viking beliefs.
● Some children can discuss how differences in Islamic and Viking beliefs are reflected in the two cultures.

Resources
Information bank on the five pillars of Islam (such as books or internet access); presentation software

Introduction
● Introduce this lesson's focus question: *How do Islamic beliefs compare with Viking beliefs?*
● Give the children, working with a partner or in a small group, a few minutes to discuss what they can remember about Viking beliefs.
● Collate children's ideas on the board.

Whole-class work
● Discuss Islamic beliefs as a class (existing knowledge is likely to vary considerably).
● Draw out the following points: Islam is based on the teachings of a man named Muhammad, who was born in AD570 at Mecca, in Saudi Arabia. People who follow the religion of Islam are called Muslims. Muslims believe that there is only one God, called Allah. They believe that Allah sent a series of prophets (messengers) to teach his message to humanity, and that Muhammad was the last and most important of these prophets. Muslims believe the holy book of Islam, the Qur'an, is the word of Allah, as revealed to the prophet Muhammad by the angel Gabriel.
● Explain that there are five duties that all Muslims are expected to carry out. These are called the Five Pillars of Islam. Ask the children if they can describe any of the five pillars.

Group work
● Organise the class into five groups.
● Give each group access to the information bank you have prepared and assign them one of the pillars of Islam to research: *Shahadah, Salat, Zakat, Sawm* or *Hajj.*
● Ask each group to work together to create a slide show about the pillar of Islam they have researched. You may want to revise the features of the presentation software children will be using.

> **Differentiation**
> ● Support: ask children to create a single slide rather than a whole slideshow.
> ● Challenge: as an extension activity, children can discuss ways in which differences in Islamic and Viking beliefs are reflected in differences between the two cultures.

Review
● Give each group an opportunity to share their slide show with the rest of the class, receive feedback, and answer questions.
● Ask: *How do Islamic beliefs compare with Viking beliefs?* Discuss ideas together.
● Ask any children who have completed the extension activity to talk about it.

Lesson objective

● To develop a chronologically secure knowledge and understanding of British, local and world history, establishing clear narratives within and across the periods they study.

Expected outcomes

● All children can describe some of the features of the social structure of early Islamic civilisation.
● Most children can explain the social structure of early Islamic civilisation.
● Some children can compare and contrast the early Islamic social structure with the social structure of modern Britain.

Resources

Photocopiable page 222 'How was early Islamic society structured?'; plain paper and colouring pencils or modelling materials (such as dough, clay or aluminium foil) or computer software with diagramming capability

2: How was early Islamic society structured?

Introduction

● Introduce this lesson's focus question: *How was early Islamic society structured?*
● Give out individual copies of photocopiable page 222 'How was early Islamic society structured?'. Allow enough time for everyone to read the text. Ask anyone who finishes reading before the time is up to write a question based on the text and keep it secret.
● Ask everyone to place their copy of the text face down, and then divide the class into groups. Ask each group a question based on the text. Include any questions children have written. Group members may confer to decide on the answer. Award 2 points for a correct answer. If a group does not answer correctly, open the question up for 1 point.

Paired work

● Ask children to work with a partner to draw a diagram showing the social structure of early Islamic society. They could create their diagram on paper, in three dimensions using modelling materials, or on a computer using a program with diagramming capability.

Differentiation
● Support: children may benefit from working with an adult or a more confident partner.
● Challenge: ask children to compare and contrast the social structure of early Islamic civilisation and the social structure of modern Britain.

Review

● Ask pairs to share and explain their diagrams, inviting the rest of the class to provide feedback. The most successful diagrams could be put on display.
● If any children have compared and contrasted the social structure of early Islamic civilisation with the social structure of modern Britain (see *Differentiation*), ask them to present what they have found out.

Week 3 lesson plans

This week's lessons focus on Baghdad. In Lesson 1 children discuss the factors influencing the location of settlements. They read a text describing early Baghdad and create a map of the city. They discuss the reasons why Baghdad was the most important city in early Islamic civilisation. In Lesson 2 children revise what they know about life in a Viking village. They research everyday life in early Baghdad, noting and discussing similarities and differences between it and Viking life. They write a diary entry for a citizen of early Baghdad.

Lesson objectives
● To develop a chronologically secure knowledge and understanding of British, local and world history, establishing clear narratives within and across the periods they study.
● To note connections, contrasts and trends over time.
● To regularly address and sometimes devise historically valid questions about change, cause, similarity and difference, and significance.

Expected outcomes
● All children can describe the factors affecting the location of settlements.
● Most children can give at least one reason why Baghdad was the centre of early Islamic civilisation.
● Some children can explain in more detail why Baghdad was the centre of early Islamic civilisation.

Resources
Photocopiable page 'Ancient Baghdad' from the CD-ROM; satellite image of Baghdad (optional)

1: Why was Baghdad the most important city in early Islamic civilisation?

Introduction
● Introduce this lesson's focus question: *Why was Baghdad the most important city in early Islamic civilisation?*

Whole-class work
● Ask: *What do people look for when they are choosing a place to build a settlement?*
● Give children a few minutes, working with a partner, to discuss this question and note down their ideas.
● Discuss the factors influencing the choice of where to build a settlement together as a class. These include site factors (what is available on or near the proposed site of the settlement) and situation (where the proposed site is located in relation to other settlements). Important site factors include a water supply, building materials, fuel, quality of soil, climate, shelter, a defensible position, and good communications (ability to travel easily to and from the site). A site with good communications might be at a bridging point in a river, or a route centre (meeting point of two valleys and/or roads).
● If possible, display a satellite map of modern Baghdad (for example from Google Earth). Zoom out so that the whole city can be seen, as well as its location in relation to surrounding geographical features.
● Ask: *What clues does this map give you to why this location was chosen to build the city of Baghdad?*
● Display photocopiable page 'Ancient Baghdad' from the CD-ROM. Read and discuss the text.

Group work
● Organise the class into pairs or small groups.
● Give each pair or group one copy of the photocopiable page.
● Ask each group to draw a map of ancient Baghdad using the information given on the photocopiable page.

> **Differentiation**
> ● Support: provide them with a simplified version of the text from the photocopiable page.

Review
● Ask: *Why was Baghdad the most important city in early Islamic civilisation?*
● Ask each group to present their map to the class. Compare and contrast the maps.

Lesson objectives
● To develop a chronologically secure knowledge and understanding of British, local and world history, establishing clear narratives within and across the periods they study.
● To regularly address and sometimes devise historically valid questions about change, cause, similarity and difference, and significance.
● To note connections, contrasts and trends over time.

Expected outcomes
● All children can describe some of the main features of daily life in the early Islamic Empire.
● Most children can compare and contrast daily life in the early Islamic Empire with life in Viking-age Britain.
● Some children can suggest reasons for the differences between daily life in the two cultures.

Resources
Information bank on daily life in the early Islamic Empire (such as, *Daily Life in Ancient and Modern Baghdad* by Dawn Kotapish, *Heinemann History Scheme Book 1: Life in Medieval Times* by Judith Kidd, Rosemary Rees and Ruth Tudor, *Great Empires of the Past: Empire of the Islamic World* by Robin S Doak and internet access)

2: How did life in the early Islamic Empire compare with life in Viking-age Britain?

Introduction
● Introduce this lesson's focus question: *How did life in the early Islamic Empire compare with life in Viking-age Britain?*
● Ask the children to discuss with a partner what they can remember about life in Viking-age Britain. Share ideas as a class.
● Draw out the facts that a large proportion of people's time was spent growing, collecting and preparing food and making and maintaining essential items such as clothing and tools. People had very little leisure time, and almost no one learned to read or write.

Whole-class work
● Ask the children to imagine they have been transported back in time to live in Baghdad in around AD900.
● Tell children they will be doing some research to find out what their day-to-day life would be like. Provide children with a list of search terms that might be useful (for online and index searches). These include: *daily life (in the) early/ medieval Islamic world/empire*.

Paired work
● Organise the class into pairs, giving each pair access to the information bank you have prepared. Ask children to conduct research to discover and note what daily life was like in the early Islamic Empire.

Whole-class work
● Ask pairs to share what they have found out about life in the early Islamic Empire.
● Work together as a class to draw up a list of similarities and differences between life in the early Islamic Empire and life in Viking-age Britain.

Independent work
● Ask children to use what they have found out to write a diary entry describing a typical day in the life of an inhabitant of Baghdad during the early Islamic Empire.
● Children could write from the point of view of a child, or of an adult character, such as a scholar or merchant.

Review
● Ask: *If you had been alive in around AD900, where would you rather have lived, a Viking village or Baghdad? Explain your reasoning.*

Week 4 lesson plans

In Lesson 1 children learn about Baghdad's House of Wisdom. They find out more about the work that was carried out there. They write a report on the significance of the House of Wisdom. In Lesson 2 children learn to read and write Arabic numerals, and then play a game of bingo using numbers written in Arabic numerals.

1: Baghdad's House of Wisdom: what was so special about it?

Lesson objectives
● To develop a chronologically secure knowledge and understanding of British, local and world history, establishing clear narratives within and across the periods they study.
● To regularly address and sometimes devise historically valid questions about change, cause, similarity and difference, and significance.

Expected outcomes
● All children can describe Baghdad's House of Wisdom.
● Most children can explain the purpose of Baghdad's House of Wisdom.
● Some children can explain the role Baghdad's House of Wisdom played in the Golden Age of Islam.

Resources
One or more non-fiction books about the Golden Age of Islam (optional); teaching assistant (optional)

Introduction
● Introduce this lesson's focus question: *Baghdad's House of Wisdom: what was so special about it?*
● Give the children information about Baghdad's House of Wisdom, for example, by hot seating in character as a scholar.
● Draw out the following: The Islamic empire was large. Scholars, philosophers and artists from all across the empire came to Baghdad's House of Wisdom seeking answers to logistical, scientific and engineering problems. They studied in the library and, importantly, discussed their problems with others. This makes the House of Wisdom the first international scholarly endeavour. It's legacy is still with us. The scholars translated texts into Arabic from many different languages, including Ancient Greek, Persian and Sanskrit – preserving knowledge that might otherwise have been lost for ever.

Whole-class work
● Ask children to recap what they have learned from the introduction about the work done at Baghdad's House of Wisdom.
● Ask a volunteer to make notes on the board that can be used for reference later in the lesson.
● Discuss the focus question: *Baghdad's House of Wisdom: what was so special about it?* Give children research time, then establish the reasons why the House of Wisdom was so important at the time and how it influenced the future of learning.
● Revise the features of a report. (It provides information about a subject, and is usually written in the present tense. The text is typically arranged in paragraphs divided by headings and subheadings, and there may be visual information in the form of photographs, illustrations, maps or diagrams.) You could use a page from a non-fiction book about the Golden Age of Islam as an example.

Independent work
● Ask individuals to write a report on Baghdad's House of Wisdom using the focus question as the title.

Differentiation
● Support: provide children with appropriate scaffolding and/or adult support.
● Challenge: ask children to consider the role that the House of Wisdom played in the Golden Age of Islam.

Review
● Organise the class into pairs, asking partners to read and comment on each other's reports, perhaps using the 'two stars and a wish' format.

Lesson objectives
● To develop a chronologically secure knowledge and understanding of British, local and world history, establishing clear narratives within and across the periods they study.
● To regularly address and sometimes devise historically valid questions about change, cause, similarity and difference, and significance.
● To note connections, contrasts and trends over time.

Expected outcomes
● All children can describe in general terms some of the contributions to mathematics made by early Islamic scholars.
● Most children can read and write numbers using Arabic numerals.
● Some children can describe the contributions Muhammad ibn Mūsā al-Khwārizmī, made to mathematics.

Resources
Photocopiable pages 'Arabic numerals' from the CD-ROM; cards prepared from the photocopiable pages

2: What does mathematics owe to early Islamic civilisation?

Introduction
● Introduce this lesson's focus question: *What does mathematics owe to early Islamic civilisation?*
● Ask: *What contributions did early Islamic scholars make to mathematics?* Give children a minute or two to discuss ideas with a partner.
● Discuss children's ideas.

Whole-class work
● Explain that early Islamic scholars made significant contributions to mathematics. They translated mathematical texts from all around the world (particularly Greece and India), synthesising and building on their ideas. Branches of mathematics advanced by Islamic scholars include geometry and trigonometry. Islamic mathematicians invented algebra and calculus, and introduced a version of the Indian number system, which our present-day number system is based on.
● Display and discuss the photocopiable pages 'Arabic numerals' from the CD-ROM. Explain that unlike Arabic letters, which are written from right to left, Arabic numerals are written from left to right.
● Remove the photocopiable pages from display and hold up one Arabic number card at a time, asking children to say the number aloud. Say a number aloud, asking the children to write it in Arabic numerals.
● Play a game of Arabic numeral bingo. Ask each child to draw a 3 by 3 grid, writing a different Arabic number between 0 and 29 in each cell of the grid. Ask a volunteer to draw an Arabic number card and read the number on it aloud, without showing the card to the rest of the class. Play progresses in the usual manner.

> ### Differentiation
> ● Support: for the bingo game, provide children with prepared bingo grids rather than asking them to write in the numbers themselves.
> ● Challenge: for homework, some children can find out about the life and work of one of the early Islamic mathematicians, Muhammad ibn Mūsā al-Khwārizmī.

Review
● Write some mental arithmetic questions on the board using Arabic numerals, asking children to write the answers using Arabic numerals. You could differentiate the questions depending on your maths groups.

Week 5 lesson plans

In Lesson 1 children research the work of three early Islamic scientists. They complete a table of information about the three scientists. They hold a debate on which of the three made the greatest contribution to science. In Lesson 2 children examine examples of early Islamic art, identifying common motifs and the role of symmetry. They create their own original tile design in an Islamic style, and then use this design to decorate a tile. Lesson 2 may take several sessions to complete.

1: What contributions did early Islamic civilisation make to science?

Lesson objectives
● To develop a chronologically secure knowledge and understanding of British, local and world history, establishing clear narratives within and across the periods they study.
● To regularly address and sometimes devise historically valid questions about change, cause, similarity and difference, and significance.
● To note connections, contrasts and trends over time.

Expected outcomes
● All children can describe some of the contributions to science made by three early Islamic scientists.
● Most children can debate the relative importance of the contribution made by each scientist.
● Some children can put forward a compelling argument in support of their point of view.

Resources
Information bank on three scientists from early Islamic civilisation: ibn Firnas, al-Battani and Razi; photocopiable page 223 'Scientists of the Islamic Golden Age'

Introduction
● Introduce this lesson's focus question: *What contributions did early Islamic civilisation make to science?*

Paired work
● Organise the class into pairs, giving each pair a copy of photocopiable page 223 'Scientists of the Islamic Golden Age' and access to the information bank you have prepared.
● Ask children to read the information about ibn Firnas on the photocopiable page. They should then use the information bank to fill in the table for the other two scientists, al-Battani and Razi.

Group work
● Divide the class into three groups, one for each of the three scientists.
● Ask each group to prepare arguments to support the assertion that the scientist they have chosen (or been given) was the one who made the greatest contribution to science.
● Ask individuals or pairs within the group to prepare a short presentation based on one of these arguments.

Whole-class work
● Conduct a class debate, with each group presenting their arguments.

Differentiation
● Support: children could prepare their arguments based on the information about ibn Firnas given on the photocopiable page.
● Challenge: children should prepare their arguments based on their research. Some children could find out about the contributions to science made by other early Islamic scholars.

Review
● Complete the debate by asking children to vote for the scientist whose achievements were supported by the most compelling arguments.
● You may wish to use the following additional questions: *Which way did you vote? Did you find the decision about which way to vote difficult to make? Why? Why not?*

Lesson objective
● To develop a chronologically secure knowledge and understanding of British, local and world history, establishing clear narratives within and across the periods they study.

Expected outcomes
● All children can describe some forms of Islamic art, in terms of both media and motifs.
● Most children can create an original design in an Islamic style.
● Some children can create an original symmetrical design in an Islamic style using a variety of accurately drawn geometrical shapes.

Resources
Information bank showing examples of Islamic art and design (from the internet or books); media resource 'Islamic tile patterns' on the CD-ROM; art sketchbooks; art pencils; colouring pencils; erasers; rulers; drawing compasses; protractors; clay; clay modelling tools and equipment; coloured glazes; access to a kiln

2: What forms did early Islamic art take?

Introduction
● Introduce this lesson's focus question: *What forms did early Islamic art take?* Revise the art and design terms media and motif.
● Display the images you have collected showing examples of Islamic art and design. Ask the children to look for any recurring themes, forms, patterns or colours, and discuss these with a partner.
● Discuss ideas together as a class. Talk about the predominance of pattern over representation, and the importance of symmetry. Discuss the types and orders of symmetry used.

Independent work
● Children will need the images close at hand for the rest of the lesson.
● Ask the children to copy one or more Islamic motifs of their choice into their sketchbooks.

Whole class work
● Display the media resource 'Islamic tile patterns' from the CD-ROM and discuss the features of the tile designs.
● Ask the children to create their own original design for a tile in the Islamic style.

Independent work
● Give children time to create their own tile design in their sketchbooks and colour it in.
● Ask those who finish their design to make the tile they have designed, in clay. This will need to be done in stages over several sessions: cutting out the tile, firing it, creating the design using coloured glazes, and firing the tile a second time.
● If you do not have a kiln in school, you may be able to make arrangements with a local secondary school to use their kiln.
● If working with clay is not practicable, children could create their 'tiles' using other media, such as printing, painting or digital imaging.

Differentiation
● Support: children should create their designs using rulers alone.
● Challenge: children should create geometrically accurate symmetrical designs based on circles (for example, using compasses) and regular polygons (for example, using protractors to measure angles).

Review
● Ask the children to explain to a partner what they know about Islamic art and design.

Week 6 lesson plans

In Lesson 1 children explore early Islamic architecture, and then design and make a model of Baghdad's House of Wisdom. This lesson is likely to take several sessions to complete. If you are short on time, you could 'steal' some sessions from design and technology. In Lesson 2 children devise historically relevant questions about early Islamic civilisation, and then research answers to their questions, evaluating their sources for reliability. They agree on a method of presenting their results, and work together to produce a whole-class presentation, which they share with a specific audience.

1: What was early Islamic architecture like?

Lesson objective
● To develop a chronologically secure knowledge and understanding of British, local and world history, establishing clear narratives within and across the periods they study.

Expected outcomes
● All children can describe features of early Islamic architecture.
● Most children can describe early Islamic architecture using suitable technical terms.
● Some children can discuss the relationship between early Islamic architecture and the local environment and culture.

Resources
Examples of Islamic architecture from books or the internet; model making materials and tools

Introduction
● Introduce this lesson's focus question: *What was early Islamic architecture like?*
● Give children a couple of minutes to discuss the focus question with a partner, and then ask children to share their discussion with the rest of the class.
● Display some examples of Islamic architecture.
● Discuss the features of Islamic architecture, for example, use of stone as a building material, arches, domes, minarets, courtyards, and pools. Discuss how the buildings are highly decorated, using gilding, mosaics, carvings, latticework, and bright colours.

Group work
● Organise children into small groups.
● Give groups the task of designing a model of a Baghdad's House of Wisdom. Explain that the House of Wisdom was destroyed many centuries ago. They will need to imagine what it might have looked like, based on what they know about it and about early Islamic architecture.
● Tell children their designs should include a floor plan, an exterior view, and a list of materials and equipment they will use to make the model.
● You might want to provide children with a list of construction materials to choose from, or give them a completely free choice about the materials they will use. You might ask children to make their model within a particular range of dimensions, or allow them to choose the scale.
● Give groups enough time to make their models.

Differentiation
● Challenge: ask children to consider how the local environment and culture influence Islamic architecture. For example, ask: *Why are pools and courtyards common features of Islamic architecture?* (To provide cool air and shade in a hot climate.) *Why are buildings decorated using geometric patterns?* (Because they represent the perfection and infinity of Allah.)

Review
● Ask each group, through discussion, to nominate one model (not their own) to be displayed outside the classroom to a wider audience (for example, in the school entrance hall). Ask a spokesperson from each group to tell the class which model they nominate and explain why.

■ SCHOLASTIC
www.scholastic.co.uk

Lesson objectives
● To develop a chronologically secure knowledge and understanding of British, local and world history, establishing clear narratives within and across the periods they study.
● To regularly address and sometimes devise historically valid questions about change, cause, similarity and difference, and significance.
● To understand how our knowledge of the past is constructed from a range of sources.

Expected outcomes
● All children can devise historically valid questions about early Islamic civilisation.
● Most children can research answers to their questions, evaluating the sources they use for reliability.
● Some children can curate research results.

Resources
Books about the Golden Age of Islam and/or computers with access to the internet; other resources will vary

2: What else would we like to find out about early Islamic civilisation?

Introduction
● Introduce this lesson's focus question: *What else would we like to find out about early Islamic civilisation?*
● Revise or explain the term *curate* (to organise or manage; used especially for organising exhibits in an art gallery or museum).

Paired work
● Ask: *What questions would you like to ask about early Islamic civilisation?* Organise the class into pairs and give children time to discuss and write down their questions.

Whole-class work
● Ask pairs to share their questions, creating a class list. Help children to adapt their questions if necessary so that they are specific, and cover one of the historical concepts of change, cause, similarity and difference, and significance. The questions in the list need to be distinct from one another, so encourage children to offer only questions that are not covered by questions already on the board.
● If conducting online research, revise effective internet search techniques, e-safety considerations and how to evaluate the reliability of online sources of information.
● Discuss possible ways of presenting research results and agree on a common presentation approach all pairs will use in order to create a whole-class outcome.

Paired work or Independent work
● Ask individuals or pairs to choose a question from the list to research, and make or collect appropriate notes that will help them answer their question.
● When they have found out the answer to their question they should present it using the agreed method.

Differentiation
● Support: pair children with a more confident partner during the first paired work and during the later paired or independent work.
● Challenge: ask children to collect and curate the results of everyone's research.

Review
● Share the whole-class outcome with an audience within school (for example, another class) or outside school (for example, parents). Encourage children to devise and implement a way of asking the audience for feedback.
● Discuss the feedback received, encouraging children to suggest what went well, and what they might do differently if they were to do it again.

Curriculum objective
• To regularly address and sometimes devise historically valid questions about change, cause, similarity and difference, and significance.

Resources
Interactive activity 'Early Islamic civilisation quiz' on the CD-ROM; computers (optional); example of a mind map; e-book software (optional)

Early Islam mind map

Revise
• Introduce the interactive activity 'Early Islamic civilisation quiz' on the CD-ROM.
• Organise the class into pairs, giving each pair computer access to the quiz, and give children time to answer the questions.
• Alternatively, complete the quiz questions as a whole class, using the whiteboard.

Assess
• Revise the term *mind map* and show an example. Ideally, the mind map should be one drawn by members of the class.
• Tell the children they will be creating a mind map. On the centre of the board write: *How was life in early Islamic civilisation different from life in Viking Age Britain?*
• Give the children a set length of time (for example, 25 minutes) to complete the task. Emphasise the importance of working independently for this task. Encourage the children to work fast and to include as much breadth *and* depth of information as they can.
• Ask any children who struggle with writing to write the main headings only (such as, go for breadth rather than depth). They could communicate details to you verbally later.

Further practice
• Ask children to incorporate what they have learned about early Islamic civilisation into an e-book.

Curriculum objective
• To develop a chronologically secure knowledge and understanding of British, local and world history, establishing clear narratives within and across the periods they study.

Resources
Writing materials

An early Islam report

Revise
• Working in groups, ask children to make a list of the aspects of early Islamic civilisation they have investigated.
• Discuss ideas together as a class and draw up a complete list on the board (such as, where and when early Islamic civilisation developed, the role of writing, Islamic beliefs, social structure, art, architecture, Baghdad, the House of Wisdom and the contributions to maths and science made by early Islamic scholars).

Assess
• Ask children to choose one of the aspects of early Islamic civilisation they have studied during this chapter and write a report on it. In their report they should explain as much as possible about what they know. Tell the children it is important they work independently.
• If you did the report-writing activity in Week 4 Lesson 1, the children will already have written a report about Baghdad's House of Wisdom, so make this subject off-limits.
• You might want to revise the features of a report, especially if you did not do the report writing activity in Week 4.
• If you have any children who struggle with writing you might want to assess what they know through a one-to-one conversation conducted with a teaching assistant, or which you conduct yourself later.

Further practice
• Ask children to choose another aspect of early Islamic civilisation and write a different type of text based on it (such as, a story, poem or cartoon strip).

■▲SCHOLASTIC
www.scholastic.co.uk

The role of writing in early Islamic civilisation

Arabic script had been developed before Muhammad; the oldest known text in the Arabic alphabet was written more than two centuries before the prophet was born. However, it was not until Islam began to spread that writing started to take on a central role in Middle Eastern society.

The religion of Islam is based around a holy text, the Qur'an. Muslims (the followers of Islam) believe that the Qur'an represents the words of God as revealed to the prophet Muhammad through the archangel Gabriel. One of the duties of a Muslim is to read and study the Qur'an, so the spread of Islam went hand-in-hand with the spread of literacy.

The Qur'an stresses the value of knowledge and scholarship. As a result of this, the Arab world became an intellectual centre for science, philosophy, medicine and education. The Caliphs of the Abbasid dynasty championed the cause of knowledge and established the House of Wisdom in Baghdad, where both Muslim and non-Muslim scholars sought to gather all the world's knowledge and translate it into Arabic.

Writing was the most efficient way of recording this knowledge, communicating it across the empire, and passing it down from generation to generation.

In the 8th century, the secret of papermaking spread to the Islamic world from China. Paper was a big improvement on the other writing materials that were available at the time: it was easier to manufacture than parchment, less likely to crack than papyrus, and could absorb ink. This meant that ink marks made on paper were difficult to erase, which made paper ideal for keeping records. Islamic papermakers improved production techniques to turn papermaking from an art form into a major industry. They also invented assembly-line methods of hand-copying manuscripts, which allowed books to be produced more quickly and in greater numbers than ever before.

Questions

1. Why did the spread of Islam go hand-in-hand with the spread of literacy?
2. What inspired the caliphs of the Abbasid dynasty to set up the House of Wisdom in Baghdad?
3. What technological developments allowed early Islamic civilisation to produce more books than ever before?
4. What social factors might have made producing a lot of books profitable?

I can answer questions about the role of writing in early Islamic civilisation.

How did you do?

How was early Islamic society structured?

The supreme ruler in early Islamic society was called the caliph. The word is derived from the Arabic word *khalifa* meaning 'successor', because the caliphs were regarded as successors to Muhammad.

Below the caliph was the government. The head of government was the vizier or grand vizier, who was the equivalent of a prime minister. It was the vizier's job to consult with the caliph and enforce his decrees.

Under the vizier were the emirs, who were the governors of the provinces. The emirs had a lot of power, and were very rarely challenged. Local officials would control towns and villages and answer to the emirs.

Beneath the government were ordinary citizens. At the highest level were professionals, such as merchants, teachers and doctors. Many ancient cultures valued agriculture first, but in the Islamic Middle East, trade and the prosperity it brought were considered more important. The fact that the prophet Muhammad was a merchant may also have had something to do with the high regard in which merchants were held.

The next level of social class was the *dhimmis*, the non-Muslim citizens. They had to pay a special tax. They were excused from certain duties Muslim citizens were expected to perform, and excluded from certain privileges reserved for Muslims, but otherwise they were treated equally.

At the bottom of the class system were the slaves. Slaves could gain freedom in various ways, and both the Qur'an and the Hadith (the two most important books of Islam) praised masters who freed their slaves.

Name: _____   Date: _____

Scientists of the Islamic Golden Age

- The table below gives information about one of the eminent scientists of the Islamic Golden Age, ibn Firnas.
- Read the information in the table about ibn Firnas. Fill in the table for the other two scientists, al-Battani and Razi.

Short name	ibn Firnas	al-Battani	Razi
Full name	Abbas Abu Al-Qasim ibn Firnas ibn Wirdas al-Takurini		
Place of birth	Ronda, Spain		
Dates	810–887		
Description	Inventor, physician (doctor), engineer, musician and poet		
Contributions to science	Devised a way of making colourless glass. Made glass lenses to correct vision. Designed a water clock. Invented the metronome. Attempted glider flight.		
Interesting facts	A crater on the Moon is named after him.		

I can describe some of the contributions made to science made by scientists of the Islamic age.

How did you do?

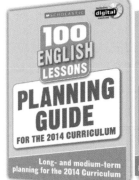 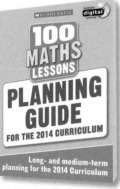 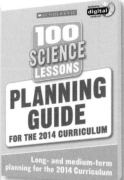  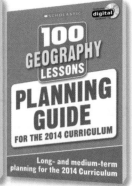
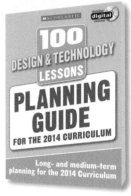 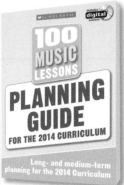  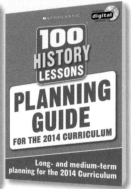